The Transition to a Colonial Economy

Weavers, Merchants and Kings in South India 1720–1800

Prasannan Parthasarathi

Boston College

D1332731

CAMBRIDGE
UNIVERSITY PRESS

CAMBRIDGE UNIVERSITY PRESS
Cambridge, New York, Melbourne, Madrid, Cape Town, Singapore, São Paulo

Cambridge University Press
The Edinburgh Building, Cambridge CB2 2RU, UK

Published in the United States of America by Cambridge University Press, New York

www.cambridge.org
Information on this title: www.cambridge.org/9780521570428

First published 2001
This digitally printed first paperback version 2006

A catalogue record for this publication is available from the British Library

Learning Resources
Centre

1307699X

Library of Congress Cataloguing in Publication data

Parthasarathi, Prasannan.
The transition to a colonial economy: weavers, merchants and kings in
South India, 1720–1800 / Prasannan Parthasarathi.
    p.   cm. – (Cambridge studies in Indian history and society; 7)
Includes bibliographical references and index.
ISBN 0 521 57042 5
1. India, South – Economic conditions – 18th century.   2. Industries – India,
South – History – 18th century.   I. Title.   II. Series.
HC437.S8 P37 2001
330.954'029–dc21   00-045441

ISBN-13 978-0-521-57042-8 hardback
ISBN-10 0-521-57042-5 hardback

ISBN-13 978-0-521-03310-7 paperback
ISBN-10 0-521-03310-1 paperback

To my parents

Contents

Tables

Acknowledgments

I have received a great deal of assistance in the completion of this book. It began its life as a doctoral dissertation and I am grateful to my committee members, David Landes, Stephen Marglin and Tosun Aricanli, for their sound support and advice. I am also deeply indebted to David Washbrook who introduced me to South Asian history and has been an adviser and close friend. Others who have assisted me in various ways over the years include R. K. Raghavan, Narendra Subramanian, Meenakshi Menon, R. Sengammal, Sujatha Rangaswami, S. S. Sivakumar, Chitra Sivakumar, David Ludden, Niranjana Candadai, Ramesh Candadai, Sugata Bose, Burton Stein, Raj Chandavarkar, Christopher Bayly, Pratap Mehta, Jeffrey James, Willem van Schendel, Bernard Lown, Louise Lown, David Quigley, Kevin Kenney, Robin Fleming, Paul Breines, Burke Griggs, Peter Noble-Cass and Mark Stansbury. I also thank the Andrew W. Mellon Economic History Fund, the Alfred D. Chandler, Jr. Traveling Fellowship and the Netherlands Organization for Scientific Research (NWO) for extending financial support for the research and writing. I must also thank the staffs of the Oriental and India Office Collection, British Library, the Tamil Nadu Archives and the Andhra Pradesh State Archives for their assistance. Finally, I am grateful for the patience, encouragement and love of Julie, Krishna and Sulakshana. I dedicate this work to my parents.

Note on Indian words and place names

In general I have used the fairly accurate transliteration of words and place names found in the late nineteenth- and early twentieth-century district manuals and gazetteers. I have endeavored to avoid both corrupt eighteenth-century forms, except in quotations of original passages, and more modern transliterations with diacritical marks in order to simplify presentation in the text. Some eighteenth-century forms of Indian words and names have been retained in cases where it is unclear what the original may have been. Much of South India was renamed and administratively reorganized from the late eighteenth century as the area came under British rule. I have in general avoided the use of British district names prior to the establishment of British authority, but in some cases have relied upon them for ease of historical exposition.

At the end of the book there is a glossary of Indian and Anglo-Indian words used in the text, together with other words that may require explanation. These terms appear in italic at their first occurrence in the text.

Note on money

South Indian coinage consisted of gold, silver and copper, respectively *pagodas, fanams* and *cash*. In the Northern Sarkars, there was also another copper coin, *dub*. Through much of the century, 1 pagoda exchanged for 8 or 9 British shillings and 3 to 3.25 silver rupees. Although there was great local variation and many varieties of coins, in 1790 the following exchanges prevailed between the different South Indian currency units:

In the Northern Sarkars: 2,880 cash = 36 fanams = 1 pagoda
In Cuddalore: 3,520 cash = 44 fanams = 1 pagoda.

Abbreviations

APSA	Andhra Pradesh State Archives, Hyderabad
CEHI	*Cambridge Economic History of India*
FSDC	English East India Company, *Fort St. David Consultations*
FSGDC	English East India Company, *Fort St. George Diary and Consultation Book*
IESHR	*Indian Economic and Social History Review*
JIH	*Journal of Indian History*
MAS	*Modern Asian Studies*
MPP	Madras Public Proceedings
OIOC	Oriental and India Office Collection, British Library, London
TNA	Tamil Nadu Archives, Chennai

Introduction

Low wages and a degraded status for laborers are undeniable features of contemporary South Asia. In the case of India, substantial numbers of workers are subject to endemic hunger and chronic insecurity as they receive incomes which are both uncertain and insufficient to meet their minimum needs for food, clothing and shelter. The position of laborers, be they industrial or agricultural, urban or rural, men or women, is further weakened by the fact that some 40 percent of the population live below the poverty line and supply for employers a vast "reserve army of unemployed."[1] The situation in Pakistan and Bangladesh is largely similar.

In the opinion of many historians, these conditions are not novel, but have characterized the subcontinent for several centuries. Support for this view may be found in the accounts of European visitors, who since the fifteenth century have described the working people of India as scantily clad, undernourished, poorly paid and subject to the capricious abuses of their political and economic superiors.[2] Historians have often too easily accepted the accounts of these visitors. W. H. Moreland, drawing upon these sources, concluded that in the sixteenth century "the masses lived on the same economic plane" as in the early twentieth century.[3] The opinions of European travelers inform Irfan Habib's magisterial account of the decline of the Mughal Empire, which he traced to peasant revolts in protest against endemic state oppression and consequent poverty.[4] And K. N. Chaudhuri has written of the poverty of weavers in eighteenth-century India, which, in his opinion, accounted for the competitiveness of Indian cloth exports.[5] Tapan Raychaudhuri, writing in the *Cambridge*

---

[1] For a portrait of conditions of work in contemporary India see Jan Breman, *Footloose Labour: Working in India's Informal Economy* (Cambridge, 1996).
[2] For a survey of these descriptions see W. H. Moreland, *India at the Death of Akbar* (London, 1920; repr. Delhi, 1990), pp. 265–70.
[3] Moreland, *India at the Death of Akbar*, p. 270.
[4] Irfan Habib, *The Agrarian System of Mughal India* (Bombay, 1963), chap. 9.
[5] K. N. Chaudhuri, *The Trading World of Asia and the English East India Company* (Cambridge, 1978), p. 274.

Economic History of India, and Christopher Bayly have concurred with this view.[6]

Despite this apparent consensus, there is growing evidence, at the moment from eighteenth-century South India, that laborers have not always been impoverished. David Washbrook has argued recently that in the late eighteenth century "pariahs" possessed secure claims to incomes and were in a very strong position in the social and economic order. S. S. Sivakumar and Chitra Sivakumar have estimated that the real earnings from agricultural work for *adimai* or dependent cultivators in Chingleput were three times higher in 1795 than in 1976. I have shown that in the late eighteenth century wages in South India compared very favorably with those in Britain. Although contemporary poverty is undeniable, these contributions suggest that a low standard of living was not a long-standing feature of India, but emerged in the nineteenth and twentieth centuries.[7]

I argue in this work that poverty and low wages were a product of colonial rule. Of course, the association between poverty and colonialism has a long legacy in India and is found in the writings of early nationalist critics of British rule. A very clear statement is contained in the classic work of Romesh Dutt, who traced a decline in standards of living to the nineteenth-century deindustrialization of the subcontinent and the narrowing of sources of wealth which followed:

India in the eighteenth century was a great manufacturing as well as great agricultural country, and the products of the Indian loom supplied the markets of Asia and of Europe. It is, unfortunately, true that the East Indian Company and the British Parliament . . . discouraged Indian manufactures in the early years of British rule in order to encourage the rising manufactures of England . . . millions

---

[6] Tapan Raychaudhuri, "The Mid-Eighteenth-Century Background," in Dharma Kumar (ed.), *CEHI*, vol. II, *c. 1757–c. 1970* (Cambridge, 1982), p. 8; C. A. Bayly, *Indian Society and the Making of the British Empire* (Cambridge, 1988), p. 37.

[7] David Washbrook, "Land and Labour in Late Eighteenth-Century South India: The Golden Age of the Pariah?," in Peter Robb (ed.), *Dalit Movements and the Meanings of Labour in India* (Delhi, 1993); S. S. Sivakumar and Chitra Sivakumar, *Peasants and Nabobs* (Delhi, 1993), p. 14; Prasannan Parthasarathi, "Rethinking Wages and Competitiveness in the Eighteenth Century: Britain and South India," *Past and Present*, no. 158 (1998). There is also evidence that the nutrition and well-being of South Indian laborers declined in the second half of the nineteenth century. See Lance Brannan, John McDonald and Ralph Schlomowitz, "Trends in the Economic Well-Being of South Indians under British Rule: The Anthropometric Evidence," *Explorations in Economic History*, 31 (1994). These findings also have implications for the Subaltern Studies project. The focus of the Subaltern historians has largely been on the colonial period. However, it is likely that the self-understanding of subaltern groups was very different in the pre-colonial period, given the vastly different social, political and economic conditions. Thus appeals to factors such as primordialism are insufficient to explain the actions of subaltern classes. Rather the evolution of subaltern consciousness must be analyzed in close relation to social, political and economic circumstances.

of Indian artisans lost their earnings; the population of India lost one great source of their wealth.[8]

According to Dutt, as a consequence of deindustrialization there was an increased dependence upon agriculture, which also came under severe pressures with British rule, chiefly because of the high level of taxation. In our own times Amiya Bagchi is an eloquent proponent of these views.[9]

Nationalist writers have always had their interlocutors. For many decades they came from the ranks of supporters of British rule in India. Agreeing with nationalist analysts, these writers saw British rule as a fundamental break with the pre-colonial past, but they wrote favorably of that rule. Morris D. Morris, who is typical of this position, saw colonialism, and the "westernization" and "modernization" it initiated, as inaugurating a new era of prosperity in India. The British, in this interpretation, brought peace, order and the rule of law which laid the foundations for nineteenth-century growth.[10]

More recently, as a consequence of new scholarship on eighteenth-century South Asia, nationalist interpretations of colonialism and its impact have come under fresh attack. Prior to this work of revision, the eighteenth century was widely considered to be a period of chaos, anarchy and decline. Historians of Mughal India subscribed to this view, as anarchy was seen as a natural consequence of the decline of empire.[11] For imperialist historians, the narrative of eighteenth-century chaos justified the imposition of British rule. Recent scholarship has rejected both these views and recast the eighteenth century as a period of great dynamism and change. It was a time of commercial expansion, with the establishment of market centers and growth in the use of money.[12] It was also a period of profound political change. States in South Asia were transforming themselves to adjust to the new commercial environment. Attempts were made to develop bureaucracies and to rationalize systems of revenue collection.[13] According to Burton Stein, these were responses to the new military demands of the period, most importantly the rise of standing

---

[8] Romesh Dutt, *The Economic History of India*, vol. I, *Under Early British Rule*, 2nd edn. (2 vols., London, 1906; repr. Delhi, 1990), pp. vi–vii.

[9] For a concise statement, see Amiya Bagchi, *The Political Economy of Underdevelopment* (Cambridge, 1982), pp. 78–82. Also see Amiya Bagchi, "De-industrialization in India in the Nineteenth Century: Some Theoretical Implications," *Journal of Development Studies*, 12 (1976), pp. 135–64.

[10] Morris D. Morris, "Towards a Reinterpretation of Nineteenth-Century Indian Economic History," *Journal of Economic History*, 23 (1963), pp. 606–18.

[11] An eloquent statement may be found in Habib, *Agrarian System*, p. 351.

[12] C. A. Bayly, *Rulers, Townsmen and Bazaars: North Indian Society in the Age of European Expansion, 1770–1870* (Cambridge, 1983); Frank Perlin, "Proto-Industrialization and Pre-Colonial South Asia," *Past and Present*, no. 98 (1983), pp. 30–95.

[13] Frank Perlin, "State Formation Reconsidered", *MAS*, 19 (1985), pp. 415–80.

armies, which placed greater fiscal pressures on states in the subcontinent.[14] In Northern India the combination of expanding commerce and changing states led to the rise of a new "middle class" of merchants, bankers and literate groups who stood between the state and agrarian society.[15] From these revisions of the eighteenth century the origins and nature of colonialism themselves have been reinterpreted.

Colonial rule, according to the revisionists, was not an abrupt break with late pre-colonial India, but in many respects was shaped by that past. First, the dynamism of pre-colonial commerce and economic activity shaped and limited colonial transformation and rule. In other words, Indian society was not formless clay that the British could mold as they wished, but possessed its own centers of power and trajectories of change. These not infrequently led, in Christopher Bayly's words, to the "frustration of Europe."[16] Second, many policies of the early colonial state were not revolutionary, but have been identified as continuations of precolonial practices. The canonical example comes from South India and is that of the Mysore state under the rule of Hyder Ali and Tipu Sultan. The Mysore state's attempts to command a larger share of resources within its territories by settling revenue demands directly with the cultivators themselves were the inspiration, according to Burton Stein, for the English East India Company's *ryotwari* system. Other Mysorean policies, such as the elimination of the *poligars*, who stood between the ruler and the agrarian producer, were also replicated by the Company.[17] Finally, colonial rule, according to the revisionists, was not solely a product of British actions and activities, but was established with the aid and assistance of Indians. In particular, Indian bankers and merchants lent financial support to the English East India Company, which was critical for the expansion of its political power.[18] To sum up, according to the revisionists, colonial rule was in several respects a continuity with the pre-colonial order and was not, contrary to both nationalist and imperialist accounts, a profound break with that past.

[14] Burton Stein, "State Formation and Economy Reconsidered," *MAS*, 19 (1985), pp. 387–413.

[15] Bayly, *Rulers, Townsmen and Bazaars.*

[16] Bayly, *Rulers, Townsmen and Bazaars*, p. 253. The power of late pre-colonial Indian society is also reflected in the vitality into the nineteenth century of many eighteenth-century commercial relations. See David Ludden, "Agrarian Commercialism in Eighteenth Century South India: Evidence from the 1823 Tirunelveli Census," *IESHR*, 25 (1988), pp. 493–519.

[17] Stein, "State Formation and Economy Reconsidered."

[18] Bayly, *Rulers, Townsmen and Bazaars*, chap. 6; Bayly, *Indian Society*, chap. 2; Lakshmi Subramanian, *Indigenous Capital and Imperial Expansion* (Delhi, 1996). Eugene Irschick's dialogical approach to colonial culture is consistent with these emphases on indigenous roots to colonialism. See his *Dialogue and History: Constructing South India, 1795–1895* (Berkeley and Los Angeles, 1994).

As should be evident, these recent contributions to the history of eighteenth-century South Asia have focused largely on the state, commerce and finance. Far less is known about laborers, the framework of production and the conditions of work. From these perspectives, which are those explored in this work, the rise of colonial rule in South India appears far less continuous with the pre-colonial past. In its policies towards laborers the colonial state reveals its European antecedents as colonial authorities drew not upon the customs of South Indian statecraft but upon English practices. As a consequence, under colonial rule laborers in South India came under immense disciplinary authority and in the process came to lose the economic and political power that they had possessed prior to British rule. This decline in the status and position of laborers, although largely unknown and unexplored,[19] led to a decline in wages and living standards from the late eighteenth century. Therefore, poverty in South Asia did not originate with deindustrialization, as an earlier stream of writings argued, but with the profound political reordering which accompanied British rule.

These conclusions have been reached from a study of weavers in eighteenth-century South India, who were the first to feel the disciplinary weight of the colonial state. South India in the eighteenth century was one of the leading manufacturing regions in the world and the cotton textiles of the region were famous worldwide.[20] Merchants in West Africa demanded them in exchange for slaves, the spice marts of Southeast Asia had an enormous appetite for them, and the consumers of Europe created a "calico craze" from the moment they were introduced on a large scale in the late seventeenth century. Well into the eighteenth century cotton textiles were the main point of contact between the English East India Company and South Indians. With the Company's ascendance to political power, this point of contact came increasingly to be focused upon weavers as the English sought to reduce the prices of the textiles. And it

[19] There have been signs in previous studies that the British applied coercion, especially against weavers, but the novelty of British practices has not been apparent as very little is known about the situation of weavers prior to British rule. See for instance D. B. Mitra, *The Cotton Weavers of Bengal* (Calcutta, 1978); Hameeda Hossain, *The Company Weavers of Bengal* (Delhi, 1988); S. Arasaratnam, "Trade and Political Dominion in South India, 1750–1790: Changing British–Indian Relationships," *MAS*, 13 (1979), pp. 19–40 and "Weavers, Merchants and Company: The Handloom Industry in Southeastern India 1750–90," *IESHR*, 17 (1980), pp. 257–81. David Washbrook has pointed to some profound changes with the coming of British rule, but at the same time wants to insist on continuity with the pre-colonial order on the terrain of the logic of capitalism. See his "Progress and Problems: South Asian Economic and Social History c. 1720–1860," *MAS*, 22 (1988), pp. 57–96.

[20] According to estimates, in 1750 South Asia as a whole accounted for 25 percent of the world's manufactures. See Paul Bairoch, "International Industrialization Levels from 1750 to 1980," *Journal of European Economic History*, 11 (1982), p. 296.

was for this reason that weavers were the first to bear the brunt of British power.

Weaving in pre-colonial India, and the trade and production of cotton cloth, cannot be studied in isolation from agriculture, however. The cotton itself was a product of agriculture and much of the textile manu-facturing work – from the cleaning and preparation of the cotton to the spinning of the yarn – was done by agriculturalists. Finally, the com-petitiveness of South Indian textiles on world markets, as I have shown elsewhere, rested upon the enormous productivity of South Indian agri-culture.[21] I argue in this work that the productivity of South Indian agriculture derived from the economic and political power of laborers. In pre-colonial South India, conceptions of the moral order which kings were to create and uphold set stringent limits on the use of force and coercion against laborers, in particular against their freedom to migrate. In the absence of methods by which labor could be disciplined, invest-ment came to be enormously important for attracting and spatially fixing laborers. Agricultural improvement made it possible for political authori-ties and agrarian elites to satisfy producer demands for high and secure incomes. The end result was great dynamism in agriculture and a highly productive agricultural production regime. The Company, and later colonial state, did not share this moral universe. Under British rule state power was used to fix laborers and a powerful incentive for investment in late pre-colonial South India came to be eliminated. The result was stagnation in agriculture. Therefore, colonialism in South India had devastating consequences not only for the standard of living of laborers but also for the dynamism of the economy as a whole.[22]

Although this work takes issue with the revisionist claim for continuity from pre-colonial to colonial India, it finds renewed evidence for the other central revisionist contribution, that of indigenous sources for colonialism. From the perspective of laborers, the indigenous sources of support for British power broaden considerably to include merchants and dominant classes in agriculture. Cloth merchants and *mirasidars* were among the first to grasp the novelty of the Company state and to seek it out to discipline weavers and agrarian producers. This interlocking of colonial authority and dominant Indian groups may explain the resilience of colonialism in India.

---

[21] The price of grain, at this time the primary source of calories for laborers throughout the world, was twice as expensive in Britain as in South India. As a consequence, although real wages may have been higher in South India than in Britain, money wages were far lower. Thus cloth prices were far lower than in Europe. See Parthasarathi, "Rethinking Wages and Competitiveness," *Past and Present*.

[22] This account may be contrasted with the conventional focus on the drain, which is central to nationalist accounts, as the culprit.

The term South India has been used in several ways in historical scholarship. In its broadest usage, it has been employed to refer to the whole of peninsular India.[23] A more limited definition is used in this study and it corresponds closely to that of Burton Stein.[24] South India as defined here refers to peninsular India south of the Raichur Doab on the west and Ganjam on the east. (Modern Kerala has been excluded on the grounds that it had no cotton cultivation and little textile production to speak of.) Strictly speaking, the region is southeastern India, but for the sake of simplicity, it will be referred to as South India.

Stein has adopted this definition of South India on the basis of social, cultural and political features which came to be shared throughout the region. According to Stein:

a portion of the southern peninsula may be demarcated on the basis of persistent and important interrelationships over most of the medieval period. In political, cultural, and social terms all of Tamil country and the southern parts of Karnataka and Andhra may be seen as bound together by the movement of peoples of all kinds – from Brahmans to the most vulnerable of landless folk – cult practices, and shifting patterns of overlordship. The outcome of these diverse interactions was a region which, while complex in language, some aspects of social structure, and cultural forms, was a uniformity which sets it off from other, physically contiguous territories.[25]

This sharing of cultural, social and political features continued into the eighteenth century. To them may be added others drawn from the manufacture of cotton textiles and the circumstances of the manufacturers.

South India, as defined here, encompassed the major weaving centers of peninsular India. These centers supplied local as well as export markets and weavers throughout the region produced very similar sorts of cloth. Although there would have been countless local variations, the many centuries of cultural and social interaction had created broad similarities of taste in the region. The standardization of production would have been even more striking in the case of cloth supplied to the European Companies. The bulk of the cloth demanded by the Companies, as well as European private traders, consisted of only a few varieties. The most important were calicoes of standard dimensions and counts. In the eighteenth century the sort of calico known as *longcloth* was manufactured in coastal villages from Ganjam, in the northeast, to Tinnevelly, at the southern tip of the subcontinent, a distance of some 800 miles. Many of

---

[23] See, for example, K. A. Nilakanta Sastri, *A History of South India* (Delhi, 1966), chap. 2.
[24] Burton Stein, *Peasant State and Society in Medieval South India* (Delhi, 1980), chap. 2.
[25] Stein, *Peasant State*, p. 57.

these villages would also have been populated by the same weaving castes. In addition, throughout the region, weavers received advances from merchants for the financing of production and the contractual terms for these advances were broadly similar.

The interior districts were an integral part of this South Indian region because of their importance as the producing zones for cotton. As chapter 2 will show, the cotton utilized by weavers on the coast came from great distances in the interior of South India. Here were found districts whose ecological and political features led to specialization in the cultivation of cotton and the trade in this product became a crucial link between coastal and interior South India.

South India as defined here was also linked by the movement of textile manufacturers. There is a great deal of evidence that weavers, spinners and other textile specialists had a long history of movement and migration within the region. In the interior, weavers moved about freely between the Baramahal, Mysore and the Ceded Districts and this movement continued well into the eighteenth century. Another important axis of migration was from Andhra to the Tamil country, which may have been part of the larger southward migration of Telugu-speaking peoples which began in the late medieval period.[26]

[26] A striking feature of textile production in eighteenth-century South India was that the knowledge and skills of weavers declined as one moved from north to south. Some of the finest muslins in the world were produced in South India at this time and one of the major centers was Chicacole, close to the northern tip of the South Indian region defined here. By contrast, ordinary calico, a very mediocre quality cloth, was the finest cloth produced in Tinnevelly, at the southern end of the region. Centers of fine cloth manufacture were to be found in the Tamil country, but these were in areas settled by Telugu migrants. The most prominent of these lay in the environs of Kanchipuram and Arni in the northern Tamil country and the muslins manufactured in these places were reputed to rival those of Bengal. The weaving, however, was carried out by Telugu weavers and the spinning by Telugu-speaking *parayars* who used techniques virtually identical to those used in Chicacole. For a description of techniques in Arni see G. Bidie, *Catalogue of Articles of the Madras Presidency and Travancore Collected and Forwarded to the Calcutta International Exhibition of 1883* (Madras, 1883). For Chicacole see E. B. Havell, *Reports on the Arts and Industries of the Madras Presidency Submitted by Mr. E. B. Havell during Years 1885–88* (Madras, 1909), p. 25.

1   Weavers and merchants 1720–1760

It is no easy matter to reconstruct the relationship between weavers and merchants in the early eighteenth century.[1] Much of the material in the European Company records, the major source for the social and economic history of the period, deals largely with the Companies' external trade and their commercial activities in South India. However, the ninety years of documents, from 1670 to 1760, which comprise the English East India Company's Fort St. George and Fort St. David Consultations and upon which this chapter is based, also contain occasional glimpses of local social and economic life. Some of the most valuable insights are found during crises in cloth production. At these times the English interrogated their merchants to understand the reasons for the shortfalls in cloth production and delivery. On occasion, Company servants themselves ventured into the weaving villages. These moments are veritable gold mines for the historian.

In this chapter, the early eighteenth-century sources are supplemented wherever possible with material from later in the century. The later material is much more plentiful and far more detailed, but I have used such evidence carefully. It is not used to introduce new elements to the picture or argument and it is only drawn upon when it is consistent with evidence from the first half of the century. I have used it to fill out the picture – to give it flesh and blood, so to speak. The skeleton, however, has been constructed from early eighteenth-century material.

Much of the material on merchants and weavers in the English East India Company records pertains to weaving villages that supplied cloth to the Company at Madras and Fort St. David (near Pondicherry). This material, which was drawn from a large number of villages dispersed over a wide area of the Tamil country and eastern Andhra, indicates that the relations between merchants and weavers throughout the area were broadly similar. In addition, evidence from other parts of South India –

---

[1] This point has been made by Arasaratnam, "Weavers, Merchants and Company," p. 258.

dating from both the early and late eighteenth century – suggests that these relations were found widely.

The Weavers

Although in recent times South India has become famous for its silks, especially the lush, silk saris of Kanchipuram, these cloths are of recent origin and they began to be manufactured only in the nineteenth century. Before 1800 cotton and wool were the major fibers in South India, with cotton accounting for much of the total textile production. While cotton cloth was manufactured in many parts of South India, the production of woolens (in the form of blankets or cumblies) was concentrated in the cooler and higher elevations of the interior where herds of goat could be reared. This weaving was done largely by *kurumbars* who shepherded the goats, sheared the wool, prepared the yarn and wove the cloth.

The majority of cotton weavers in South India were professional weavers; that is, work at the loom represented their sole source of earnings. However, a small number of South Indians took up weaving in order to supplement earnings from other pursuits. This latter group was largely found in the dry or plains areas of South India and their small numbers suggest that they accounted for only a small fraction of total cloth production.[2] Many were primarily agriculturalists who followed weaving seasonally.[3] For them, weaving not only represented some additional income, but may have also provided some insurance to help weather bad times. As was also the case with spinning, weaving was work which could be taken up even in times of drought when work in agriculture was either unavailable or held out little prospect of success. Others who worked at the loom on occasion included barbers, *chucklers* (cobblers), *dhers* (tanners) and scavengers.[4]

These weavers, being of low skill, tended to produce coarser varieties of cloth. This production supplied the needs of the weaver and his family as well as outside customers who by and large tended to be located in the immediate vicinity of the weaver. Of these part-time or seasonal weavers, the majority worked their looms only upon receiving orders for cloth and

---

[2] In dry areas agriculture was rain-fed, and thus seasonal. This may be contrasted with wet areas where agriculture was based on river water and extensive irrigation systems. For a discussion of this distinction see David Ludden, *Peasant History in South India* (Princeton, 1985), pp. 20–1.

[3] Francis Buchanan, *A Journey from Madras through the Countries of Mysore, Canara and Malabar* (3 vols., London, 1807), vol. I, p. 218.

[4] Bellary District Records, 1804, vol. 398, pp. 191–8, TNA; "Sundry Information about Weaving in Dindigul Taluk, Measurements, and Nature of Dyeing," n.d., Mackenzie Collection, Shelf No. D-3014, Government Oriental Manuscripts Library, Madras University.

at that time they were often given the yarn as well.[5] It was not uncommon – especially in cotton-growing areas – for peasants to obtain their cloth by giving the yarn that had been spun in the household to these weavers, who were then paid for their services. Agriculturalists who engaged in weaving would have produced cloth for the use of their families, but given the small numbers of these peasant-weavers, it must have been rare for South Indian peasants to produce the cloth they wore.

For professional weavers, work at the loom was a full-time occupation. It is this group which is the focus of this work. These artisans produced a wide variety of cloths for both local and long-distance markets, ranging from the coarse counts that clothed the South Indian poor to the very fine muslins of Arni which in the nineteenth century were compared favorably with the more famous muslins of Dacca. The majority of these full-time weavers were drawn from the four main weaving castes in South India: the *kaikolar, devanga, sale* and *seniyar.* Although the majority of men in these caste groups followed the occupation of weaving, there were no-table exceptions. Kaikolars in the Baramahal, for example, were also employed as merchants and as agriculturalists.[6] Similarly, all professional weavers were not drawn from only these four castes. The finest weavers in the Baramahal, one of the largest weaving centers in South India, were a group of "untouchables" – *manniwars.* They were reputed to weave the finest cloth in the district.[7]

Although information on loom technology in South India is not abundant, we do know that a variety of looms were to be found. Vertical looms were distributed quite widely and used for the production of carpets. Draw looms, with their elaborate apparatus of weaver working in conjunction with a "drawboy," were utilized in the manufacture of fancy patterned cloths. However, the loom which easily accounted for the bulk of cloth production, and was therefore the workhorse in South Indian weaving, was the pit loom.[8]

The pit loom is a very simple horizontal loom, but several of its features made it ideal for South Indian conditions. First, weavers in South India were often on the move and the pit loom made this possible. The loom itself was relatively light, simply a few pieces of wood tied together, and it could easily be disassembled, transported and reassembled. According to

[5] "Sundry Information about Weaving in Dindigul Taluk, Measurements, and Nature of Dyeing," Mackenzie Collection, Shelf No. D-3014.
[6] English East India Company, *The Baramahal Records,* Section III: *Inhabitants* (Madras, 1907).
[7] English East India Company, *The Baramahal Records,* Section VII: *Imposts* (Madras, 1920), p. 27.
[8] Vijaya Ramaswamy, "Notes on Textile Technology in Medieval India with Special Reference to the South," *IESHR,* 17 (1980), pp. 227–41.

Abbé Dubois, who resided in South India in the late eighteenth and early nineteenth centuries, "It is by no means a rare sight to see one of these weavers changing his abode, and carrying on his back all that is necessary for setting to work the moment he arrives at his new home."[9] Second, the hole under the loom where the weaver sat and worked the pedals – the pit – created the proper humidity for cotton weaving. Cotton weaving is much better performed in humid conditions which prevent the yarn from becoming brittle and snapping. Finally, the pit loom provided a comfortable seating posture for the weaver.[10] In the early nineteenth century an English East India Company servant noted that two types of pit looms were used in South India and that "the same loom which weaves the coarsest cloth cannot be used in the construction of the finer sorts." No additional details are given, however.[11]

The pit loom and other tools accounted for only a small fraction of the total capital needed in weaving. According to a Company servant, these items could be obtained for five or six pagodas, a sum which was the equivalent of about three months' earnings for a weaver of middling quality cloth.[12] Such a figure is consistent with the simplicity of both the loom and the tools used in ancillary activities. Warping, for instance, was done with sticks stuck into the ground and reeling was done with a simple wooden flywheel. The bulk of the capital in weaving went to the purchase of materials, most importantly yarn which was the single largest expenditure in cloth production.

Most weavers purchased their yarn with funds that they received from cloth merchants as an advance, but on occasion yarn merchants and head weavers were known to supply such money. In the early eighteenth century there is no evidence that temples or kings – both of which for several centuries had been important sources of capital in the South Indian economy – were engaged in advancing money to weavers. However, later in the century, a number of South Indian states entered the cloth trade and provided advances to weavers in order to finance production.

The servants of the English East India Company argued that weavers were reliant upon merchant advances because they were too poor to purchase yarn for themselves.[13] I have shown elsewhere that the poverty of weavers was a construction of European observers and that it is not supported by evidence on weaver incomes.[14] It is likely that many weavers

---

[9] Abbé J. A. Dubois, *Hindu Manners, Customs and Ceremonies*, trans. Henry K. Beauchamp, 3rd edn. (Oxford, 1924), p. 36.
[10] I am indebted to Shakeb Afseh for the last two observations.
[11] Tinnevelly Collectorate Records, 1811, vol. 3587, pp. 428–37, TNA.
[12] Chingleput Collectorate Records, 1793, vol. 445, p. 54, TNA.
[13] *FSGDC*, 1672–8, p. 74; *FSGDC*, 1693, p. 100.
[14] See my "Rethinking Wages and Competitiveness."

possessed the funds to work as independent producers and finance production for themselves, but preferred to receive advances from merchants. By entering into such a relationship, weavers forced merchants to
bear some of the risks associated with cloth production. These risks
included uncertainties in the prices of yarn and cloth, shortages of yarn,
droughts and localized shortfalls of grain. A merchant who made an
advance to a weaver had to share the burden of losses resulting from
economic fluctuations and this gave weavers an enormous measure of
security. Such off-loading of risk through creating ties of dependence was
found in many areas of economic life in pre-colonial South India and was
one of its central features.[15]

The weaver household

About one-third of the merchant advance went to the weaver as payment
for manufacturing a piece of cloth. Weavers spent much of this on food
and other necessities for themselves and their families, but a small
amount was used for the maintenance of looms and tools. The loom
strings, which had to be replaced every two months, represented the
costliest item of maintenance.[16] The remainder of the advance was used
to purchase materials. Of these, yarn was the major expense, but small
sums were also needed to purchase pieces of cloth and small quantities of
rice and oil for sizing the warp.

While the weaver worked his loom, his wife and children were typically
hard at work preparing the yarn for the next piece. Weavers who had
small families had to hire laborers ("coolies") to do this preparatory
work, which reduced the income of the weaver and his household. This
led a late eighteenth-century Company servant to remark that large
families yielded higher incomes for weavers.[17] The preparation of the yarn
consisted of warping, sizing and readying the bobbins for the shuttle. The
warping and sizing were usually done outdoors under the shade of trees,
but the weaving itself was done inside the weaver's house where light was
provided by a small hole in the wall.[18]

[15] The off-loading of risk was especially important in agriculture where agrarian elites and
revenue and political authorities shouldered burdens through guarantees of minimum
incomes to producers and advances (*taccavi*) for financing production and agricultural
improvement. These are discussed in the following chapter.
[16] South Arcot Collectorate Records, Cuddalore Consultations, 1779, vol. 81, pp. 206–7,
TNA.
[17] South Arcot Collectorate Records, Cuddalore Consultations, 1779, vol. 81, pp. 206–7,
TNA. Godavari District Records, 1803, vol. 832, p. 412–26, APSA. It was reported that
longcloth required seven or eight people to prepare the thread: MPP, 1791, vol. P/241/
26, p. 2836, OIOC.
[18] The Paterson Diaries, vol. 9, p. 137, OIOC; MPP, 1791, vol. P/241/26, pp. 2791–3,

For most counts of cloth the preparation of the yarn took as many days as the weaving itself.[19] For this reason it would have been difficult for a weaver to earn a sufficient income by producing a piece, selling it and then using the proceeds to purchase yarn for the next round of production. Therefore, to be able to maintain sufficient earnings, a weaver had to always have on hand enough yarn for two pieces of cloth so that weaving and yarn preparation could take place simultaneously. In order to do this, weavers required a sizable advance. In 1768 weavers who produced ordinary varieties of longcloth earned two pagodas a month, a sum which could purchase about 250 pounds of rice. The same weavers always had on hand at minimum an advance of four pagodas, but often far more.[20]

Boys were trained in the art of weaving within the household and family. The first step in the long training process was to assist in the preparation of the yarn, which introduced a young boy to the proper techniques for handling yarn. Preparing the bobbins was especially valuable as it was an opportunity for a young child to learn how to reconnect the yarn when it broke. From here the boy would have progressed to more difficult tasks, culminating with weaving itself. A Company servant observed that in the homes of muslin weavers in the *jagir* (Chingleput), teenage boys developed their skills by weaving turbans.[21] The narrow width of turbans (they were among the narrowest cloths manufactured in South India) may have made them ideal cloths on which to learn the proper techniques for throwing the shuttle and beating the weft.

The weavers' reputation for easy mobility suggests that they led simple lives and had few possessions. A typical weaver's house was constructed with mud walls and a thatched roof.[22] In 1698 and 1768 weavers who migrated to Company settlements received five pagodas for the construction of such a dwelling.[23] This figure may be contrasted with the cost of merchants' houses. A Company *kanakkapillai* (accountant) in Madras sold his house in 1714 for 397 pagodas.[24] In 1716 the house of a Company merchant at Fort St. David was estimated to be worth 100 pagodas.[25] The weavers' diet was also simple and consisted chiefly of grain.

OIOC; Edgar Thurston, *Monograph on the Silk Fabric Industry of the Madras Presidency* (Madras, 1899), p. 12.

[19] MPP, 1790, vol. P/241/16, pp. 340–1, OIOC.
[20] South Arcot Collectorate Records, Cuddalore Consultations, 1768, vol. 66, pp. 211–12, TNA.
[21] MPP, 1791, vol. P/241/26, p. 2833, OIOC.
[22] According to Abbé Dubois, weavers worked in "thatched huts built of mud, twenty to thirty feet long by seven or eight feet broad." See his *Hindu Manners*, p. 81. Some of the highly skilled and wealthier, and thus more sedentary, muslin weavers of Kanchipuram and surrounding towns lived in houses constructed from stone and roofed with tiles.
[23] FSGDC, 1698, p. 121; South Arcot Collectorate Records, Cuddalore Consultations, 1769, vol. 67, p. 58, TNA.
[24] FSGDC, 1714, p. 87.   [25] FSGDC, 1716, p. 98.

In very prosperous times weavers on the coast may have eaten rice, and even then most likely the cheaper grades, but much of the time, and certainly in times of trouble, the grains of choice for weavers were less expensive millets. In the dry areas of interior South India, however, millets were the staple grain for weavers as well as much of the population as a whole.

Table 1.1 contains information on food consumption by caste or occupation for the inhabitants of the Baramahal (a dry district) in the late eighteenth century. According to this information, brahmins were easily the best fed group in the Baramahal. They consumed a disproportionate share of many food items, especially the highly prized luxury foods, and the quantity, variety and richness of their diets are striking. Brahmins made up only 6.7 percent of the sample, but they consumed 25 percent of the rice, 55 percent of the wheat, and 21.2 percent of the *ghee* and *gingelly* (sesame) oil. The brahmin diet was also superior to those of merchants and trading groups who, however, possessed diets which were far richer and more varied than those of laboring groups.

Weavers were the most prosperous of the laboring groups represented in the table. They were able to afford more rice, pulses and spices than those from other occupations and they were even in a position to purchase a few luxury items such as ghee. It is likely that weavers obtained these items, as well as the others contained in table 1.1, from markets and shops, but they were also supplemented with the produce of their own gardens which yielded, in the words of an English Company servant, "a few brinjalls chillies, etc. vegetables which they chiefly live upon."[26] The wives and children of weavers were probably in charge of these patches as weavers had to preserve the suppleness of their hands and fingers for their work at the loom. Weavers did agricultural and other hard physical labor only when times were desperate. Weavers were also fond of *betel* and tobacco and these they claimed were essential for them to carry on their work. According to a petition from the weavers and painters of Madras: "if we have not or can't be permitted by reason of a hurry of Business which sometimes happens to get our victuals We can chearfully bear it if we have but Beetle and Tobacco."[27] When purchasing these items weavers were extremely sensitive to their prices. In 1701 and 1733 many weavers left Fort St. David, where there were heavy taxes on both, and settled at French and Dutch factories where these items could be obtained free of all taxes.[28]

It has been suggested that from the late medieval period weavers were polarized into master weavers, who owned many looms, and cooly

[26] South Arcot Collectorate Records, 1803, vol. 111, pp. 163–6, TNA.
[27] *FSGDC*, 1735, p. 105.
[28] *FSDC*, 1701, p. 3; *FSGDC*, 1733, pp. 184–5.

Table 1.1. *Food consumption in the Baramahal by occupational group, 1797 (figures represent percentage of each item)*

	Occupational group										
	Brahmins	Merchants or marwaris	Muslims	Labbays (traders)	Barbers and washermen	Dhair and chamar	Potmakers and burdar	Kurumbars (shepherds)	Oddars and kurchivars (tank diggers)	Julaha and kaikolars (weavers)	Inhabitants (agriculturalists?)
Proportion of sample	6.7	6.0	3.3	5.3	1.3	2.7	2.0	4.0	0.7	4.7	63.3
Rice	25	15	7.3	6.7	0.6	0.8	0.7	1.2	0.2	2.9	39.6
Ragi and bajra	2.1	3.8	2.3	5.0	1.5	3.1	2.3	4.7	0.8	5.1	69.3
Salt	7.5	6.2	4.4	8.8	1.9	2.5	2.5	4.4	0.6	3.8	57.5
Chilies	7.5	3.8	3.1	6.2	0.9	1.6	1.6	3.1	0.3	1.2	69.4
Tamarind	18	7.5	5.0	7.5	0.6	0.9	0.6	1.2	0.3	1.2	57.5
Wheat	55	25	10	10	0	0	0	0	0	0	0
Urad	18	8.8	3.8	3.8	0	0	0	0	0	3.8	62.5
Mung	55	25	7.5	3.8	0	0	0	0	0	8.8	0
Chana	31	50	6.2	0	0	0	0	0	0	6.2	6.2
Coriander	12	6.2	12	12	6.2	0	6.2	6.2	6.2	6.2	25.0
Pepper	12	6.2	6.2	12	0	0	0	0	0	6.2	56.2
Fenugreek	19	6.2	6.2	6.2	0	0	0	0	0	6.2	50.0
Turmeric	12	6.2	3.1	6.2	1.6	1.6	1.6	1.6	1.6	1.6	62.5
Onions	0	8.1	5.6	8.1	1.9	3.8	2.5	5.6	1.2	5.6	57.5
Garlic	0	11	5.0	11	1.2	2.5	1.2	2.5	1.2	3.8	60.0
Jaggery	12	6.2	3.1	3.8	0.6	1.2	0.6	1.2	0.3	1.2	64.1
Tar-gur	0	8.3	2.1	3.3	0.4	1.7	1.2	2.5	0.4	3.3	76.7
Ghee	21	11	10	10	0	0	0	0	0	4.3	43.8
Sesame oil	21	11	4.3	4.3	1.2	3.1	1.2	0.6	3.1	6.2	43.8
Betel nut	10	10	3.1	5.0	0.6	0.6	0.6	1.2	0.6	3.8	64.4
Betel leaf	8.8	8.8	3.8	5.0	0.6	0.6	0.6	1.2	0.3	3.8	66.6
Cumin	12	6.2	12	12	6.2	0	6.2	6.2	0	6.2	25.0
Coconut	16	12	3.1	6.2	3.1	3.1	3.1	6.2	3.1	6.2	37.5
Tobacco	1.2	5.6	2.8	4.4	1.2	1.9	1.6	2.8	0.6	2.8	75.0
Bhang	0	12	6.2	6.2	3.1	3.1	1.6	3.1	1.6	6.2	56.2

Reading the table: The figures for food consumption for each occupational group are read down each column and must be understood relative to the proportion of that group in the sample as a whole. For example, brahmins are 6.7% of the sample, but they consume 25% of the total rice consumed by the sample, 2.1% of the total *ragi* and *bajra* consumed, etc. The proportion of each group in the sample is not necessarily reflective of their share in the population.

Source: English East India Company, *The Baramahal Records*, Section IV: *Products* (Madras, 1912), pp. 107–8.

weavers, who worked these looms as wage laborers.[29] These claims have been supported with evidence from several temple inscriptions. It has been further argued that master weavers continued to operate in the seventeenth and eighteenth centuries and actually became more powerful and exerted greater control over their cooly weavers. Although I cannot address the arguments for the medieval period, I have found no support for the existence of master weavers in the eighteenth century and the evidence I have come across suggests that nearly all weavers owned their looms.[30] In 1771 the English conducted a detailed loom survey of weaving villages in Chingleput. The data show that 1,572 (83.4 percent) of weavers owned one loom; 272 (14.4 percent) owned two looms; 34 (1.8 percent) owned three looms; 6 (0.3 percent) owned four looms; and one household owned nine looms.[31] These figures show that a large majority of weavers owned one loom and that an overwhelming number (98 percent) owned only one or two looms.

The main piece of evidence for the existence of master weavers in post-medieval South India comes from a Dutch East India Company census of households and looms in five weaving villages in late seventeenth-century Northern Coromandel. However, these data are highly aggregated and give the total number of households and the total number of looms in each village. The ratio of weaving households to looms is the same for all five villages – three to four – which suggests that these numbers were estimates and not actual enumerations. Nevertheless, they do indicate that some weaving households must have owned more than one loom and from this the existence of master weavers has been inferred. However, such a conclusion should not be reached too hastily. The structure of weaver families and households must be considered as well. The predominance of one loom households in the Chingleput survey suggests that the typical weaver household was a nuclear family, but other family structures were also to be found among weavers in South India. For example, in the late eighteenth century an English Company servant came upon a weaving household in the Northern Sarkars which owned half a dozen looms. It was not the household of a master weaver, however, but

[29] Vijaya Ramaswamy, "The Genesis and Historical Role of the Masterweavers in South Indian Textile Production," *Journal of the Economic and Social History of the Orient*, 28 (1985), pp. 294–325.
[30] Another problem with Vijaya Ramaswamy's work is that she uses the terms master weaver, head weaver and principal weaver interchangeably. The terms head weaver and principal weaver are found in the English records. Neither can be equated with Vijaya Ramaswamy's category of master weaver. I have nowhere in the English records come across the term master weaver and I do not believe it was used by the English. As will be discussed later in this chapter, head weaver is a literal translation of a term found in Tamil and Telugu.
[31] MPP, 1771, vol. 106B, pp. 1062–130, TNA.

that of a weaver, his sons and a nephew who were all weavers. Aggregate figures do not capture such variations in weaver family structures.

The rhythms of weaving

Weaving in South India was ruled by rhythms. Many aspects of the working lives of weavers – including the distribution of work and leisure over the year, the pace and intensity of work and the length of the working day – followed set, seasonal patterns. It is likely that weavers rose at dawn in order to work in the cool and greater humidity of the early morning. Early rising may explain why weavers were "according to established custom" in the habit of being "two or three hours in the day idle."[32] There is evidence that weavers stepped up the pace of work at their looms at times of heavy demand. In 1723, in response to English Company complaints about the quality of the cloth, the merchant suppliers said:

the very large demand lately made has occasion'd the running the Cloth off the Loom so fast 'tis not practicable to keep them justly to the goodness of the muster. That they can always provide the quantity and much more, but that when they do so they cannot pretend to engage for the Goodness, Since it is certain that the People working in a hurry must be more careless and negligent than when they have more time; so that when this place provided 1000 Bales per annum it was very easy to keep them up to the Musters, but that now the demand is encreas'd to four times that quantity it is not reasonable to expect it should be equal in goodness.[33]

Sacrificing quality and intensifying the pace of work was also a way in which the growing demand for cloth in the seventeenth and eighteenth centuries was satisfied.

The climate in South India imposed limits on the working year for weavers. During the rainy season, between October and December in South India but with some geographical variation, weaving came to a standstill for about a month.[34] In Kongunad such a work schedule is reflected in the fact that festivals for the left-hand caste, of which weavers were an integral part, were concentrated in the months of the monsoon.[35] In Masulipatnam, as well, textile manufacturers celebrated a number of festivals at the monsoon period.[36] During the rains, the yarn preparation,

[32] South Arcot Collectorate Records, Cuddalore Consultations, 1772, vol. 71, p. 134, TNA.
[33] FSGDC, 1723, pp. 91–2.
[34] MPP, 1792, vol. P/241/30, pp. 196–201, OIOC.
[35] The relationship between work and ritual calendars in Kongunad is discussed at greater detail in the next chapter.
[36] Masulipatnam District Records, Commercial Consultations, 1790, vol. 2840, p. 12, APSA.

which was done outdoors, could not be performed. However, the heavy rains of the northeast monsoon penetrated even inside houses and kept weavers from their looms. In 1791 an English Company servant reported that weavers in the jagir (Chingleput) were unable to work during the monsoon because their "looms filled with water." This was no doubt a reference to the loom pit.[37] There were also other features of the South Indian climate that imposed limits on weaving. In the jagir the best months for weaving were October and December through March since there were no land winds in those months. During the rest of the year it was not uncommon for severe winds to break the warp yarns that were fixed in the loom. Weavers tied knots to reconnect the broken ends, which diminished the quality of the cloth. Company servants observed similar winds in Nellore.[38]

The annual work schedule for weavers was also determined by the demand for cloth, which was not distributed evenly through the year. In South India, as in Europe, it is likely that much of the work of weaving was performed close to the times when cloth had to be delivered.[39] Factors such as shipping schedules and sailing times determined the timing of demand for export markets and these in the Indian Ocean were dependent upon the monsoon winds.[40] Traditionally, Asian shipping in the Indian Ocean set sail from the southeastern Indian coast for Southeast Asia between early September and mid-October. European shipping, however, followed the September sailing time, but also added a second departure between January and March. Therefore, the entry of Europeans into the Indian Ocean may have lengthened the weaving season by creating another peak period of weaving to fill the departing European ships.

South Indian festivals, religious holidays and ritual activities set the calendar for local demand. The summer months, especially May and June, would have been a period of heavy demand. In part this was due to the concentration of weddings in these months. Although the wedding season extended from January 15 to July 15, May and June were the peak months as there was a lull in agriculture.[41] Cloth, and in abundant supplies, was absolutely essential at weddings for the numerous prestations which accompanied the ceremony and the run up to the wedding season would have undoubtedly kept many a weaver hard at work at his

---

[37] MPP, 1792, vol. P/241/30, p. 345, OIOC.
[38] MPP, 1791, vol. P/241/26, p. 2832, OIOC.
[39] For the unevenness of production in Europe see E. P. Thompson, "Time, Work-Discipline and Industrial Capitalism," *Past and Present*, no. 38 (1967), pp. 56–97.
[40] Sanjay Subrahmanyam, *The Political Economy of Commerce: Southern India, 1500–1650* (Cambridge, 1990), pp. 48–9.
[41] Dubois, *Hindu Manners*, pp. 213–14 and 217.

loom. In addition, the renewal of annual contracts in the rice-growing valleys, at which time a gift of cloth was made, took place in late June and early July. This would have represented an additional source of demand at the time of wedding activity. A second major period for local cloth demand was in late September and early October during the festival of *Dasara*. The presentation of new cloth was essential to the celebration of this major holiday.[42]

Weavers had a variety of strategies for coping with disruptions in demand. In 1782 the English had no money to finance cloth production in Vizagapatnam, which led many of the poorer weavers to "quit their native villages to seek livelyhood in distant countries by following occupations foreign to the one they brought upon."[43] This passage gives no information on the occupations followed by these weavers, but evidence suggests that it was common for weavers at times of low cloth demand to take up soldiering. By the late eighteenth century this created a serious shortage of weavers and the English Company prohibited weavers from joining its armies.[44] At times of crisis weavers also took to producing coarser varieties of cloth, largely for local markets. The returns were lower and the credit terms were probably more stringent for these inferior fabrics, but the demand was more reliable.[45] Movement in the opposite direction, up the quality ladder, was far rarer. The additional skill necessary to move up even one rung in quality was substantial, which limited entry into the ranks of the more highly skilled weavers.

The merchants

Of the cloth merchants who advanced funds to weavers for the production of cloth, the most extensive and detailed information is available for those who acted as intermediaries to the European Companies. Many merchants competed for the privilege of supplying cloth to these Companies as this position as "Company merchant" brought with it major political and economic benefits.[46] In the case of the English East India Company, merchants who sought this position were required to possess extensive knowledge of the major weaving centers as well as security or

[42] Dubois, *Hindu Manners*, p. 569. *Deepavali* was also celebrated shortly after Dasara and cloth may have played an important role in that festival as well.
[43] MPP, 1782, vol. P/240/55, p. 826, OIOC.
[44] MPP, 1786, vol. P/240/64, p. 1858, OIOC; MPP, 1786, vol. P/240/65, pp. 2245–52, OIOC.
[45] *FSGDC*, 1693, p. 119; *FSGDC*, 1694. p. 122; *FSDC*, 1743, pp. 22–3. Also see South Arcot Collectorate Records, Cuddalore Consultations, 1786, vol. 86, pp. 12–13, TNA.
[46] This section is an introduction to the merchants and cloth traders who supplied cloth to the English East India Company. A more detailed discussion of merchants and their position in the South Indian political economy appears in chapter 5.

standing in the community of merchants and bankers. The latter served as collateral for the money the Company advanced to their merchants for the purchase of cloth.[47] The merchants who satisfied these criteria were a diverse group and they came from a variety of social and economic backgrounds. In Northern Coromandel, the merchants were mainly Telugu speakers. Telugu speakers were also present in Madras and Fort St. David, but south of the Palar River, Tamil merchants were more numerous. In the early eighteenth century, even a Gujarati merchant engaged to provide cloth at Madras. Many of these merchants came from the traditional South Indian mercantile castes, *komaties* and *chetties*, but there were also merchants from other backgrounds. There were even a few weavers who rose to the status of merchants. Merchants were also drawn from both sides of the great social divide in South India, the right- and left-hand castes.[48]

Merchants also varied widely in the size of their capital and the scale of their commercial activities. Some Company merchants ran large mercantile empires and a few who supplied cloth at Madras owned ships and were themselves involved in the cloth trade to Southeast Asia. However, the majority of Company merchants ran small operations. The merchants of Masulipatnam and Madras in general were more substantial men, which was reflected in their connections to the broader trading world of the Indian Ocean, than were merchants to the north or south of these places. The Masulipatnam and Madras merchants, for instance, were able to find buyers for the broadcloth imported by the English. This cloth was very expensive and beyond the reach of all but the richest in South India. A major market for English broadcloth was the court in the kingdom of Golconda, but even after the fall of Golconda, the Madras merchants were able to vend these textiles as well as other European goods. The Fort St. David merchants, by contrast, were never able to find a market for these luxury goods.[49] There were also substantial differences in the quantity of cloth that merchants could supply to the Company. These differences are reflected in the structure of Company joint-stocks, which were associations formed by groups of merchants to supply cloth. In 1680 the shares in a newly formed joint-stock were distributed among sixty-seven merchants at Fort St. George, but two merchants held 25 percent of the shares, and supplied a quarter of the

[47] *FSGDC*, 1700, p. 61.
[48] S. Arasaratnam, *Merchants, Companies and Commerce on the Coromandel Coast* (Delhi, 1986), pp. 215–20. Also see *FSGDC*, 1694, p. 123; *FSGDC*, 1707, p. 54; *FSGDC*, 1717, p. 7; *FSGDC*, 1718, p. 27. For a discussion of the right- and left-hand divide, see also Arjun Appadurai, "Right and Left Hand Castes in South India," *IESHR*, 11 (1974), pp. 216–59.
[49] *FSGDC*, 1712, p. 91; *FSDC*, 1740, p. 69.

cloth investment, and forty-three merchants held only 31 percent of the total shares.[50]

Relations between merchants and weavers

The belief that laborers in pre-colonial South Asia were the victims of relentless oppression by their political and economic superiors is deep-seated in historical consciousness. It is a commonplace image that state authorities taxed laborers with impunity, that merchants cheated them at every turn and that laborers were defenseless against these depredations.[51] Such views gave rise to the conclusion that weavers in eighteenth-century India were poverty-stricken and helpless in their dealings with merchants and kings.[52] However, relations between weavers and merchants in eighteenth-century South India bear little resemblance to this widely accepted picture. Far from being oppressed and defenseless, what follows shows that weavers were in a very strong and secure position within the South Indian economic and political order. In many respects, the position of South Indian weavers was superior to that of their counterparts in England.[53]

The strong position of weavers was in part a product of the very high demand for South Indian cloth, which translated into very high demand for the services of weavers. This, in turn, placed them in a powerful bargaining position. However, these market conditions cannot fully account for the position of weavers. As we shall see shortly, after 1770, although cloth demand remained buoyant, the power of weavers diminished considerably. The decline in weaver power at the close of the eighteenth century was a result of the social and political changes which accompanied the rise of British rule in South India. Therefore, the powerful position of weavers was due not simply to the market but to the social and political order in pre-colonial South India.

Cloth merchants obtained their goods by making advances of money to weavers. This system satisfied the needs of both parties. Weavers were supplied with working capital, and along with it protection from market fluctuations, and merchants obtained cloth of the proper quality and in the appropriate quantity. It was extremely difficult, and perhaps even impossible, for a merchant to meet the requirements of distant markets, and especially those of European Companies, by buying in country

---

[50] *FSGDC*, 1680–81, pp. 48–9. For a similar breakdown also see *FSGDC*, 1698, p. 86.
[51] This despotic view of the state is explored in greater detail in chapter 5.
[52] See Chaudhuri, *Trading World*, p. 274 and Raychaudhuri, "The Mid-Eighteenth-Century Background," pp. 17 and 33.
[53] See my "Rethinking Wages and Competitiveness."

markets and fairs. Such markets were suited to local needs, but were unable to supply cloth in sufficient quantity or of proper quality for the highly specific demands of various export markets.[54] Many cloth merchants, especially those who supplied the European Companies, resided in port towns along the coast and made advances and procured cloth through a network of agents or brokers in the major weaving centers.[55]

When the advance was made an oral contract was struck between the weaver and the merchant or his broker.[56] This contract specified the size of the advance, the price and quality of the cloth and its date of delivery. In the opinion of the English East India Company's servants, the price of cloth was determined in some automatic fashion by the prices of cotton and rice. These servants assumed that the incomes of weavers were fixed by custom and that the price of cotton set the cost of materials, most importantly yarn, and that the price of rice determined the earnings of the weaver.[57] My findings suggest that the weavers' incomes were not fixed, but were determined by a process of bargaining over cloth prices. The results of this bargaining process also determined the profits of the merchant. From this perspective, increases in cloth prices, which through much of the eighteenth century accompanied increases in cotton and rice prices, were not automatic, but the product of successful weaver efforts to push up prices to compensate for their higher costs. Merchants, of course, resisted these weaver attempts to pass on costs.

The material given in table 1.2 provides evidence that the price of rice was not the determinant of weaver incomes. The table has been constructed from detailed surveys of costs in cloth manufacturing that were conducted by the English East India Company in 1790. The first two columns of the table report the income received by weavers for manufacturing several counts of longcloth at Ingeram and Madapollam, two English factories in the Northern Sarkars. The third column gives for each count the ratio of the weavers' incomes at the two factories. If the incomes of weavers were determined by the price of rice, this ratio should be the same for each count of cloth and should simply be the ratio of rice prices at the two factories. These ratios, however, range widely from 0.97 to 1.24, which indicates that the price of rice alone did not determine the incomes of weavers. Rather, as the records of the English East India Company themselves suggest, the incomes of weavers were determined

[54] Chaudhuri, *Trading World*, pp. 254–5.
[55] *FSGDC*, 1675, p. 73; *FSGDC*, 1688, pp. 130–1; *FSGDC*, 1693, p. 119.
[56] The reluctance of weavers in Salem to enter into written contracts with the East India Company suggests that the typical contract was oral. See MPP, 1792, vol. P/241/34, pp. 2611–32, OIOC.
[57] This formulation is also found in Arasaratnam, "Weavers, Merchants and Company," p. 269 and Chaudhuri, *Trading World*, pp. 265–7.

Table 1.2. *Returns to weavers for longcloth, 1790*

Punjam	Returns to weavers			Returns to merchants	
	Ingeram	Madapollam	Ratio	Ingeram	Madapollam
14	0,12,7	0,11,65	1.02	0,4,40	0,6,60
16	0,20,47	0,19,10	1.08	0,4,4	0,7,54
18	0,28,10	0,23,50	1.19	0,4,58	0,8,16
22	1,0,0	1,1,10	0.97	0,7,16	0,7,74
24	1,1,55	0,33,60	1.12	0,8,8	0,8,31
36	4,15,25	3,20,65	1.24	1,27,0	1,27,16

Note: Returns are given in pagodas, fanams, cash.
1 pagoda = 36 fanams and 1 fanam = 80 cash.
Ratio = (returns to weaving at Ingeram)/(returns to weaving at Madapollam).
Source: MPP, 1790, vol. P/241/16, pp. 343-4, OIOC.

by bargaining between merchants and weavers and the relative power of the two parties.

The profit the merchant received for each count of cloth, which is also given in table 1.2, further indicates that there was a process of bargaining. The profit to the merchant varied widely between the two factories, suggesting that these rested on the success or failure of merchant negotiating power. In fact, the profit of the merchant was the product of two bargains over price. The first took place between merchants and the English East India Company and the second between merchants and weavers. The difference between these two prices was profit to merchants. Or to put it more accurately, the price merchants negotiated with weavers determined the potential size of their profits. To achieve this potential, however, merchants had to enforce the conditions of their contracts with weavers, which was no easy matter. The form of contracts combined with fluctuations and uncertainties in South Indian economic life to make it extremely difficult for merchants to compel weavers to abide by their agreements. In particular, merchants had enormous difficulties enforcing quality standards and collecting outstanding weaver debts. These problems were persistent and they made merchant profits at best precarious and at worst altogether nonexistent.[58]

---

[58] In contrast to K. N. Chaudhuri who thought the advance system "divided the financial risks equally between the producer and the distributor," these problems suggest that the distributor shouldered a greater burden of the risk. See Chaudhuri, *Trading World*, p. 257, n. 69.

The cloth quality problem

The merchant advance typically consisted of money. With these funds weavers purchased materials, most importantly yarn.[59] This arrangement gave weavers enormous power to select the yarn that they used in their cloth and, therefore, over the quality of the final product. Their control over yarn purchases also gave weavers the power to set their earnings and weavers could easily increase their incomes by simply spending less on yarn. This could take the form of using less yarn per piece, which resulted in pieces which were short of the proper measure or pieces which were thin and loosely woven. Or weavers could buy less expensive counts of yarn which yielded poor-quality, coarse cloth. In both cases, weaver incomes were further swelled by the fact that poor-quality cloth took less time to weave. To maintain their profits, merchants had to detect such deficiencies in quality and then reduce the price given to the weaver, but neither of these was easily done in the late pre-colonial South Indian context.

Weavers developed sophisticated schemes to conceal defects in their cloth. A common weaver practice, judging from the frequency of English complaints, was to mix both good and poor yarns in a single piece of cloth. At times weavers had no choice about the matter as the proper yarn could not always be found in sufficient quantities. However, the prevalence of the practice suggests that weavers also deliberately substituted coarse yarns for fine in order to increase their earnings. In addition, the different quality yarns were not mixed randomly within a piece, but with great forethought and planning to minimize the chances of detection. This entailed carefully locating the finer yarns in the outside folds of the cloth, which were more visible and easier to inspect. The coarser yarns were then placed in the inside folds, which were less accessible and less likely to be examined by a merchant or his brokers.[60] This scheme was most effective with longcloth which, as its name indicates, was extremely long, usually running to 34 to 36 yards in length. Its great size made it costly and laborious to unfold and properly examine several thousand pieces.

Weavers also possessed other subterfuges to trick the sorters who were in charge of inspecting their cloth. A particularly effective one was to cover thin or defective areas with *congee* (rice starch), oil or other materials, which, according to the Cuddalore Council, even "deceive the best sorters."[61] Weavers also used cow dung, which blended in with the

---

[59] There were a very few exceptions to this general rule and these are taken up in subsequent pages.
[60] *FSGDC*, 1693, p. 46; MPP, 1762, vol. P/240/20, pp. 174–5, OIOC.
[61] South Arcot Collectorate Records, 1764, vol. 161, pp. 14–15, TNA.

brown color of unbleached cloth, to conceal holes or areas that had been darned. These defects would be discovered only months later after the cloth had been bleached and washed. By then the weaver was long forgotten and the washerman blamed for the holes which had suddenly appeared in the cloth.

Although it was no easy matter for merchants to detect poor-quality cloth, this in many ways was only the beginning of the quality battle with weavers. The identification of poor quality had to be followed by the taking of deductions, or abatements, in the price given to the weaver, but weavers were in a powerful position to resist such abatements. Weavers were protected by the customs of the contracting system which gave them valuable privileges and rights. With these, weavers were able to rebuff merchant demands for lower prices. These weaver privileges were a product of fundamental asymmetries in the weaver–merchant contract.

Asymmetries of contract

Contracts in South India extended to weavers several privileges which merchants were denied. The most important was the prerogative to cancel a contract, which weavers could do at any time by refunding the advance to the merchant. In 1701, for example, merchants supplying the English East India Company contracted with large numbers of weavers and advanced the sum of five pagodas to each. After the contract was concluded, however, merchants supplying the Dutch East India Company lured the weavers to their employ with an offer of advances of ten pagodas. The weavers canceled their contracts with the English Company merchants, which they did by returning the advance. To retain the weavers the English Company's merchants were forced to match the larger Dutch advances.[62] Merchants, on the other hand, did not possess the right to break a contract. Nor could they demand the return of an advance. Entering into a contract with a weaver obligated a merchant to accept the weaver's cloth. To refuse a piece of cloth was in effect a forfeiture of the advance.[63]

This asymmetry of contract made it extremely difficult for merchants

[62] *FSGDC*, 1701, p. 57.
[63] *FSGDC*, 1723, p. 92 and *FSGDC*, 1724, p. 117. In 1738 Ananda Ranga Pillai entered in his diary: "[The Governor] explained that, owing to the slackness of business at Mocha, he no longer needed these articles. I told him that it would be impossible now to cancel the orders given to the weavers, because money had already been advanced to them, and some had commenced sending in their cloths. He desired me to do what I best could in the matter, and I agreed. I subsequently wrote in evasive terms to the weavers at Porto Novo, Chennamanayakkan palaiyam, etc., that the stuffs were not required, and that they need not weave or send them for some time." *The Private Diary of Ananda Ranga Pillai* (12 vols., Madras, 1904), vol. I, p. 55.

to take price abatements for poor-quality cloth. In these situations, as the merchant could not refuse the cloth, his only option was to negotiate with the weaver for a reduction in price. A late eighteenth-century servant of the English East India Company has supplied a terse description of this feature of contracts between merchants and weavers: "It was the Custom to receive from the weavers all the cloths they made making a proper deduction for the lower numbers as they [the weavers] were unable to take back such as might not be fit."[64] It was no easy matter for merchants to force weavers to reduce their prices, however. Rather than submitting to merchant demands for lower prices, the weaver freedom to terminate a contract meant that weavers were free to sell their finished cloth to any buyer and with the proceeds of the sale refund the advance to the merchant.[65] And in eighteenth-century South India there were no shortages of buyers for cloth. In addition to the European Companies and Asian merchants, many private traders operated in the weaving villages of South India. These buyers, as they did not want to run the risk of making advances to weavers, were willing to accept poor-quality cloth and able to give high prices. Therefore, the combination of the contract asymmetry and ready outlets for cloth meant weavers were under no pressure to accept merchant price abatements or to submit to merchant quality demands.

Evidence from the early nineteenth century indicates that contracts between merchants and agrarian producers also contained this asymmetry:

They [private traders] can extend their offers for cotton beyond what a person regularly advancing and running all risks can or at least has a right to expect[.] [T]he state of the season and demand which is then made for cotton regulates the market and should the individual who has advanced his money object to the price demanded by the cultivator excuses are not wanting to put him off or return his money which the cultivator is enabled to do by disposing of his produce to the highest bidder.[66]

Debt

Previous writers have suggested that weavers were tied to merchants by debt.[67] However, the mere existence of a debt does not imply obligations

---

[64] MPP, 1771, vol. 106B, p. 1006, TNA.
[65] See, for example, *FSGDC*, 1704, p. 92; *FSGDC*, 1713, p. 136.
[66] Tinnevelly Collectorate Records, 1811, vol. 3572, pp. 239–62, TNA. Weavers were also victims of this asymmetry when spinners to whom they had advanced funds for spinning yarn sold it for a greater profit to other buyers. See MPP, 1791, vol. P/241/26, pp. 2816–17, OIOC.
[67] Chaudhuri, *Trading World*, pp. 261–2; Arasaratnam, "Weavers, Merchants and Company," pp. 272–3.

on the part of the borrower. Nor is tying or bondage the necessary outcome of debt. These conditions are products of the political and legal framework in which a debt is situated. The political and legal framework in eighteenth-century South India did not lead to debt bondage. In fact, it was quite the opposite: in the political environment of late pre-colonial South India it was no easy matter for merchants to recover weaver debts.[68] This is not to imply that merchants had no interest in tying weavers to themselves. This they certainly sought to do. However, the means of attachment was not debt, but the guarantee of a steady stream of advances, which weavers sought in order to be assured of regular employment. For example, in 1694 merchants at Vizagapatnam appealed to the English for advances of money to keep the weavers at work. Otherwise, they said, the Dutch would employ them.[69] Similarly, in 1697, the Company merchants at Madras said that they had to keep the weavers supplied with money if they were to be kept from working for others.[70] Additional examples may be cited from the eighteenth century.[71]

Merchants employed large sums of capital to supply cloth to the European Companies. The risks of losses were high as advances were distributed to large numbers of weavers dispersed over dozens of towns and villages. Merchants took precautions to minimize their risks, such as keeping advances to a minimum during times of economic and political turmoil as at these times weavers were liable to eat the advance: rather than using merchant funds to purchase materials, weavers purchased food.[72] However, during times of trouble, merchants also came under pressure to make advances in order to prevent weavers from migrating to other areas.[73] For this reason, along with the fact that downturns in the market could not always be anticipated, despite the best of precautions weavers frequently amassed debt.

The accumulation of weaver debts was potentially disastrous for merchants as there were no legal or institutional mechanisms with which they could enforce repayment.[74] The only way for them to recover their

---

[68] *FSDC*, 1748, p. 34.   [69] *FSGDC*, 1694, p. 78.   [70] *FSGDC*, 1697, p. 2.
[71] See *FSGDC*, 1679–80, p. 21; Arthur T. Pringle (ed.) *The Diary and Consultation Book of the Agent Governor and Council of Fort St. George, 1683* (Madras, 1894), p. 70; *FSGDC*, 1695, p. 13; *FSGDC*, 1701, p. 29; *FSGDC*, 1720, p. 30.
[72] *FSGDC*, 1719, p. 41.
[73] MPP, 1764, vol. P/240/22, pp. 16–17, OIOC. Compounding the pressures on merchants were obligations to care for weavers in various ways. These were necessary to maintain a long-term relationship; see MPP, 1776, vol. 115B, pp. 393–9, TNA.
[74] According to a Company account: "The weavers being accustomed to squander what property comes into their possession will if forced (as they have been) to receive the advances of others, soon forget their old debts to distant merchants who have not authority to enforce the completing of their engagements." MPP, 1792, vol. P/241/30, pp. 78–81, OIOC. S. Ambirajan has observed that in pre-colonial India there was "no organized judiciary to secure recovery of loans." See his *Classical Political Economy and British Policy in India* (Cambridge, 1978), p. 120.

money was to make further advances and to allow weavers to gradually work off the sum,[75] but such a procedure was made uncertain by the mobility of weavers. It was not uncommon for weavers who had accumulated debt to simply pack up their looms and possessions and move elsewhere. A community of weavers was made responsible for the debt obligations of any single individual who absconded with merchant money, but this, of course, would be useless if the whole community was to migrate.[76]

Weaver mobility

For at least a century the traditional picture of India has consisted of the self-sufficient village community, which remained fixed and changeless even through turmoil in the political superstructure.[77] In recent years, however, evidence has mounted that there was a great deal of spatial mobility in pre-colonial South Asia. As David Washbrook has put it: "Evidence from regions as diverse as Maharashtra, Bengal, Bihar and the South suggests that 'cultivating' or 'peasant' society itself may have been highly mobile and by no means tied to its village communities from time out of mind."[78] In fact, Christopher Bayly has shown that the traditional and static village did not always characterize India, but was a product of the nineteenth-century colonial transformation.[79]

Weavers were an important part of this peripatetic population. Migration was integral to weaver subsistence and survival strategies and evidence indicates that they resorted to it frequently in the seventeenth and eighteenth centuries.[80] Migration, or its threat, was also an important weaver tactic and bargaining chip during conflicts with merchants and states. And it was a threat that had to be taken seriously as weavers were not hesitant about exercising their powers of movement. As the Madras Council noted: "The weavers when disgusted leave lighted Lamps in their Houses and remove to some other part of the Country, so that whole Towns are deserted in a Night."[81] Even if weavers were in debt, merchants were unable to control or restrict their movement.[82] States too were unable to place limits on weaver migration, and weavers used their

---

[75] See, for instance, MPP, 1766, vol. P/240/24, pp. 32–3, OIOC.
[76] Weavers were "mutually answerable for each other." MPP, 1771, vol. 106B, pp. 856 and 1052, TNA.
[77] Of course, we are indebted to Marx for several classic images of the village community.
[78] Washbrook, "Progress and Problems," p. 67.
[79] Bayly, *Rulers, Townsmen and Bazaars*, chap. 7.
[80] Chaudhuri, *Trading World*, p. 252.
[81] Despatches to England (Fort St. George), 13 January 1736, pp. 2–3, cited in Chaudhuri, *Trading World*, p. 252.
[82] *FSGDC*, 1672–78, p. 73; *FSGDC*, 1706, p. 22; *FSDC*, 1739, p. 13.

mobility to escape oppressive treatment at the hands of rulers and revenue authorities.[83]

Weavers also migrated to escape adverse conditions and bad times. In times of drought and famine, which were often localized, weavers moved to areas where grain was cheaper.[84] It was also not uncommon for weavers to relocate when armies were approaching.[85] Such migration was a widespread response to dearth and danger, especially in dry areas, and was not practiced only by weavers. The magnitude of movement in South India suggests that weavers, as well as the population as a whole, possessed networks which kept them abreast of conditions in various locales.

It was not difficult for weavers to migrate at a whim. They had few possessions and their houses were worth very little. Weavers also had no shortage of places to go. Because they enriched state coffers they were received with open arms by rulers throughout South India. States competed to attract weavers and offered inducements such as funds for the construction of houses and loans of money. Weavers directly added to state revenues by paying loom taxes, but their indirect contribution to revenue collections was probably even greater through the stimulation weavers gave to commercial activity. Weavers were actively involved in market exchange and the higher levels of trade in the items they demanded – cotton, yarn and foodstuffs – would have translated into higher customs collections. By the late seventeenth century for some rulers revenues from the trade stimulated by cloth manufacturing had become essential for state finances. A dispute in 1684 between the English and Lingapa, the Raja of Kanchipuram, is instructive in this regard. The origins of the dispute are not clear, but it concerned a sum of 7,000 pagodas which was due to the Raja from the English. Judging from the Company records, it also appeared to be a routine disagreement until Lingapa, in an attempt to pressure the Company, imprisoned several merchants who were purchasing cloth for the English in Kanchipuram. In retaliation, the Company put a stop to cloth purchases in his territories.[86] In less than four months Lingapa, feeling the pinch of declining customs collections, conceded defeat and released the merchants. Thereafter his attitude towards the Company was far more accommodating.[87]

---

[83] See also Ravi Ahuja, "Labour Unsettled: Mobility and Protest in the Madras Region," *IESHR*, 35 (1998), pp. 381–404.

[84] *FSGDC*, 1690, pp. 29–30; *FSGDC*, 1692, p. 33; *FSGDC*, 1694, p. 134; *FSGDC*, 1712, p. 27; *FSGDC*, 1719, p. 36.

[85] *FSDC*, 1748, p. 153.

[86] Arthur Pringle (ed.), *The Diary and Consultation Book of the Agent Governor and Council of Fort St. George, 1684* (Madras, 1895), pp. 84, 112.

[87] Arthur Pringle (ed.), *The Diary and Consultation Book of the Agent Governor and Council of Fort St. George, 1685* (Madras, 1895), p. 4.

Weaver solidarity

A final reason for the strong position of weavers in the political and economic order of South India was their powerful networks of solidarity. These allowed weavers to not compete against each other and to present a united front in their dealings with merchants and kings. As a consequence, weavers were able to maximize the prices they received for their cloth, to receive sizable advances, and to benefit from the security of merchant support during bad times. By contrast, as we shall see shortly, merchants were unable to limit competition among themselves for the services of weavers.

An important source of weaver solidarity was *jati* or caste. Jati forged a sense of corporate identity through links of marriage and through joint participation in religious and ritual life, much of this revolving around the temple. Although little is known about marriage patterns in pre-colonial South India, a reading of the Baramahal Records, especially the third section which describes the social and religious practices of the inhabitants of the Baramahal, suggests that for many groups the choice of marriage partners in eighteenth-century South India was determined by the principle of endogamy.[88] Therefore, a weaving community had solidarities that were based on the memory of marital alliances from the past, the lived experiences of alliances in the present, and the anticipation of alliances in the future.

A second way in which jati gave weavers a sense of solidarity was through temple and ritual life. Inscriptional evidence indicates that weavers were active in South Indian temple life, especially in the giving of prestations to temples. In the early medieval period, these gifts were made both individually and collectively, but by Vijayanagar times, individual gifts were rare as collective gifts came to predominate. These collective gifts typically were made by a single weaver jati, but there are also instances in which several weaver jatis joined together to pool their resources for a prestation, at times in conjunction with other artisanal groups. The practice of collective donations to temples continued to be followed in the seventeenth and eighteenth centuries.[89] Thus, through their relationships with temples, weavers affirmed their corporate and caste connections.

The solidarities formed by jati did not exist solely on a local scale, but also created a regional world of weaver corporate activity and cooperation. In medieval times the major South Indian weaving castes possessed

---

[88] English East India Company, *The Baramahal Records*, Section III: *Inhabitants*.
[89] Vijaya Ramaswamy, *Textiles and Weavers in Medieval South India* (Delhi, 1985), pp. 41, 97–8, 159–60.

regional caste organizations and ethnographic investigations have confirmed the existence of such networks in the twentieth century.[90] This
suggests that these regional caste networks and links operated in early
modern South India which implies that in the eighteenth century caste
would have given weavers a sense of solidarity that functioned at not only
the level of the locality but also at that of the region.[91]

A second source of solidarity for weavers derived from space or territory. For weavers in South India an individual's connection to a particular
space was part of a group's shared relation with that place. This collective
experience is reflected in the fact that migration and movement were
undertaken by groups and only very rarely by individual weavers. In the
eighteenth century weaver migrating groups ranged in size from twenty
families to nearly two hundred. The weavers in these groups were also
typically drawn from a single jati. In this way migration intersected with
and affirmed solidarities of jati. In addition, a migrating group always
included at least one head weaver, which takes us to another central pillar
of weaver social organization.

Weaving villages in South India had powerful corporate structures.
Crucial to the operation of these corporate bodies were head weavers who
served as village and community leaders. In 1771 on a tour of the jagir,
which consisted of territory recently ceded to the Company by the Nawab
of Arcot, a Company servant found that weaving villages were divided
into *payketts*.[92] A paykett, which consisted of several villages, had great
economic significance as it was "a district in which cloth or any other
article of trade are provided."[93] However, a paykett also possessed great
social and political importance. The following passage indicates that
kinship relations often connected weavers of a paykett:

It seems that the inhabitants of the village of Manambaddy and Chumbaucum
have had a quarrel subsisting between them for a number of years and they never

---

[90] Ramaswamy, *Textiles and Weavers*, pp. 38–40; Edgar Thurston, *Castes and Tribes of
Southern India* (7 vols., Madras, 1909), vol. III, pp. 35–6; Mattison Mines, *The Warrior
Merchants: Textiles, Trade, and Territory in South India* (Cambridge, 1984), chap. 5.
[91] The regional vision of weavers is explored further in chapter 4.
[92] As far as I have been able to discover, the term paykett as a political and territorial unit
was used only in the jagir, although it may have also been found in the Baramahal where
weavers were also organized territorially (see MPP, 1792, vol. P/241/34, pp. 2611–32,
OIOC). It should be noted that the jagir encompassed a sizable area. It extended from
Nellore to North Arcot and included both Telugu and Tamil populations. The territorial
organization into payketts was thus used over a wide area. In the Northern Sarkars, the
mootah may have been analogous to the paykett (see MPP, 1793, vol. P/241/39,
pp. 1630–1, OIOC). Evidence suggests that these types of territorial and political divi-
sions were widespread in South India. See Nicholas Dirks, *The Hollow Crown: Ethnohistory of an Indian Kingdom* (Cambridge, 1987), pp. 205–7 and 256–67.
[93] MPP, 1771, vol. 106B, p. 855, TNA.

visit each other or intermarry or even eat and drink together. It seems that
Chumbaucum is excommunicated by all the villages of the payket.[94]

The same servant added that the weavers in each paykett also had fixed
leaders, who were known under various titles, but served as the heads of
the weavers in that paykett. As he explained:

The title of Nattwar properly belongs to the general heads of representatives of the
inhabitants, but by use is improperly applied to the Heads of the Weavers in the
Southern Payketts, some of them being considerable landholders, as the late
Nattwar of the Puddapa weavers was also Nattwar of the inhabitants.
Their proper term [for these heads] in the Malabar [Tamil] language which is that
of these Payketts is Perrea Deana Caurun and in the Telinga [Telugu] tongue
which is that of Arnee and Conjiveram, Peddina Caundoo and they are so called
in those Districts where the weavers never hold land.[95]

These head weavers mediated between ordinary weavers and merchants
and political authorities. They also played pivotal roles in the revenue
collection system, often taking responsibility for collecting the taxes due
from weavers.

W eaver social and political organization extended below the level of the
paykett to that of individual villages. At this lower level there existed
another layer of head weavers who were the leaders of weavers in each
village or town. In the Company servant's words: "Besides the Nattwar of
the Paykett there are also other Nattwars to every town and village who
interfere in the distinct concerns of their respective districts with the same
trust and authority as the greater Nattwars exercise in the affairs of the
whole district."[96] The social and political organization of weavers lent
them forms of community which operated at several levels. And in
relation to merchants and states, the several layers of head weavers were a
source of leadership and helped to forge weaver collective solidarity.
However, this emphasis on solidarity should not obscure the fact that
differences and conflicts also existed within weaver corporate structures.
This issue will be pursued in later chapters.

A final source of weaver solidarity and corporate identity derived from
their working lives. It was not uncommon for several weavers with their
families to pursue their tasks together. According to Edgar Thurston:
"The several processes of twisting and untwisting threads, preparing
skeins, etc., make combined labor a necessity in the weaving industry;
and wherever one finds a weaver settlement, he must find there a large
number of these people."[97] From work, it was only a small step to form
solidarities based on occupation. The existence of such a collective

---

[94] MPP, 1771, vol. 106B, p. 1034, TNA.   [95] MPP, 1771, vol. 106B, p. 855–6, TNA.
[96] MPP, 1771, vol. 106B, p. 856, TNA.   [97] Thurston, *Castes and Tribes*, vol. VI, p. 276.

identity was pointed to in the discussion of prestations to temples, which on occasion were carried out jointly by several weaving jatis. The occupational solidarity of weavers emerges even more clearly in an alliance that was formed by the four main weaving jatis in Northern Coromandel during a conflict with the English East India Company.[98] This alliance, which will be discussed in greater detail shortly, reveals that weavers perceived themselves as sharing interests which derived from a common position in the South Indian social, political, economic and ritual order.

Although merchants possessed corporate identities, and these also were often based on caste and kinship, they were far less successful in combining their forces against weavers. The dramatically different situations of weavers and merchants are captured in a Tamil proverb, according to which "the Chetti (merchant) lost by partnership, while the weaver came to grief by isolation."[99] The very high demand for cloth in South India often forced merchants not to cooperate, but to compete with each other for the labor of weavers, which had the effect of driving up cloth prices and weaver earnings. The English and Dutch East India Companies were alarmed by this situation and sought to foster merchant cooperation. In Europe, merchants were highly successful in forming combinations to discipline laborers and bargain effectively with producers. To replicate these practices in South India, the servants of the English and Dutch East India Companies persuaded their merchant suppliers to organize themselves into joint-stock companies which were to serve many of the same functions as employer combinations in Europe. These joint-stocks, however, were racked by dissension and disputes and dissolved rather quickly.[100]

This chapter has shown that weavers possessed a variety of methods with which they maintained their earnings. These included pushing up cloth prices, reducing cloth quality and absconding with merchant advances. All of these actions reduced profits for merchants, who were often helpless in the face of them. Merchants could not form a united front to place pressure on weavers. Nor did they have access to political institutions with which they could discipline and control weavers. A major crisis of the South Indian political economy in the late 1720s and 1730s illustrates well the disadvantages under which merchants labored. In these decades, cloth merchants' profits were squeezed between the

---

[98] MPP, 1775, vol. 113B, p. 365, TNA. Also see Arasaratnam, "Trade and Political Dominion," p. 34. Further details on the conflicts between weavers and the English are given in chapters 3 and 4.
[99] Thurston, *Castes and Tribes*, vol. VI, p. 276.
[100] Joseph Brennig, "Joint-Stock Companies of Coromandel," in Blair B. Kling and M. N. Pearson (eds.), *The Age of Partnership: Europeans in Asia Before Dominion* (Honolulu, 1979).

powerful claims of weavers and the pricing policy of the English East
India Company. Many merchants went bankrupt and a number were
forced to abandon the cloth trade altogether.

The crisis of the 1720s and 1730s

South Indian merchants provided cloth to the European Companies on
the basis of a contract. Merchant suppliers to the English East India
Company were no exception and their contracts were the products of
protracted negotiations, at times dragging on for several months, over the
prices, qualities and quantities of the various types of cloth. A central
feature of these contracts was a penalty clause which the Company could
invoke if a merchant failed to abide by the conditions of the contract. The
English, as did other Europeans, insisted upon this penalty, which was
typically set at 20 or 25 percent of the total value of the contract, as an
inducement to merchants to meet their contractual obligations. In addition, the penalty would provide some compensation to the Company if
merchant failures led to costly disruptions in their very tight shipping
schedules.[101] However, the penalty was excused in extraordinary circumstances such as famine or war.[102]

Upon concluding their contracts with the English, the merchants contracted with weavers and distributed advances. In the early eighteenth
century cloth merchants, as they rarely received capital from the Company, raised much of their finance from South Indian bankers. The
Company paid the merchants for cloth as it was delivered, but often with
some delay, which forced the merchants to act as creditors to the Company. By these arrangements, the Company bore none of the risks associated with cloth procurement. The penalty provision compensated the
Company for failures in cloth supply and merchants bore all the risk of
making advances to weavers. For several decades merchants encountered
few difficulties with this arrangement, but this was to drastically change in
the 1720s.

The first signs that the merchants were headed for trouble came in
1723 and 1724 with a sharp deterioration in the quality of the cloth. The
Company pressed the merchants to cut their prices, but the merchants
refused on the grounds that the extraordinarily high demand for cloth
made it difficult to obtain pieces of the proper quality.[103] The Madras
merchants added that they "take what they can get for that now when

[101] *FSDC*, 1711, p. 74; Chaudhuri, *Trading World*, p. 71.
[102] For examples of contracts see *FSDC*, 1696, p. 31; *FSDC*, 1701, pp. 10–12; *FSDC*.
 1706, pp. 31–3.
[103] *FSDC*, 1723, pp. 30 and 60.

they complain to the weaver that the cloth is not good, he tells them if they won't buy, others will, so that to comply with their contract, they are oblig'd to take in a great deal which they are sensible ought to be better but that they can get no other."[104] Merchants at Fort St. David encountered similar problems and they reported that weavers simply refused to produce better quality cloth and the merchants said that "there was no way to oblige them to it but to let them [starve]."[105]

In response, the Company began to reject much of the merchants' cloth in the belief that this would compel the merchants to bring in better quality stuff. The merchants, however, had little incentive to improve quality because they sold the rejected cloth to other buyers at prices which were virtually the same as those of the Company.[106] In order to discipline the merchants, in early 1725 the Company invoked the penalty clause, citing the merchant failures to meet their contractual obligations in the previous year. The Company demanded as a penalty 22,000 pagodas from the Fort St. David merchants and 8,000 pagodas from the Fort St. George merchants. The penalty was lower at Fort St. George because those merchants continued to purchase the Company's broadcloth.[107] Despite these penalties, many merchants in both factories entered into new contracts to supply cloth in 1725. The Fort St. George merchants were able to meet this contract, but those in Fort St. David were unable to and they suffered an additional penalty of 10,000 pagodas.[108]

These penalties were extremely damaging for merchants in both places. In Fort St. David a few merchants declared bankruptcy and the remainder found themselves in very precarious financial positions.[109] In Fort St. George, the penalty destroyed the credit standing of the merchants and they found themselves unable to obtain loans from South Indian banking houses. As a consequence, the Company had to supply money to the merchants for the provision of cloth.[110] These events of the mid-1720s, however, were merely a prelude to even more disastrous merchant setbacks. In the late 1720s and early 1730s, cloth merchants fell victim to an agricultural crisis in South India. Prices for grain and cotton skyrocketed and merchant profits were squeezed between the weavers' ability to pass on their rising costs and the Company's low cloth procurement prices. Unlike weavers, who were able to protect their earnings, merchant profits dwindled steadily and in some cases they disappeared altogether.

---

[104] *FSGDC*, 1724, pp. 1–2.   [105] *FSGDC*, 1724, p. 168.   [106] *FSGDC*, 1724, p. 95.
[107] *FSGDC*, 1725, pp. 24–5.   [108] *FSGDC*, 1726, p. 25.
[109] *FSDC*, 1726, pp. 12 and 37–8.   [110] *FSGDC*, 1727, pp. 47, 53 and 62.

Table 1.3. *Rice prices at Fort St. George, 1720–40*

	Price (pagodas per garce)
June 1720	38
January 1722	30
September 1727	54
January 1728	90
August 1728	55
February 1729	80
June 1729	96
August 1729	110
September 1729	114
May 1730	50
January 1732	70
January 1734	80
November 1735	72
January 1736	54
January 1737	66
April 1737	88
April 1739	50
February 1740	44

Note: 1 garce = 9,600 pounds in weight.
Source: FSGDC, various years.

The agricultural price rise

Little is known about prices in eighteenth-century South India.[111] Only scattered price data are available in European records and as a consequence only fragmentary price series may be constructed. In table 1.3 I have assembled rice prices at Fort St. George between 1720 and 1740. These show that there was a dramatic increase in grain prices from the mid-1720s. There is evidence from these decades for an inflation in cotton prices as well. The reasons for these price increases are not entirely clear, but there are indications that poor monsoons produced a series of crop failures. Even Tanjore, traditionally the granary of the south, suffered poor harvests in 1732 and 1733.[112] Arguments have also been put forward that this crisis marked a secular decline in agriculture resulting from the breakdown of irrigation systems.[113] At the moment, evidence in support of the latter view is limited.

[111] A major contribution is Tsukasa Mizushima, *Nattar and Socio-Economic Change in South India in the 18th–19th Centuries* (Tokyo, 1986), pp. 284–99.
[112] S. Arasaratnam, "The Dutch East India Company and Its Coromandel Trade 1700–1740," *Bijdragen tot de Taal-Land-en Volkendunde,* 123 (1967), p. 338.
[113] Bhaskar Jyoti Basu, "The Trading World of Coromandel and the Crisis of the 1730s," *Proceedings of the Indian History Congress,* 42nd Session, Bodh-Gaya (1981), pp. 333–9.

Table 1.4. *Cotton, yarn and cloth prices, 1726–31*

	Cotton (pagodas per 100 Dutch pounds)	Yarn (pagodas per 100 Dutch pounds)	Ratio of the price of cotton to the price of yarn	Ratio of the price of yarn to the price of cloth
Porto Novo				
1726	$4\frac{1}{6}$	$9\frac{1}{6}$	0.45	0.29
1727	$4\frac{3}{4}$	$9\frac{1}{4}$	0.51	—
1728	$5\frac{1}{4}$	$9\frac{3}{4}$	0.54	—
1729	5	$9\frac{1}{4}$	0.54	—
1730	$5\frac{5}{6}$	$11\frac{1}{2}$	0.51	0.34
1731	6	12	0.50	0.28
Sadraspatnam				
1726	$3\frac{2}{3}$	$8\frac{2}{3}$	0.42	—
1727	$4\frac{2}{3}$	$9\frac{1}{2}$	0.49	—
1728	$4\frac{3}{4}$	10	0.48	—
1729	5	10	0.50	—
1730	7	$13\frac{1}{2}$	0.52	—
1731	$7\frac{1}{2}$	$13\frac{1}{2}$	0.56	—

Note: Cloth prices are pagodas per *corge*.
Sources: Cotton and yarn prices are from S. Arasaratnam, "The Dutch East India Company and its Coromandel Trade 1700–1740," *Bijdragen tot de Taal-Land-en Volkenkunde*, 123 (1967), p. 339. Cloth prices for Porto Novo are from table 1.5.

To maintain the real value of their earnings, textile producers responded to the price increases with demands for higher prices for their goods. The result was rising yarn and cloth prices. However, all producers were not equally successful in passing on costs and weavers had far greater success than spinners. In table 1.4 I have assembled cotton and yarn prices from 1726 to 1731 at Porto Novo and Sadraspatnam. The table also includes the ratio of the price of cotton to the price of yarn. This figure represents the proportion of material (in this case cotton) costs in the final cost of yarn. This ratio increased between 1726 and 1731 which indicates that the cost of cotton accounted for a larger fraction of the final price of yarn. Thus the returns to spinning as a share of the final price of yarn fell in this period. This may be contrasted with weaving, for which I have made a similar calculation. Although the data are very limited, the ratio of the price of yarn to the price of cloth appears to have remained stable between 1726 and 1731. Thus, unlike spinning, in weaving material costs as a proportion of the final price of cloth were constant. Therefore, weavers were more successful than spinners in pushing up prices to maintain their earnings, which indicates that weavers were in a better position than spinners to set the price for their products and pass on cost increases.

The difference between weavers and spinners was not due to differences in the demand for yarn and cloth. Since the demand for cloth would have determined the demand for yarn, the major input into cloth production, the demand for these two goods would have been more or less identical. Therefore, the varying ability of spinners and weavers was due not to conditions in the market, but to those in the social worlds of weaving and spinning and, in particular, in the organization of producers. In this respect there were vast differences between spinners and weavers. Spinners were dispersed, unorganized and weak. They possessed no means to influence the price of yarn and simply took the market price as given. It was also easy for individuals to move in and out of spinning, which further weakened their positions. In the poor agricultural conditions of the 1720s and 1730s the ranks of spinners were undoubtedly swelled which would have had the effect of driving down the earnings of all spinners.

In sharp contrast, the price of cloth was determined by bargaining between weavers and merchants. Weavers were tightly organized and had the bargaining power to pass on cost increases by demanding and receiving higher prices for their cloth. As a result of weaver pressures cloth prices rose by 50 percent between 1725 and 1732 (see table 1.5). Unlike earlier price increases, which were temporary upswings from a stable price, the price increase of the late 1720s and earlier 1730s resulted in a permanent increase in cloth prices. Weavers also supplemented their earnings in these crisis years by reducing the quantity of yarn in each piece and by switching to less expensive yarns, which cut their costs. Evidence for this comes from the legions of complaints in these years about the thinness of the cloth and the coarseness of the yarns.[114] Weavers further maintained earnings by reducing the dimensions of their cloth. They were increasingly delivering longcloth in lengths of 33 or 34 yards instead of the stipulated 36 yards.[115]

Weavers had great success in raising their earnings during the crisis. Nevertheless, there is evidence that a number of weavers died. It is possible that this was because the increase in earnings could not keep pace with the rise in grain prices. However, the more likely culprit is that grain was simply unavailable at any price due to widespread shortages. The lack of grain may have been due initially to poor harvests, but shortfalls in supply would have ignited speculative behavior which would

---

[114] *FSGDC*, 1732, p. 24; *FSGDC*, 1733, p. 148; *FSGDC*, 1735, p. 16.
[115] *FSDC*, 1733, pp. 18–19.

Table 1.5. *Longcloth prices at Cuddalore, 1698–1790*

Year	Price (pagodas per corge)	Year	Price (pagodas per corge)
1698	27.5	1743	47
1700	34	1744	46
1701	36	1745	46
1702	36	1746	45
1704	31.5	1747	42
1706	31.5	1748	42.5
1707	31.5	1749	46
1708	31.5	1750	46
1709	30	1768	43.5
1710	30	1769	43.5
1725	31.5	1770	44
1730	33.5	1772	42
1731	42.75	1774	42
1732	46	1775	42
1733	39	1776	43
1734	39.5	1777	43
1735	39	1786	46
1737	41.5	1790	43

Note: These prices are for longcloth ordinary. In 1737 the name of the cloth was changed to longcloth worriarpollam (udaiyarpolliam), but the quality of the cloth remained at 8 *call*. The prices for 1737–50 include the merchant brokerage fee.
Sources: 1698–1750, FSDC, various years; 1768–90, Cuddalore Consultations, South Arcot Collectorate Records, various years, TNA.

have further exacerbated shortages. In seventeenth- and eighteenth-century South India grain merchants, anticipating further price rises, often held back supplies. For example, in 1694 the grain traders at Madras lodged rice and paddy "in their godowns [and] refused to sell expecting a better price," which served to push up the price of rice even further.[116] Such speculatively generated shortages of grain would have made ineffective even the most successful weaver efforts to drive up their money incomes. In these conditions, the weavers' only option was to migrate to areas where grain was available and there is a great deal of evidence that weavers did precisely this. Such migration only compounded merchant losses as many of these weavers were in possession of merchant advances when they migrated.[117] Nevertheless, the troubled times claimed many victims, and weavers were among them.

[116] *FSGDC*, 1694, p. 135.   [117] *FSGDC*, 1731, pp. 96–8.

The Company response

In the crisis of the 1720s and 1730s merchants came to be squeezed between weavers and the Company. Weavers protected their incomes by passing on cost increases to merchants, but the Company's pricing policy prevented merchants from doing the same. Since 1720, when restrictions were erected in Britain on imports of calicoes, the prices that Indian cloth fetched in London had been stagnant, which made it imperative for the Company to hold down procurement prices in India.[118] The Company bargained hard with merchants and consistently settled upon prices that were below those given by other buyers. The consequences of this were disastrous for merchants, who between 1725 and 1735 regularly contracted for cloth at prices which proved to be unremunerative. They formulated two responses to their dilemma, but both led ultimately to merchant losses.

The first merchant response was not to fulfill their contracts. Despite Company pressures to deliver cloth, the merchants brought in very few pieces in 1729, 1730 and 1731. For these failures, the Company exacted penalties in 1731 and 1732. After this a number of merchants were wary of doing further business with the Company and ended their tenures as Company merchants. However, a sizable number continued to venture the risk.[119] The second response, which the merchants adopted after the imposition of the Company's penalties, was to bring in cloth. However, this was not viable since the Company's prices were far below those demanded by the weavers and again many merchants suffered heavy losses.[120] It was not only merchants supplying the English who lost large sums. The merchants catering to the French Company also suffered substantial losses in the early 1730s.[121]

Why did these cloth merchants continue to contract for cloth despite persistent losses? Why did they not exit from the cloth trade? Part of the answer to these questions lies in the many incentives the English Company offered to the merchants who continued to contract. In 1725, the Company offered to reduce the penalty on the Madras merchants from 90,000 pagodas to 30,000 pagodas if they contracted again.[122] Similarly, in 1726, the Fort St. David merchants were told that their penalty would be canceled if they brought in 3,000 bales of cloth that year.[123] In 1728, the Madras merchants fell short of their contract by 1,700 bales and the Company told them that the penalty would be excused if they completed

[118] Chaudhuri, *Trading World*, p. 293.
[119] *FSDC*, 1730, pp. 8–9; *FSDC*, 1731, pp. 15–16; *FSDC*, 1732, pp. 21 and 24.
[120] *FSDC*, 1732, pp. 6 and 17–18; *FSDC*, 1733, pp. 17 and 35.
[121] *FSGDC*, 1733, p. 118.   [122] *FSGDC*, 1725, p. 24.   [123] *FSGDC*, 1724, p. 27.

the contract by September 1729.[124] The merchants once again failed to deliver the cloth, but they avoided the penalty by entering into another contract.[125] Such incentives were repeated in the 1730s.[126]

Merchants also were forced to contract with the Company because of the loss of their standing within the South Indian financial community. As a consequence of the penalties imposed upon them in 1725 and 1726, these cloth merchants were unable to raise money in local credit markets and the Company became their only source of credit. In the words of the Fort St. George Council:

[the merchants'] credit (which formerly when the Company trusted them thus largely was so good that they could not only find money for the investment, but ever were able to raise any sums in town and lend the same for the Company) is now so sunk by the distrust the Company shew of them that no body will lend them any money and it therefore lies solely on the Company to do it. That the large penalties inflicted on them in the year 1725 has compleated the loss of their credit in the town since no body dares to lend them any money lest another accident of the same kind should disable them to pay what should be so lent.[127]

The Company's credit was available only to those merchants who contracted to supply cloth. Ostensibly this credit was to be used only for the provision of cloth, but the merchants also relied upon Company funds to finance their private trade. The Company suspected that merchants were misusing its money and later in the century it sought to put a stop to it.[128] The merchants' inability to raise credit also explains why the Company was willing to advance money to them. In previous years, the Company had been reluctant to advance its own money and forced the merchants to draw upon their own resources. On a few occasions, when credit in South India was tight, the Company extended credit to merchants, but in exchange it demanded lower cloth prices. However, after the loss of the merchants' reputation, the Company had no option but to loan funds to the merchants if it wanted to procure cloth in South India. And this was to lead the Company to become ever more entangled in the political and economic life of South Indians.

[124] *FSGDC*, 1729, p. 24.   [125] *FSGDC*, 1729, pp. 63–4 and 71.
[126] *FSGDC*, 1730, p. 29; *FSGDC*, 1735, p. 75.   [127] *FSGDC*, 1736, p. 80.
[128] *FSGDC*, 1731, p. 103.

2   Agriculture and cotton textiles

The dominant position of Indian cotton textiles in world markets was a consequence of a combination of their fine quality and their very low prices. The fine quality was due to the skill of the Indian manufacturer, but in theory could be reproduced elsewhere. More difficult to match, however, was the low price for cloth. To put it simply, much of the world was unable to manufacture cloth for less. Since the late seventeenth century observers have attributed the cheapness of Indian cottons to the exploitative and oppressive conditions under which Indian laborers toiled. We have seen, however, that weavers in eighteenth-century South India were in a very strong position in their dealings with merchants. It is now difficult to sustain old conceptions of the degraded position of laborers in eighteenth-century South Asia.

I have argued elsewhere that the competitive position of Indian cotton cloth arose not from cheap labor but from agriculture. To summarize the argument, the price of grain was far lower in South India than in Europe. Grain prices in Britain, for instance, were twice as high as in South India. Although in real terms wages in South India were comparable to, or perhaps even higher than those in Europe, the low price for grain meant that money wages were far lower. And with this, the prices of Indian textiles were far lower. Or to put it another way, the price level was far lower in India than in Britain.[1]

The basis for lower grain prices in South India was the greater productivity of South Indian agriculture. Adam Smith, always a keen observer, reached the same conclusion in his *Wealth of Nations*:

In rice countries, which generally yield two, sometimes three crops in the year, each of them more plentiful than any common crop of corn, the abundance of food must be much greater than in any corn country of equal extent... The precious metals, therefore, would naturally exchange in India ... for a much greater quantity of food than in Europe. The money price ... of food, the first of all necessaries, [would be] a great deal lower in the one country than the other.[2]

---

[1] See my "Rethinking Wages and Competitiveness."
[2] Adam Smith, *The Wealth of Nations*, Canaan edn. (2 vols., Chicago, 1976), vol. II, pp. 228–9.

The superior productivity of South Indian agriculture cannot be attributed simply to the climatic or geographical features of the region. The limitations of such an explanation are evident from the fact that in the late nineteenth century the agricultural productivity of England had far surpassed that of South India. Rather, as this chapter will argue, the superior agricultural productivity of eighteenth-century South India rested upon high rates of investment in agricultural improvement, including the clearing of high-quality land, the construction of irrigation, and manuring, crop rotation and other practices to preserve the fertility of the soil. Such investments date back several centuries in South India and were promoted by kings and temples and were closely linked to statecraft and temple and ritual life.[3] However, high rates of investment in agriculture, especially in the seventeenth and eighteenth centuries, were also propelled by the strong position of laborers in the South Indian political and economic order. Investment in agricultural improvement was a way to attract and fix laborers in the conditions of scarcity and intense competition for laborers which existed in the late pre-colonial period.

The investment process in agriculture

Previous studies of South India have divided the agricultural landscape into ecological zones. David Ludden classified Tinnevelly into the tripartite division of wet, dry and mixed area. Christopher Baker divided the whole of the Tamil country along similar lines.[4] While this ecological approach has been enormously valuable, I would like to depart from it, for the moment, and emphasize an important feature of the agrarian economy which was shared across ecological zones in South India: the mobility of the direct producer.

The mobility of the producer is perhaps most obvious in the dry zones where in several parts of South India a period was set aside every year during which producers moved. In the Ceded Districts, this period lasted from early April to the middle of July. At this time, known as the *kalawedi* season, producers moved from their villages, and even *taluks*, and took up land in other places.[5] The same custom was practiced in the Baramahal, where, according to a description from Alexander Read, producers "are

---

[3] See, for instance, the following by Burton Stein: "The Economic Functions of a Medieval South Indian Temple" and "The State, the Temple and Agricultural Development: A Study in Medieval South India," in his *All the Kings' Mana: Papers on Medieval South Indian History* (Madras, 1984).

[4] Ludden, *Peasant History*, pp. 52–9; C. J. Baker, *An Indian Rural Economy 1880–1955: The Tamilnad Countryside* (Delhi, 1984), pp. 85–97.

[5] Burton Stein, *Thomas Munro: The Origins of the Colonial State and his Vision of Empire* (Delhi, 1989), p. 114.

commonly hired for the year, or the season only, [and] are at liberty to move where they please, in quest of new service, during the 'Calliwaddies', or spring months."[6] Similar movement of cultivators was also reported in North Arcot and in Chingleput. In the latter place, Lionel Place estimated that every year around 13 percent of the population shifted villages.[7]

Mobility of the producer is perhaps less obvious in the wet areas, where the class involved in many of the direct activities of cultivation, *adimai* in Tamil, has often been portrayed as tied to the land or to an agricultural superior, either as slave, serf, bonded laborer or in other unfree forms.[8] Gyan Prakash has demonstrated that these are profound misreadings of this relationship.[9] Even observers who operated within the discourse of slavery noted some features of the adimai system which could not be contained within that discourse:

A parriah, the slave of his landlord, may with his permission, enlist in the army, or in the service of an European gentleman, as a servant (and many have done so without their permission), exercising all the rights of free men. Indeed, even if he remains with his master as a slave, I apprehend that, as regards all acts between him and strangers, he possesses the same rights as free men.[10]

Lionel Place, collector of the jagir in the 1790s and an early chronicler of conditions in agriculture, also noted some peculiarities of the system:

The servant engages in the service of a cultivator at the beginning of the year on the customary terms of the village to which he is conciliated ... [H]is servitude expires with the year; during which it seldom happens that he is guilty of desertion if those terms are faithfully observed towards him, many from good treatment acquire an attachment to their masters whom no inducement could almost prevail with them to desert ... [T]hus long residence creates attachment, and a kind of inherent right which it is for the Interest of both not to violate.[11]

---

⁶ Board's Collections, No. 752, F/4/17, pp. 22–3, OIOC. (Photocopy consulted at Tozzer Library, Harvard University.)
⁷ North Arcot District Records, 1801, vol. 23, pp. 5–76, TNA; Washbrook, "Land and Labor," p. 44.
⁸ Cultivation in wet areas was also carried out, sometimes with the assistance of adimai, by a class of peasants known as *poragoodies*, some of whom were peripatetic.
⁹ Gyan Prakash, *Bonded Histories: Genealogies of Labor Servitude in Colonial India* (Cambridge, 1990), pp. 1–12. Also see Washbrook, "Land and Labor."
¹⁰ Minutes of Evidence Taken Before the Select Committee on the Affairs of the East India Company, vol. 1, Public (London, 1832), p. 575.
¹¹ Board of Revenue Proceedings, 1796, vol. 144, pp. 543–4, TNA. Place also reported that in a village near Madras the adimai "Had been defrauded by their masters of the hire which was due to them, while working on the tank; and from the injustice thus done to them many have deserted and others could not be prevailed upon to engage with them." Place to Board of Revenue, 28 January 1796, Board's Collections, no. 940, OIOC; Place to Board of Revenue, 28 June 1796, Board's Collections, vol. 36, OIOC, cited in Irschick, *Dialogue and History*, p. 78.

These passages suggest that the adimai were not immobilized, but rather enmeshed within a complex system of rights and obligations. If the holders of superior rights in agriculture did not fulfill their obligations, mobility was one possible response. This option was symbolized in the desertion ritual which accompanied the annual renewal of the relationship. In this ritual the adimai left the village in which they had resided in the previous year and their agricultural superiors would beseech them to return.[12]

One of the most important obligations of agricultural superiors was to maintain the security and productivity of the agricultural production regime, that is, to invest in agriculture. The link between investing and retaining laborers is revealed by Place himself, who observed the following series of events at Maduranticum:

> Previous to the repair of the tank – it is not known how long – the lands had been uncultivated, but so soon as this work was completed, the descendants of many families who had formerly been the hereditary servants of the Brahmins claimed, and were admitted to their inheritance, although in the intermediate time they had taken up other occupations, and might be supposed to have forgot it.[13]

In this case, as soon as investment was carried out, and the tank restored, producers returned to the site and reclaimed a hereditary right.

Mobility of laborers in agriculture also meant competition for them. Thomas Munro observed this competition in the Ceded Districts during kalawedi season when village headmen offered low revenue rates to attract cultivators.[14] Furthermore, investment in agricultural improvement would have made it possible to offer the favorable conditions – most importantly more productive land and more secure production systems – that would attract hands for the business of cultivation. As a consequence, investment in agriculture was an integral part of political practice in South India. It was not only village headmen who competed to attract laborers, however. As agrarian producers were able to move freely from one political entity to another, the diffusion (or segmentation or decentralization) of political authority also led to competition between states for laborers, which has been illustrated for the case of weavers. Investment in agriculture, as a method to compete for producers, was then institutionalized in the political practices of states in South India.

[12] For a more detailed description of this ritual see Sivakumar and Sivakumar, *Peasants and Nabobs*, p. 31.

[13] W. H. Bayley and W. Huddleston, *Papers on Mirasi Right Selected from the Records of the Madras Government* (Madras, 1862), pp. 47–8. This passage gives two important features of the adimai situation. First, the adimai held a right to a share of the produce, which was a form of property and could be inherited. Second, the producer was not attached permanently to a piece of land, but possessed some freedom of movement.

[14] Stein, *Munro*, p. 114.

Two sorts of evidence suggest a powerful link between political authority and investment in South India. The first comes from the spatial
distribution of agricultural activity which reveals that agricultural activities requiring heavy investment were concentrated in areas of major
political authority. Such a pattern emerges clearly in the case of cotton
cultivation where the more capital-intensive cultivation of cotton was
found within the confines of important political entities. The second
comes from texts on statecraft which were produced in early modern
South India. These show that investment in agriculture was integral to
kingship in South India.

The state and investment

According to works on statecraft produced in early modern South
India, the treasury was the cornerstone of the successful state. The
Rayavacakamu, a Telugu text produced in the late sixteenth or early
seventeenth century, proclaimed the treasury to be one of the seven limbs
of the state, along with the king, minister, ally, country, fort and army.[15] A
full treasury was absolutely essential for the pursuit of both politics and
military adventures:

> It can turn enemy into friend,
> friend into servant,
> and servant into loyal son –
> Wondrous are the ways of money!
> From even the worst of perils

> it can lead a king to safety:
> Sowing dissension in the enemy's camp
> is the best expedient for a desperate king![16]

In addition, a full treasury could give a sovereign peace of mind: "That
king can lay his hand on his breast and sleep peacefully . . . who increases
his treasury by multiplying his income and lessening expenditure."[17]

These works state explicitly that the prosperity of the sovereign is to
come through the prosperity of the ruled. The following advice was given
in the *Rayavacakamu*:

> To acquire wealth:
> make the people prosper.
> To make the people prosper:

---

[15] Philip B. Wagoner (trans.), *Tidings of the King* (Honolulu, 1993), p. 89.
[16] Wagoner, *Tidings of the King*, pp. 151–2.
[17] A. Rangasvami Sarasvati, "Political Maxims of the Emperor-Poet, Krishnadeva Raya,"
JIH, 4 (1926), pp. 72–3.

justice is the means.
O Kirti Narayana!
They say that justice
is the treasury of kings.[18]

The creation of a prosperous kingdom could only redound in favor of the sovereign. According to the *Amuktamalyada*, a Telugu text attributed to the Vijayanagar Emperor Krishnadeva Raya (reign from 1509 to 1529): "(The people of) a country wish the welfare of the king who seeks the progress and prosperity of the country. One should not think it is no serious matter."[19] Not only will he be the object of goodwill but he will also fill his treasury. In the words of the *Rayavacakamu*: "If the king acts in accordance with *dharma*, the rains will fall at least three times in every month, causing the earth to produce abundantly. If the palace then takes the taxes that are its due without being unjust, the palace will prosper, and cash will flow into the treasury in great quantities."[20]

According to these South Indian works on statecraft, a sovereign could create wealth and increase prosperity in two ways. The first was through the promotion of commerce. In the *Amuktamalyada*, two verses are devoted to merchants and trade, and they direct the king to "improve the harbours of his country and so encourage its commerce"; "arrange that foreign sailors who land in his country . . . are looked after"; "Make the merchants of distant countries . . . attached to yourself." According to the *Rayavacakamu*, a king should "increase his wealth by means of . . . merchant traffic on land and sea."[21]

The second was to support agricultural expansion and improvement. The *Amuktamalyada* imparted the following instructions to the sovereign: "The extent of a state is the root cause of its prosperity. When a state is small in extent then both virtue (*Dharma*) and prosperity (*Artha*) will increase only when tanks and irrigation canals are constructed." Investment in agriculture was recommended not only on instrumental or economic grounds, but also as a means to increase *dharma*.

The same type of recommendations were made in the *Rayavacakamu* which instructs the king to "beget the 'sevenfold progeny', which are a son, a treasure, a temple, a garden, *an irrigation tank*, a literary work, and a village established for brahmans." And elsewhere it states:

A broken family, damaged tanks and wells,
a fallen kingdom, one who comes seeking refuge,

---

[18] Wagoner, *Tidings of the King*, p. 95.
[19] Rangasvami Sarasvati, "Political Maxims of Krishnadeva Raya," p. 64.
[20] Wagoner, *Tidings of the King*, pp. 94–5.   [21] Wagoner, *Tidings of the King*, p. 90.

cows and brahman, and temples of the gods –
supporting these is four times as meritorious![22]

Similar sentiments are expressed in Revenue Regulations issued by Tipu
Sultan in Mysore. Twelve of the Regulations' 127 articles deal with
measures for the promotion and expansion of agriculture. In article two,
the *aumil* [revenue official] is instructed to:

ascertain in what *Reyuts'* houses there are a number of men, and but few ploughs;
and having enquired into the circumstances of such *Reyuts*, shall oblige those who
are in good circumstances to increase the number of their ploughs; and in order to
enable the *Reyuts* who are needy to purchase ploughs and to cultivate the lands, he
shall give *Tucavee*, at the rate of three or four pagodas for every plough.[23]

If the tax farmer was unable to collect the sum he had engaged for, he was
to "procure new *Reyuts*, whom he shall provide with new ploughs, and by
advancing *Tucavee* to them, enable them to complete the cultivation, so
that the amount specified in the engagement be realized."[24]
    Individuals who undertook investments were to be granted land tax-
free: "If any person shall, at his own expence, dig tanks, wells, &c. . . . a
quantity of ground shall be given to him as *Inaumkutcodukee*; and if no
such custom shall prevail at the place in question . . . land [shall] be given
to him as *Enaum [inam]*."[25] Revenue reductions were also to be offered as
an incentive to expand cultivated area: "Land which has lain fallow ten
years shall be delivered to *Reyuts* to cultivate, upon *Cowle*; the first year
they shall be exempt from paying any revenue, and the second year they
shall only pay half the customary assessment; but the third year the full
amount thereof shall be collected from them."[26]
    Very much in the spirit of earlier writings on statecraft, Mysore actively
sought to promote agricultural improvement. With such improvement
cultivators and producers in agriculture could be attracted and fixed
within the confines of the kingdom. Thus, the productivity and dynamism of agriculture in late pre-colonial South India were rooted in part in
the power and mobility of the producers themselves. The pattern of
cotton cultivation further reveals the connections between investment,
political authority and labor.

---

[22] Wagoner, *Tidings of the King*, pp. 90, 155. Emphasis added.
[23] Burrish Crisp, *The Mysorean Revenue Regulations* (Calcutta, 1792), in C. B. Greville,
    British India Analyzed (London, 1793), article 2.
[24] Crisp, *Mysorean Revenue Regulations*, article 10.
[25] Crisp, *Mysorean Revenue Regulations*, article 36.
[26] Crisp, *Mysorean Revenue Regulations*, article 15.

The pattern of cotton cultivation

Cotton was cultivated in South India under two very different regimes. I have labeled these intensive and extensive.[27] According to figures from the early nineteenth century, yields from intensive cultivation were at least double those from extensive cultivation.[28] More reliable data from late nineteenth-century Coimbatore confirm the superiority of intensive cultivation, which yielded $62\frac{1}{2}$ pounds of cleaned cotton per acre as opposed to $22\frac{1}{2}$ pounds from extensive.[29] Intensive cultivation, however, required far greater inputs of both capital and labor. Descriptions of the two cultivation regimes, which are given in Appendix 2.1, make this clear. Intensive cultivation was carried out on the rich and loamy black soils of South India while extensive cultivation was carried out on thinner and lighter red soils.

Cropping patterns in South India are commonly attributed to ecological conditions, such as soil type and the availability of water.[30] Soil was certainly a factor in the distribution of extensive and intensive cultivation. Ninety-six percent of the soil in Dindigul is red and virtually all cotton cultivation was extensive.[31] Red soils also predominated in other areas of major extensive cultivation, including South Arcot, Trichinopoly and the Baramahal. However, the availability of soil alone cannot explain the distribution of intensive and extensive cultivation.

Much of the intensive cultivation in South India was found in Tinnevelly, Madurai, Coimbatore and the southern Deccan plateau, part of which came to be known as the Ceded Districts in British India.[32] However, the relative proportion of intensive cultivation varied widely between these four areas and this variation cannot be explained solely by the distribution of soil types. In Coimbatore and Tinnevelly intensive cultivation accounted for only a small fraction of total cotton cultivation; most cotton in these districts was grown extensively. However, the predominance of extensive cultivation was not owing to shortages of black soil. On the contrary, abundant quantities of black soil were available in

---

[27] The rest of this section is largely based on detailed surveys of cotton cultivation conducted by the English East India Company between 1790 and 1820. The purpose of the surveys was to collect information to form policies for the promotion of cotton cultivation. The Company's original motive was to reduce cotton imports into its territories in order to reduce the drain of specie. In the nineteenth century, however, the Company was attempting to increase the output of cotton to meet the growing demand for cotton in China.

[28] Coimbatore Collectorate Records, 1812, vol. 605, pp. 204–26, TNA; Godavari District Records, 1798, vol. 847, pp. 156–65, APSA; English East India Company, *The Baramahal Records*, Section IV: *Products* (Madras, 1912), p. 106.

[29] F. A. Nicholson, *The Coimbatore District Manual* (Madras, 1898), p. 235.

[30] See Ludden, *Peasant History*, pp. 51–67; Baker, *Rural Economy*, chap. 1.

[31] W. Francis, *Madura District Gazetteer* (2 vols., Madras, 1914), vol. I, p. 12.

[32] For simplicity I will refer to this area as the Ceded Districts.

both places. In Coimbatore, much of the area of this black soil was cleared only in the nineteenth and twentieth centuries.[33] In Tinnevelly, in the mid-eighteenth century, Jean-Baptiste Tavernier found that the black soils in the northern part of the district were heavily forested.[34] These forests were cleared from the early nineteenth century and between 1811 and 1862 cotton production in Tinnevelly increased ten-fold.[35]

Red soils were also abundant in the Ceded Districts and Madurai, but in contrast to Coimbatore and Tinnevelly, in these areas virtually all cotton cultivation was located on black soils.[36] In fact, in Madurai and the Bellary Division of the Ceded Districts no cotton was cultivated at all on red soils. The only extensive cultivation in the Ceded Districts was in the Kurpah (Cuddapah) Division and even there it represented only a small fraction of total cultivation. Thus the distribution of intensive and extensive cultivation in these four areas – Coimbatore, Tinnevelly, Madurai and the Ceded Districts – indicates that the location of soil types was not the only determinant of cropping patterns. The major factor behind these patterns was the availability of capital, which could then attract its supply of labor.

While extensive cultivation required very little outlay of money, intensive rested upon the expenditure of abundant supplies of capital. Funds were needed for clearing and plowing the heavy black soils and for the close supervision which intensive cultivation demanded. According to Thomas Munro, in the Ceded Districts a portion of the capital necessary for cultivation on black soils was provided by political and revenue authorities in the form of taccavi, or advances for the financing of production:

These lands, after having lain waste eight or ten years, cannot be broken up without a large plough drawn by six yokes of bullocks, and they must afterwards be cleared of the roots of the long grass [nut grass] with which they are overrun, by a machine drawn by seven or eight yokes. The expense of setting a single plough in motion is about 150 pagodas, so that it can only be done by substantial ryots, or by the union of two or three of those whose means are less. A considerable portion of the bullocks employed are from Nellore, and it is absolutely necessary that the yoke next to the plough be of that breed. It is for the purchase of that yoke, which usually costs from 20 to 24 pagodas that the ryots require tuckavi [taccavi].[37]

[33] Coimbatore Collectorate Records, 1812, vol. 605, pp. 204–26, TNA; Baker, *Rural Economy*, pp. 93–5.

[34] Jean-Baptiste Tavernier, *Travels in India*, trans. V. Ball, ed. W. Crooke (2 vols., London, 1925), vol. I, p. 216. Cited in Baker, *Rural Economy*, p. 81.

[35] Cotton cultivation increased from 4,000 *candies* in 1811 to nearly 40, 000 in 1862. The source for the 1811 figure is Tinnevelly Collectorate Records, 1811, vol. 3572, pp. 239–62, TNA. The source for 1862 is J. Talboys Wheeler, *Handbook to the Cotton Cultivation in the Madras Presidency* (London, 1863), p. 211.

[36] Madurai Collectorate Records, 1812, vol. 1156, pp. 145–50, TNA; Bellary District Records, 1813, vol. 426, pp. 9–20, TNA.

[37] Quoted in J. D. B. Gribble, *A Manual of the District of Cuddapah* (Madras, 1875), pp. 201–2. Munro made these observations in 1806. Taccavi is a government loan. With

The Ceded Districts and Madurai formed the core regions of major political entities. Being politically important, they were the focus of state activities to improve agriculture, which also served to attract labor. The final goal of this investment was, of course, to increase the revenue potential of the realm. Thus the presence of states here supplied the capital for the clearing and cultivation of black soils. In contrast to Madurai and the Ceded Districts, Coimbatore and Tinnevelly were outside major South Indian political centers. From its settlement in medieval times Coimbatore was a frontier region.[38] Only in the nineteenth and twentieth centuries did Coimbatore's status change as it became a dynamic and booming agricultural, and later industrial, center. Tinnevelly held a similar position. Until the nineteenth century the focus of investment in Tinnevelly was paddy cultivation in the valley of the Tambraparni.[39]

To sum up, the locales where cotton was cultivated intensively had not only black soils, but also a political superstructure which supplied credit to support a capital- and labor-intensive production regime. The foundations for intensive cotton cultivation in the Deccan were laid from at least the late medieval period with the rise of the Vijayanagar state. The capital of Vijayanagar was in the southern Deccan – in the heart of what became a major cotton-producing area – which led to the economic vitalization of that region. The patronage of the Vijayanagar state led to the pushing out of the frontier and a great expansion in cultivated area in the Raichur Doab and also south of the Tungabahdra in Rayalaseema.[40] These trends continued in the seventeenth and eighteenth centuries after the decline of Vijayanagar in 1565. The work of Stein has shown that the areas which formed the core of the Vijayanagar Empire – especially the Ceded Districts – were heavily contested by a number of smaller states which emerged under the rule of poligars. The conflicts between these states and the consequent military pressures forced the competing states to supply credit for agricultural improvement.[41]

The rise of Vijayanagar had consequences for the drier areas of South India far beyond the immediate center of the empire. Before Vijayanagar the important political centers in South India were located in the river

these loans, revenue and political authorities bore some of the risks associated with agricultural operations in South India and this may be seen as akin to the advance system in weaving. For a discussion of the importance of the state contribution to investment, see Satish Chandra, "Some Institutional Factors in Providing Capital Inputs for the Improvement and Expansion of Cultivation in Medieval India," *Indian Historical Review*, 3 (1976), pp. 83–98.

[38] M. Arokiaswami, *Kongunad* (Madras, 1956) and Baker, *Rural Economy*, pp. 93–5.
[39] Ludden, *Peasant History*, chaps. 1–3.
[40] Burton Stein, *Vijayanagar* (Cambridge, 1989), chap. 4.
[41] Stein, *Vijayanagar*, chap. 5. For further information on poligars, albeit in the Tamil country, see K. Rajayyan, *Rise and Fall of the Poligars of Tamilnadu* (Madras, 1974).

valleys.[42] However, concomitant with the rise of the Vijayanagar Empire was a massive southward migration of Telugu-speaking peoples under the auspices of the Vijayanagar state. These migrants established a series of Nayaka kingdoms in the plains of the Tamil country, which produced an economic boom in the dry areas of this region. The most important and powerful Nayaka kingdom had its capital at Madurai and the political and military aspirations of the Madurai Nayaka led to a project of agricultural improvement. The state sought to increase the revenue base to finance the higher levels of political and military expenditures. And it appears that the Madurai Nayaka financed the expansion of cultivation on black soils, which made it possible for cotton cultivation within the kingdom to be confined to these soils. David Ludden has found that the settlement of the black soil areas in northern Tinnevelly was undertaken under the auspices of the Madurai Nayaka.[43]

To sum up the discussion thus far, agriculture was a major arena for investment in late pre-colonial South India. Therefore, the high productivity of agriculture in South India was not due to "natural" advantages of climate or soil, but rather to high rates of investment which were sustained through a complex mediation between competition for labor and political authority. The success of statecraft in late pre-colonial South India was dependent upon populating ones territories and the simplest route to this was investment in agricultural improvement. Expenditure of capital, in other words, created its supply of labor.

From cotton to yarn

In late pre-colonial South India the shortage of producers in agriculture and their mobility put them in a strong position in the political and economic order. The position of these producers, especially those located in dry areas, was further strengthened by the availability of work. There were abundant opportunities for seasonal work, as well as work during periods of crisis in agriculture, and this gave peasants and other agrarian producers a great measure of independence. An important source of non-agricultural work was the preparation of cotton for weaving. Agricultural producers, and in particular women, did much of the processing of

---

[42] See Stein, *Peasant State and Society,* chap. 2.
[43] Ludden, *Peasant History,* p. 51. The importance of capital for cultivation of black soils may also help to explain why Telugu migrants to the Tamil country chose to settle in black soil regions. Burton Stein has speculated that the migrants may have possessed technical knowledge to make those soils productive. David Ludden has attributed the location of Telugu migrants to the fact that in Tinnevelly the black soil areas were the only uninhabited areas in the district. However, an additional reason may have been the capital requirements of cultivation on black soils. The Telugu migrants – through their connections to the Nayaka states – may have been able to command the capital necessary to clear and cultivate these lands.

cotton, which transformed it from its raw state to yarn, at which point it was ready for the weavers' looms.

Cotton cleaning

The first stage in the preparation of cotton was a thorough cleaning. This was a two-step process. In the first step the cotton lint was separated from the seed. In the second a finer cleaning was performed to remove dirt, twigs, leaves and other foreign matter that was stuck to the lint. As seeds accounted for about three-fourths of the weight of the raw cotton, they were always removed before cotton was transported. Cotton growers also sought to remove the seeds themselves as they were valuable feed for cattle.

Peasant women separated the lint from the seed in their homes during lull periods of the day, week or year.[44] Women in cotton-cultivating families often did this work, but cotton pickers also cleaned the cotton which they had received as their wages for picking. Both these groups usually sold the cleaned cotton to merchants, but, on occasion, these women also performed the second, finer cleaning and spun the cotton into yarn themselves. The yarn was then sold to merchants or given to a weaver for manufacture into cloth. A woman performing both steps could clean about five pounds of raw cotton a day.[45]

Cotton cultivators and pickers also sold their raw cotton to merchants, who either employed women to clean it or sold it in its uncleaned state directly to spinners. The spinners would have cleaned the cotton themselves before spinning it into yarn. In northern Mysore, according to Francis Buchanan, the women hired by merchants as cotton cleaners received 4 fanams for working up 100 pounds of raw cotton and the yield was 25 pounds of cleaned cotton.[46] Buchanan provides no further details, but it was likely that the merchants operated a putting-out system in which women performed the work in their homes. An American cotton planter in Tinnevelly attempted to employ women in a centralized cotton cleaning workshop, but gave up after finding it extremely difficult to employ women outside the home.[47]

In the southern Maratha country there was a very simple technique for separating the lint from seed. The raw cotton was placed on a flat stone and the cleaner, sitting on a stool, used her feet to roll an iron bar over the

---

[44] Notes on the Culture of the Bourbon Cotton in the Province of Tinnevelly by a Resident Planter, c. 1815, Board Miscellaneous – Coimbatore District, TNA.
[45] Tinnevelly Collectorate Records, 1811, vol. 3572, pp. 239–62, TNA; Buchanan, *Journey*, vol. II, p. 222.
[46] Buchanan, *Journey*, vol. III, p. 317.
[47] Notes on the Culture of the Bourbon Cotton in the Province of Tinnevelly by a Resident Planter, c. 1815, Board Miscellaneous – Coimbatore District, TNA.

cotton. The seed was separated from the cotton lint and rolled out to the front of the stone, and the cleaned cotton fell under the stool. While performing this operation the cleaner wore flat wooden soles on her feet.[48] In Mysore and in the Tamil and Telugu districts, the *churka*, a more sophisticated device, was used. The instrument consisted of two rollers with a small gap between them. Turning a hand crank set the rollers to rotate in opposite directions and raw cotton was fed into the gap. The cotton lint passed through the opening, but the seeds, as they were too large, were left behind.[49] Using a churka a woman in Tinnevelly could clean $9\frac{3}{8}$ pounds of raw cotton – which yielded 2 pounds of cleaned cotton – a day.[50] The churka was made of wood and in the 1820s sold for $5\frac{1}{4}$ rupees.[51] The device drew high praise from the American cotton planter in Tinnevelly, according to whom, "The simplicity and efficiency of [the churka] cannot be too much admired, notwithstanding all the rage for the improvement of it."[52] In the early nineteenth century the English East India Company made several attempts to introduce the American cotton gin, but with little success. The American gin did not work well with the short staple cottons of South India.[53]

The first cleaning of the cotton only removed the seed. Dirt, leaves and other foreign matter often stuck to the cotton during picking, transporting and even during the first cleaning step. This material was removed in a finer and more thorough cleaning, which was akin to the carding of wool in England. The fine cleaning was always done as close as possible – both spatially and temporally – to the spinning since cotton tended to attract dirt during handling. The practice of transporting cotton before performing a thorough cleaning may explain why during the nineteenth century buyers in London found Indian cotton to be extremely dirty. Only the first cleaning step – the removal of the seed – would have been carried out on cotton that was exported.[54]

---

[48] Wheeler, *Handbook*, pp. 16–17.
[49] Guntur Collectorate Records, 1835, vol. 3991, p. 40, APSA; Wheeler, *Handbook*, p. 17.
[50] Notes on the Culture of the Bourbon Cotton in the Province of Tinnevelly by a Resident Planter, *c.* 1815, Board Miscellaneous – Coimbatore District, TNA.
[51] Elijah Hoole, *Madras, Mysore, and the South of India: A Personal Narrative of a Mission to those Countries* (London, 1844), p. 253.
[52] Notes on the Culture of the Bourbon Cotton in the Province of Tinnevelly by a Resident Planter, *c.* 1815, Board Miscellaneous – Coimbatore District, TNA. For additional praise, see John Briggs, *The Cotton Trade of India* (London, 1840), p. 43.
[53] See Wheeler, *Handbook*, p. 34.
[54] Abundant evidence for complaints from London about the dirtiness of Indian cotton is provided in Wheeler, *Handbook*. This explanation is also more satisfactory than previous ones which have pointed to the sharp dealings of Indian merchants: "Cotton buying in the Bombay of the 1860's was frustrating business: the seller determined to cheat, the buyer equally determined to stop him. But where the European broker, with his delicate constitution and sensitive dignity, stood off in the shade and tried with the aid of native

The second cleaning was done by placing a bow – which Elijah Hoole compared to the hatter's bow used for bowing wool in England – on the cotton and hitting it with a wooden mallet. The ensuing vibrations of the bow separated the dirt from the cotton and also placed the cotton fibers in parallel for spinning. The Indian bow was reputed to clean cotton as well as any machinery in Europe[55] and Hoole reported that in the 1820s it cost seven rupees.[56] Further information on the second cleaning step is limited. In some instances it was done by the women who spun the cotton, but there was also a class of professional cotton cleaners who appear to have been drawn from the ranks of weavers. In the Tamil country each professional cleaner possessed a monopoly on cleaning within a specified territory: "[Cotton cleaners] have a sort of prescriptive right established by long custom to clean the cotton in certain ranges containing a greater or smaller number of villages in which others are not allowed to set up. Some of them have thus employment for the whole twelve months, whilst others are not employed for six months in the year."[57] Presumably, cotton cleaners who did not have employment for the whole year also worked as weavers. At Rajahmundry in the late eighteenth century a professional cotton cleaner received 12 fanams for cleaning 25 pounds of cotton.[58] After this cleaning, the cotton was ready to be spun.

Spinning

Space and time were intimately linked in pre-colonial South India. Spatial location determined important elements of social and economic life, including agrarian and ritual calendars and the rhythm of work and leisure. The characteristics of a space were, in turn, heavily shaped by ecological conditions, the crucial division being wet and dry. The wet areas were zones of paddy cultivation and they rested upon large and elaborate systems of irrigation. In the dry areas, by contrast, millets and other rain-fed crops were cultivated.[59] Although the distinction between wet and dry is an ecological one, it is by no means "natural." Rather, as

---

servants to obtain unadulterated goods of uniform quality, the Indian merchant remained out on the open floor, called, cajoled, nagged and flattered, showed the best cotton from mixed bales and lauded their purity, yielded on a bad bale to return with its brother – in short, displayed the patience of a saint to sell the wares of a thief." David S. Landes, *Bankers and Pashas: International Finance and Economic Imperialism in Egypt* (Cambridge, Mass., 1958), pp. 71–2.

[55] Briggs, *Cotton Trade*, p. 54.   [56] Hoole, *Mission*, pp. 250–1.

[57] Extracts from the Proceedings of the Board of Revenue, August 29, 1814, North Arcot District Records, vol. 29, pp. 69–174, TNA.

[58] Godavari District Records, 1798, vol. 847, p. 158, APSA.

[59] See Ludden, *Peasant History*, pp. 52–67; Baker, *Rural Economy*, chap. 1.

David Ludden has argued, it is the outcome of countless individual and social decisions made over the span of many centuries. The recent agrarian history of South India has distinguished between wet and dry zones purely with reference to agricultural life. A consideration of textile manufacturing enriches the distinctions between the zones, however. There is abundant evidence that spinning was concentrated in the dry areas of South India and, as a consequence, there were profound links between agriculture and industry in these areas. These links were broken in the early nineteenth century, an aspect of deindustrialization in South India which has received little attention. However, it undoubtedly had profound implications for agrarian and gender relations in these areas.

In the wet zones the yearly calendar was completely filled except for a brief lull in May.[60] The cultivation of paddy alone created more than enough work throughout the year, but there were also other crops to be planted and tended. In addition, irrigation systems had to be maintained, which took a great deal of time and effort.[61] In the dry areas, by contrast, there was a long agricultural off-season which lasted from mid-January to July. Ritual calendars in the dry areas reflect this agrarian rhythm. In Kongunad Brenda Beck found that ritual activities for the right-hand caste, which was composed largely of agriculturalists, were concentrated in the first six months of the year. Although Beck herself did not make the connection, this coincided with the agricultural slack season. In contrast, the ritual activities of the left-hand caste, mostly artisans, were concentrated in the last six months. This was the slack season for many artisans, most notably weavers, who were idle during the rainy season. These ritual calendars in Kongunad appear to be of long-standing. For example, a new agrarian calendar created in the nineteenth and twentieth centuries, with the expansion of garden and peanut cultivation, conflicted with the ritual calendar. However, the timing of rituals and festivals did not change.[62]

Women in the dry areas took up spinning to fill the slack periods in both the daily and annual schedules. In 1818, the Collector of Coimbatore observed that women were engaged in spinning whenever they had a

[60] A major exception to this general rule was along the Palar River in the northern Tamil country where the adimai engaged in spinning. This was because of the more seasonal nature of paddy cultivation in this area which resulted from the less secure availability of water. In addition, the dense settlement of weavers who specialized in very high-quality cloths may have created a need for specialist spinners who could cater to this need. The adimai in the northern Tamil country possessed the requisite skills to produce extremely fine yarns. See MPP, 1771, vol. 106B, p. 1012, TNA.

[61] Ludden, *Peasant History*, pp. 56–7.

[62] Brenda E. F. Beck, *Peasant Society in Konku: A Study of Right and Left Subcastes in South India* (Vancouver, 1972), p. 55; Baker, *Rural Economy*, pp. 200–14.

leisure hour.[63] In 1797, a Commercial Resident at Madapollam noted that the returns to spinning varied during the year, which suggests that spinning was a seasonal activity.[64] During the agricultural off-season, when there was little else to do, the number of women engaged in spinning would have risen. Consequently, the supply of yarn would have increased, decreasing both its price and the returns to the spinners. A Commercial Resident at Ganjam has provided additional evidence for the seasonality of spinning: "the beginning of November, the grain is ready to cut here which employs all the poorer sort of people that not withstanding cotton is plenty the weavers were forced to stand still for want of thread."[65]

According to figures from the late eighteenth century on costs in cloth production, the value added from spinning was almost equal to that from weaving.[66] In the dry districts, where it was concentrated, spinning must have contributed a great deal to total household incomes, especially for poorer cultivators. In addition, spinning played an important economic role as insurance in the dry areas. In times of drought, when earnings from agriculture were threatened and agricultural work unavailable, many women must have supported their families with their spinning, which was work that was to be had as long as cotton was available. The dry districts had not only the lowest rainfall in South India, but also the greatest uncertainty and variation in rain. According to Brian Murton, in Salem between 1770 and 1790 "full crops" were obtained only in five years; three-fourths crops in seven years; half crops in five years; three-eighths crops in two years; and one-quarter crop in one year.[67] The specter of drought and crop failure was ever present in the dry districts of South India and spinning helped peasants to survive these disasters. Reflecting its importance, in Kangayam, one of the driest taluks in the Tamil country, a spinning wheel was included in a woman's dowry, a

[63] Coimbatore Collectorate Records, 1818, vol. 611, pp. 142–3, TNA. The following observations on spinning are from sources spanning a few decades. The paucity of information on spinning imposes such a procedure. However, the available information suggests that no major changes took place in spinning, and its place in the agrarian order, until the second quarter of the nineteenth century.

[64] Godavari District Records, 1797, vol. 886, APSA.

[65] English East India Company, Letters to Fort St. David, 1750 (Madras, 1935), p. 9. Similarly in the northern Tamil country, the price of thread was 20 percent cheaper in the rainy season when the spinners were unable to get any other work. See MPP, vol. P/241/26, p. 2831, OIOC.

[66] MPP, 1790, vol. P/241/16, pp. 334–64, OIOC.

[67] Brian J. Murton, "Land and Class: Cultural, Social and Biophysical Integration in Interior Tamilnadu in the Late Eighteenth Century," in Robert E. Frykenberg, Land Tenure and Peasant in South Asia (Delhi, 1977), p. 90.

practice which was maintained until the 1960s.[68] At times of drought, when many hands turned to spinning, the returns fell:

the thread is then brought into market and sold from 3 seers [a measure of weight] to 5 and it has even been known at 7 or 8 seers the rupee, but this is only where there is, from drought or other causes little or no cultivation carried on, as was the case during the late famine; every hand was then employed to gain a scanty livelihood by spinning; hence it appears that the price of thread does not always bear a proportion to that of cotton; during the time of cultivation and harvest, it is dearer from the above reason than at any other time, although the price of cotton may be the same.[69]

Additional information on spinning is limited. This is most likely because, as women's work, it was considered a low-status activity and therefore not the subject of systematic investigation. Nor were spinning wheels taxed as were looms and the equipment and tools of other "professionals." The perception of spinning as a woman's job long outlived its economic importance in South India. In the late nineteenth century, male jail inmates were trained in various crafts, including carpet-making and weaving, but they resisted training in spinning on the grounds that it was women's work. In the jails where it was introduced, spinning was confined to the female prisoners.[70] By this time spinning had virtually disappeared from South India, but its gender categorization had not, an indication of how deeply gender perceptions may penetrate. This gender division of labor was perpetuated in missionary schools, where only girls were taught to spin.[71] These attitudes were to change in the early twentieth century after Gandhi's rise to prominence led to a small-scale revitalization of spinning. Gandhi's example even encouraged men to take it up.[72]

Almost all women in the dry areas spun yarn. The notable exceptions were women from the households of brahmins and a few other high castes such as the karakara vellalavaru in the Baramahal.[73] In many parts of South India spinning offered a means of support for widows, who probably became expert at it. Women from agricultural families generally

---

[68] Personal communication from S. S. Sivakumar, Department of Econometrics, Madras University.
[69] English East India Company, The Baramahal Records, Section IV: Products, pp. 58–9.
[70] Edgar Thurston, Monograph on the Woolen Fabric Industry of the Madras Presidency (Madras, 1898) pp. 8–10.
[71] Hoole, Mission, p. 129.
[72] Havell, Reports on the Arts and Industries of the Madras Presidency, p. 7; D. Narayana Rao, Report on the Survey of Cottage Industries in the Madras Presidency (Madras, 1929), pp. 223–7.
[73] English East India Company, The Baramahal Records, Section III: Inhabitants, p. 87.

spun the coarse qualities of yarn. The best spinners were women from "untouchable" households, which is not surprising as these were the poorest groups in South India. For them spinning would have been invaluable in its dual role as a supplement to earnings from agricultural labor and insurance during times of dearth. Telugu parayars settled in the northern Tamil country spun some of the finest yarns in South India and their production was used to weave the muslin of Arni.[74]

All spinning in South India was done using a wheel, which was un-usual. Elsewhere, in Bengal and England for example, a wheel was used for coarse yarns and a distaff for finer varieties.[75] In South India a large spinning wheel was used for most counts of yarn. Elijah Hoole reported that in the 1820s one made of teak could be purchased for $3\frac{1}{2}$ rupees.[76] A smaller and more delicate wheel was used to manufacture finer yarns such as those used in Arni muslins.[77]

Spinners obtained cotton and sold their yarn in a variety of ways. Women in cotton cultivating households often spun a part of the harvest. Those who did not grow the crop purchased cotton and spun it. Presum-ably they financed the cotton purchases themselves, but no further details are known. Both sets of women could either sell their yarn to merchants or market it themselves at local fairs or marts where weavers came to make purchases. The spun yarn could also be given to a weaver to produce cloth for the use of the spinner's household. In the Godavari district, the remuneration for spinning one *maund* of cotton into coarse (14 punjam or 7 *call*) yarn was 42 fanams and the work took two months.[78]

Merchants also operated putting out systems for spinning. Elijah Hoole came across the following in South Arcot:

I walked into his house, and found several women employed in spinning a coarse description of cotton, and another winding the yarn off the cop into hank. He told me they received raw cotton from their employer, a native manufacturer, and returned it in hank, their delivering the whole being ascertained by the weight. Out of one *vis* (about three pounds) of cotton, they spin sixteen hanks, and receive for their labor eight fanams, about fourteen-pence, English money. One woman spins only one to one and a half hank per day; and consequently earns one penny, or a fraction more, as her daily wages.[79]

In northern Mysore, Buchanan reported that women received cotton wool from merchants and spun it "for hire." The women were paid $8\frac{3}{4}$

---

[74] Bidie, *Catalogue of Articles*, pp. 43–4.

[75] For Bengal see Hossain, *Company Weavers of Bengal*, p. 37. For England, Maxine Berg, *The Age of Manufactures 1700–1820* (London, 1985), p. 140.

[76] Hoole, *Mission*, p. 253.   [77] Bidie, *Catalogue of Articles*, pp. 43–4.

[78] Godavari District Records, 1798, vol. 847, p. 158, APSA.

[79] Hoole, *Mission*, pp. 247–8.

fanams for spinning 35 *seers* of cotton into coarse yarn. If she did no other work, a woman was capable of spinning three-fourths of a seer per day, which yielded a daily wage of 1.6 pennies.[80] Weavers in the northern Tamil country also advanced cotton to spinners, but reported that it was a very risky enterprise as spinners were known to run off with the cotton.[81]

Once spun, the yarn was ready for the manufacture of plain cloths. A small fraction of yarn was dyed or bleached for the manufacture of cloth patterned in the loom. The weaving of these cloths required much greater technical sophistication than plain cloths since the yarn was weakened by the high temperatures used in dyeing and bleaching. This was why as a rule the finishing steps were performed after the cloth was woven. The weavers who produced patterned goods dyed and bleached the yarn themselves.

[80] Buchanan, *Journey*, vol. III, p. 317.   [81] MPP, 1771, vol. 106B, p. 1012, TNA.

APPENDIX 2.1

THE COTTON CULTIVATION PROCESS

The extensive cultivation of cotton

The extensive cultivation of cotton was found in many parts of South India: it was the only form of cotton cultivation in Ganjam and Vizagapatnam and accounted for virtually all cotton cultivation in the Baramahal, South Arcot, Trichinopoly and Dindigul. It was also widespread in Coimbatore, Tinnevelly, Ramnad and Godavari.[1] Two features of extensive cotton cultivation made it especially attractive to peasants. First, it required little capital or labor and absolutely no expenditure of cash: the seeds were saved from previous crops and typically all the labor was provided by the cultivating household. Second, and perhaps even more appealingly, it reduced the risks posed by the uncertainties in the timing and extent of the monsoon, which made it integral to peasant subsistence strategies.

Under extensive cultivation cotton was usually interspersed with grains and there were several reasons for this practice. First, grains took less time than cotton to yield a harvest. They thus provided income to the cultivator before the cotton pods had ripened. Second, a harvest of grain increased the output from a plot of land, giving the cultivator a higher income. Third, the inter-cultivation of grains controlled for uncertainties in rainfall. The two crops had different water requirements, which reduced the risk to the cultivator.[2] For example, in Godavari white cotton was sown with black paddy and dhal. If the rains were scanty, the paddy failed, but the cotton and dhal survived. Conversely, if the rains were abundant, the cotton and dhal failed, but the paddy succeeded.[3] A Company servant in Salem provided a similar explanation for inter-cultivation: "It is reckoned a great speculation in farming to sow cotton alone, because too much or too little rain is unfavorable for cotton, on which account a season may be favorable for cotton, but unfavorable for other productions, and vice-versa. By sowing both the farmer has a chance of getting a moderate crop of each, and almost a certainty of getting a good crop of either one or the other."[4] The crops that were inter-cultivated with cotton varied from district to district, but they were typically millets and other dry crops. In Coimbatore cotton was also inter-cultivated with dhals and oil-seeds and in Godavari, as just stated, with black paddy and dhal.[5]

In the Tamil country, *nadam*, the variety of cotton used in extensive cultivation, was a perennial, which provided peasants an extra element of security. To reach maturity, the dry grains cultivated in South India required sufficient supplies of water at several critical periods. A failure of the rains at these times would severely curtail the yield. Since it was a perennial, nadam cotton was less reliant than

---

[1] English East India Company, *Reports and Documents Connected with the Proceedings in Regard to the Culture and Manufacture of Cotton-wool, Raw Silk and Indigo in India* (London, 1836), pp. 398–421.
[2] English East India Company, *The Baramahal Records*, Section IV: *Products*, p. 106.
[3] Godavari District Records, 1798, vol. 847, pp. 156–65, APSA.
[4] English East India Company, *The Baramahal Records*, Section IV: *Products*, p. 106.
[5] Salem Collectorate Records, Board of Revenue Correspondence, 1819, vol. 3172, pp. 79–81, TNA; Trichinopoly District Records, Board of Revenue Correspondence, 1812, vol. 3670, pp. 267–72, TNA; Memorandum of Cotton Cultivation, Board Miscellaneous – Coimbatore District, *c.* 1815, TNA.

grains upon rains falling at any particular time. The nadam cotton was also a shrub, which enabled it to withstand droughts that typically killed cereals. In addition, in times of poor rainfall, the cotton yield was reduced, but, unlike grains, the cotton crop was rarely a total failure. The nadam cotton plant also lasted from three to five years. Even after a poor monsoon it would recover and yield well after the first good subsequent rain.[6]

Extensive cultivation of cotton was concentrated on red soils throughout South India, but the variety of cotton that was grown varied geographically: in the Andhra districts, *cocanadas* cotton (*Gossypium indicum*) was planted while nadam (*Gossypium nanking*) was grown in the Tamil country.[7] Quite detailed information on the techniques of extensive cultivation is available for nadam cotton in the Tamil districts and this material imparts something of the flavor of extensive growing of the plant. In particular, it shows that nadam could be cultivated in a very perfunctory manner, with little plowing, manuring and weeding, as well as with great care and attention.

Nadam cotton could be planted at any time of the year except during the height of summer (April/May) and during the northeast monsoon (November/December).[8] It was often sown between August and October, for which the plowing of the ground began between April and June. Red soils were light which meant that they could be plowed without much effort. After plowing, the fields were manured. The usual method was to pen a flock of cattle, sheep or goats for two or three days. It was said that the large flocks of sheep for which Coimbatore was famous were reared primarily for this purpose. A more thorough plowing was performed after manuring and the number of plowings was determined by the quantity of manure that had been applied. Three plowings were typical in Trichinopoly; usually five, but sometimes six or seven, in Madurai; and between four and twelve in Coimbatore.[9]

Sowing was done by broadcast between August and October and the ground lightly turned up to cover the seeds. To prevent clumping of the seeds, they were first soaked overnight in a mixture of water, cow dung and salt. As the plants matured the field was weeded several times by plowing between the rows of cotton and grain.[10] The more often the plowing was done, the higher the cotton yields. This advice was contained in a Tamil proverb from Coimbatore district: "Inter-plough your young cotton seven times and you will get a pot of money."[11]

The cotton was ready to pick six to twelve months after sowing. The nadam plant yielded cotton for three to five years and pickings were taken at six- to

[6] Nicholson, *The Coimbatore District Manual*, p. 232.
[7] Arno Schmidt, *Cotton Growing in India* (n.p., n.d.), pp. 9–19; Arno S. Pearse, *Indian Cotton* (n.p., n.d.), pp. 141–58. Neither volume has publication information, but they appear to date from the mid-nineteenth century.
[8] Translation of a Tamil Memorandum for the Cultivation of the Cotton Plant, Called Parapoon in Tinnevelly, *c.* 1815, Board Miscellaneous – Coimbatore District, TNA.
[9] Trichinopoly District Records, Board of Revenue Correspondence, 1812, vol. 3670, pp. 267–72, TNA; Madurai Collectorate Records, 1812, vol. 1156, pp. 145–50, TNA; Coimbatore Collectorate Records, 1812, vol. 605, pp. 204–26, TNA.
[10] Trichinopoly District Records, Board of Revenue Correspondence, 1812, vol. 3670, pp. 267–72, TNA; Madurai Collectorate Records, 1812, vol. 1156, pp. 145–50, TNA.
[11] Nicholson, *The Coimbatore District Manual*, p. 234.

twelve-month intervals. Picking practices under extensive cultivation varied widely. Ideally cotton should be picked soon after the pod has burst. This was the custom in Tinnevelly where the cultivator and his family picked cotton every other day for a period of six or seven weeks.[12] However, in Coimbatore, to minimize their labor, peasants waited for all the pods to burst and picked cotton only once. Both the yield and the quality of the cotton suffered by this practice as burst pods were subject to the elements. They often attracted dirt and deteriorated in quality and a short shower could completely ruin the burst pods.[13]

The intensive cultivation of cotton

In the mid-nineteenth century J. Talboys Wheeler noted that the successful and profitable cultivation of cotton in South India required investment of capital and the application of hard labor. This observation was no less valid for earlier centuries and was precisely the secret behind the intensive cultivation of cotton. Under intensive regimes, cotton cultivation practices were far more careful and rigorous than under extensive and the reward was far higher yields of cotton. In addition, the intensive cultivation of cotton was more profitable than extensive cultivation.[14] However, the capital and labor demands of intensive cultivation limited its extent.

Intensive cultivation was found in much of South India, but it was concentrated on the black "cotton" soils of Tinnevelly, Madurai, Coimbatore and the Ceded Districts. These soils required large inputs of capital. Black soils were clayey and heavy, which made clearing and plowing expensive.[15] Therefore, intensive cultivation could only be undertaken by cultivators who themselves possessed capital or had access to capital. In addition, the labor supplied by a peasant household was not sufficient to meet the demands of cultivation on black soils. This meant cultivators had to be in a position to obtain and pay hired laborers. Finally, intensive cultivation entailed greater risks than extensive. Thus cultivators had to possess sufficient means to weather crop failures.

Francis Buchanan has provided a detailed account of intensive cultivation in Coimbatore.[16] The soil was first plowed four times between mid-August and October. Manure was then applied and the field plowed again, but on occasion manure was omitted altogether.[17] Immediately after the first rains of the northeast monsoon, usually in November, the seeds were sown by broadcast. Between early December and early January the field was weeded by means of a small hoe called a *cotu*. This was more laborious, thus more costly, than weeding by plowing between the plants, which was used in extensive cotton cultivation.[18] The cotton

---

[12] Translation of a Tamil Memorandum for the Cultivation of the Cotton Plant, Called Parapoon in Tinnevelly, *c.* 1815, Board Miscellaneous – Coimbatore District, TNA.

[13] Coimbatore Collectorate Records, 1819, vol. 612, pp. 33–40, TNA.

[14] Coimbatore Collectorate Records, 1812, vol. 605, pp. 204–26, TNA.

[15] Baker, *Rural Economy*, p. 201.   [16] Buchanan, *Journey*, vol. II, p. 222.

[17] In 1812, William Garrow, the Revenue Collector in Coimbatore, wrote that for *uppam* cultivation the ground was plowed nine times, was sown by itself, and no manure was applied. See Coimbatore Collectorate Records, 1812, vol. 605, pp. 204–26, TNA.

[18] Notes on the Culture of the Bourbon Cotton in the Province of Tinnevelly by a Resident Planter, c. 1815, Board Miscellaneous – Coimbatore District, TNA.

was picked between March and June and the cotton plant usually pulled immediately from the ground. However, if there were rains in June, one more picking was taken in July and then the plant pulled.

Under intensive cultivation in Coimbatore, just as with extensive, cultivators preferred not to plant cotton alone, but they had no choice if the onset of the monsoon was delayed. Coconuts, oil-seeds, pulses and spices (including *horse-womum* and coriander) were some of the crops inter-cultivated with cotton in Coimbatore and as in extensive cultivation the reason was to control for uncertainties in rainfall.[19] Although the mixing of cotton with other crops in intensive cultivation halved the yield of cotton, for most cultivators a total crop failure due to untimely rains would have been disastrous and therefore not worth the gamble. Thus the majority opted for a lower but more secure return. In the Baramahal, farmers of the reddi caste, who were considered the best farmers in the district and among the most prosperous, were the only ones to intensively cultivate cotton without mixing it with grain.[20]

In the Deccan and Mysore, intensive cultivation used far more sophisticated and rigorous techniques than in the Tamil country. More specialized implements were utilized and far more labor was applied. For example, in the Ceded Districts sowing was done with a drill, which is much more efficient than sowing by broadcast, and much greater care and far more labor was expended in weeding and picking. All this required greater expenditure of capital and labor, but produced substantially higher yields.[21] In the Ceded Districts the major operations for intensive cultivation also commenced with the northeast monsoon. However, on fields that had been recently cultivated, thus already cleared, thorns and roots from the previous season were removed with a harrow several months earlier, usually in May or June. (As all manure was saved for grain cultivation in the Ceded Districts, no manure was applied to those fields planted with cotton.) The exact timing of sowing and plowing was dictated by the monsoon, but these steps were typically performed between mid-August and mid-September, after the soil had been moistened by a rain shower. Sowing and plowing were combined in a single operation and were done using a drill plow. As the name suggests, this implement was a combination drill and plow and consisted of three harrows and three bamboo drill *tutees*. A drill corresponded to each harrow and seeds were sown simultaneously in three separate channels. If cotton was mixed with grains, which was common, the sowing was done two or three weeks earlier than when cotton was cultivated by itself.

The sown seeds were covered by means of an instrument called a *goontika* which was a type of rake drawn by bullocks. The field was raked, harrowed and cleared of weeds at regular intervals by means of an instrument called a *junta*, which was drawn by bullocks between the rows of plants. As the plants matured

---

[19] Coimbatore Collectorate Records, 1809, vol. 604, pp. 25–8, TNA; Buchanan, *Journey*, vol. II, p. 327.
[20] English East India Company, *The Baramahal Records*, Section IV: *Products*, pp. 106–7.
[21] The following description of intensive cultivation in the Ceded Districts is drawn from Bellary District Records, 1813, vol. 426, pp. 9–20, TNA. Intensive cultivation on black soils in Mysore was very similar to that in the Ceded Districts. See the descriptions of Francis Buchanan.

and the junta could not be maneuvered safely between them, laborers were hired to remove weeds and grass with hoes. This had to be done frequently as weeds grew abundantly on black soils.

The cotton was ready to be picked after about five months. The exact time varied by locale within the Ceded Districts, but picking generally commenced in February or March and continued till May. Three pickings were taken with a two- to three-week interval between each. The first was the largest and most important of the three. Under intensive cultivation, unlike extensive, the cotton was picked by hired labor. The pickers were mostly women and children and their wages consisted of a share of their pickings. For the second and third pickings, which were smaller and also more difficult than the first, the wage share was one-third to one-half times greater than the share for the first picking.

APPENDIX 2.2

THE COTTON TRADE IN SOUTH INDIA

Table 2.1 gives the cotton output by district in South India around 1800. The table shows that much of the cotton cultivation was concentrated in only a few areas, largely in the interior districts. The major weaving centers, by contrast, were located on the coast, where very little cotton was cultivated. Because of this, there was a very large trade in cotton. In the seventeenth and eighteenth centuries cotton and yarn were among the most important items of internal commerce in South India.

The major trade routes for cotton originated in the Deccan, which was the main center of cotton cultivation; more than half of the cotton production of South India came from this area. In addition to the Ceded Districts cotton was cultivated widely in the Raichur Doab and the southern Maratha country. The cotton routes from the Deccan went east to supply the looms in the Northern Sarkars and south to supply the northern Tamil country and Mysore. Cotton cultivation in coastal Andhra and Mysore was not sufficient to meet local demand. The northern Tamil districts produced no cotton at all and thus were completely reliant upon cotton imported from the Deccan.

Table 2.1. *Cotton production and consumption in South India, c. 1814*

District	Cleaned cotton production (candies)
Ganjam	1,000
Vizagapatnam	750
Rajahmundry	250
Masulipatnam	very little
Guntur	3,041
Nellore	very little
Chingleput	none
Cuddalore	601
Tanjore	736
Trichinopoly	630
Madurai/Dindigul/Ramnad	1,980
Tinnevelly	2,360
Coimbatore	4,457
Ceded Districts (Kurpah Div.)	2,750
Ceded Districts (Bellary Div.)	10,156
From Raichur Doab	13,000
From other Deccan sources	1,865
Total	43,576

Sources: See Appendix 2.3.

The cotton trade from the Deccan to the Andhra coast dates from at least the early seventeenth century. Joseph Brennig has argued that in the 1630s the trade increased substantially to meet growing Dutch demand for cloth. To meet this greater demand, the transport of cotton by boats on the Godavari and Krishna was replaced by caravans of pack bullocks, which were organized by the nomadic *Banjara* community. After selling their cotton on the coast, the Banjaras purchased salt for sale in the interior. Brennig has speculated that from the Deccan the caravans followed a route which took them along the valley of the Godavari River.[1] The precise source of this cotton in the Deccan in the seventeenth century remains unclear, but Sanjay Subrahmanyam believes it to be the region extending from Nanded to Aurangabad.[2] On the coast, the imported cotton was considered superior to the local cotton. It was of a "more delicate texture," considerably cleaner, and more easily spun into yarn.[3]

Late eighteenth-century and early nineteenth-century sources provide more detailed information on this trade. Cotton continued to be carried by Banjara caravans to a number of destinations on the coast. An important market was at Vizagapatnam where English Company servants estimated around one thousand candies of cotton were brought for sale every year. Banjara caravans also carried cotton to the Guntur region.[4] An English Company servant also reported that Banjaras came from Sadah and sold cotton at Rajahmundry. Late eighteenth-century sources report that merchants residing on the coast in Yerranagoodam and Anantapilly were also involved in the cotton trade to Rajahmundry and financed the transport of cotton from the interior.[5]

The trading methods of the merchants were very different from those of the Banjaras. It cost the Banjaras 17 pagodas to purchase a candy of cotton and transport it to the coast: 9 pagodas for the cotton, $7\frac{1}{2}$ pagodas for customs and $\frac{1}{2}$ pagoda for gunny sacks to hold the cotton. On the coast they sold the cotton at 18 pagodas per candy. The Banjaras could afford to sell at such a small mark-up because they owned their cattle. Since cotton merchants did not own cattle, their costs of transport were higher. Thus they were often forced to store cotton on the coast in warehouses until the price was more favorable. For example, in January 1798, shortages had driven cotton prices up by 25 percent and merchants were selling off stocks of cotton that they had accumulated in the two previous years.[6]

Early nineteenth-century sources also contain estimates of the size of the trade. In 1795 865 candies of cotton were imported from the Deccan to Rajahmundry: 505 candies were brought by Banjara caravans and the remainder by merchants.[7] In 1803 an East India Company Commercial Resident estimated that 5,000

[1] Joseph Brennig, "Textile Producers and Production in Late Seventeenth Century Coromandel," *IESHR*, 23 (1986), p. 337.
[2] Sanjay Subrahmanyam, "Rural Industry and Commercial Agriculture in Late Seventeenth-Century South-eastern India," *Past and Present*, no. 126 (1989), p. 87.
[3] Godavari District Records, 1797, vol. 886, APSA.
[4] Guntur Collectorate Records, 1797, vol. 979, pp. 662–7, APSA.
[5] Godavari District Records, 1798, vol. 847, pp. 156–65, APSA.
[6] Godavari District Records, 1798, vol. 847, pp. 156–65, APSA.
[7] Godavari District Records, 1798, vol. 847, pp. 156–65, APSA.

candies of cotton were sold annually at Hinghaun Ghaut, an important Deccan cotton mart for the Banjara trade to the Northern Sarkars.[8] The Deccan also supplied cotton to the northern Tamil country and Mysore. There is evidence for this trade from the late seventeenth century, but it may have been much older.[9] Raichur had been a center for cotton cultivation since at least the twelfth century.[10] By Vijayanagar times it appears cotton was carried from the Raichur Doab along an overland trade route to the Tamil country.[11]

Around 1800 much the same route was followed. Cotton and yarn from the Maratha domains on the north bank of the Krishna and the Raichur Doab were carried through Bellary, where none of it was sold, and taken to Mysore, Nellore and the major cotton market at Walajapet.[12] Some of the cotton carried to Mysore was later re-exported to Salem.[13] Early nineteenth-century figures indicate that this trade was very sizable: 10,500 candies in 1806; 15,781 candies in 1813; and 12,781 candies in 1814–15. Thus the average annual trade for these years was 13,000 candies or more than three tons. Half of this quantity was in cotton and half in yarn. Cotton from the Ceded Districts followed the same routes and went to the same markets. Estimates of the quantity exported from the Ceded Districts range from 6,360 candies in 1806 to 4,400 candies in 1813 and 1814–15. The average of these years is 5,065 candies.[14] Thus the combined trade from the north bank of the Krishna and Raichur Doab and the Ceded Districts averaged 18,000 candies (or nearly five tons) in the early nineteenth century, which would have made it one of the largest bulk trades in the Indian subcontinent at this time. It was more than 50 percent larger than the cotton trade from Bundelkhand and central India to Bengal (before the start of the export trade to China), which Christopher Bayly reports as 190,000 United Provinces maunds (11,400 South Indian candies) in 1789.[15] At an average bullock load of 9 maunds (0.45 candy), the southward trade from the Deccan would have required 40,000 bullocks annually. While in Bangalore Francis Buchanan noted that the best cattle were reserved for the cotton trade, which is not surprising given that the distance covered was some 250 miles.[16]

The southward trade from the Deccan dwarfed the trade east to coastal Andhra. This is reflected in the trading methods. The southerly trade was not organized or financed by Banjaras. The trade was a major bulk trade under the control of large merchants residing in the Deccan. In the early eighteenth century,

---

[8] Godavari District Records, vol. 832, February 1, 1819, p. 105, APSA, cited in Brennig, "Textile Producers," p. 337.
[9] *FSGDC*, 1690, p. 30.
[10] Meera Abraham, *Two Medieval Merchant Guilds of South India*, (New Delhi, 1988), p. 163.
[11] See Stein, *Vijayanagar*, Map 1, p. xiii.
[12] Bellary District Records, 1806, vol. 401, pp. 164–71, TNA.
[13] Salem Collectorate Records, Board of Revenue Correspondence, 1819, vol. 3172, pp. 79–81, TNA.
[14] Bellary District Records, 1806, vol. 401, pp. 164–71, TNA; Bellary District Records, 1813, vol. 426, pp. 9–20, TNA; English East India Company, *Reports and Documents Connected with Cotton-wool*, p. 414.
[15] Bayly, *Rulers, Townsmen and Bazaars*, p. 235.
[16] Buchanan, *Journey*, vol. I, p. 205.

this trade was organized by "Lingum and Canary" merchants who annually brought 130,000 to 150,000 pagodas worth of cotton to be sold at the fair at Laudepettah.[17] In the early nineteenth century Francis Buchanan supplied more details on the merchants who controlled this trade:

> The importation of cotton wool to Bangalore is very great and is carried on entirely by the *Pancham Banijigaru*. It comes mostly from the dominions of the *Marattahs*, and the *Nizam* [of Hyderabad]; and is brought hither by the merchants from Naragunda, Navalagunda, and Savonuru in the Duab; from Jalalu, the district in which Gajendraghur is situated; and from Hubuli, in which stands Darwara, all of which belong to the former: and from Balahari and Advany, which belong to the latter power. All the merchants are natives of these places, and in the Marattah country are very well protected. They sell by wholesale to the traders of Bangalore, who retail it out in the town and neighbourhood.[18]

In the late seventeenth century Madras was also supplied with cotton from Ricolta in Visiaporee country and from Chicacole, which was near Ganjam.[19] But evidence from the Fort St. George Consultations suggests that the latter no longer supplied cotton to Madras after the early eighteenth century and the Deccan became the sole source of cotton to the northern Tamil country. The establishment of European factories at Ganjam and Vizagapatnam in the early eighteenth century may have led to higher local demand for the Chicacole cotton and brought the export of cotton to an end. In fact, by the early eighteenth century the trade had reversed and the Vizagapatnam factory was reliant upon supplies of cotton from Madras. This cotton was sent from Madras by coastal shipping.[20]

From Madras moving south in the Tamil country brought one closer to cotton cultivating regions. The English valued their factory at Fort St. David for precisely this reason.[21] The main centers of cotton cultivation in the Tamil country were Coimbatore, Madurai, Ramnad, Dindigul and Tinnevelly. All of these, except Dindigul, were also cotton export centers. The figures in table 2.1 show that Coimbatore and Tinnevelly were the most important of these. Coimbatore cotton was exported in all directions. Both cotton and yarn were sent north to the Baramahal (Salem), which had a thriving weaving industry, but little cotton cultivation. Coimbatore cotton also went east to supply looms on the coast and it may have been the main source of cotton since at least the late seventeenth century for the major weaving centers in Cuddalore, Porto Novo and Pondicherry. Cotton from Coimbatore was also transported west over the Ghats to Malabar, but this was a minor trade. Finally, Coimbatore cotton was carried south to Trichinopoly, Madurai and Tinnevelly.[22] The southeastern coast was also supplied with cotton from Madurai, Ramnad and Tinnevelly. Merchants

---

[17] *FSGDC*, 1734, p. 3.   [18] Buchanan, *Journey*, vol. I, p. 203.
[19] *FSGDC*, 1672–8, p. 6.
[20] *FSGDC*, 1692, p. 47; *FSGDC*, 1711, p. 88; *FSGDC*, 1731, p. 102.
[21] *FSGDC*, 1733, p. 191.
[22] Coimbatore Collectorate Records, 1809, vol. 604, pp. 25–8, TNA; Coimbatore Collectorate Records, vol. 611, 1818, pp. 177–8, TNA; Coimbatore Collectorate Records, vol. 606, 1813, pp. 88–90, TNA; English East India Company, *The Baramahal Records*, Section IV: *Products*, p. 69.

based in Tanjore came to these districts annually and purchased and transported cotton to Nagore, Chidambram and other weaving centers in the Tanjore delta. However, none of these trades can be compared in volume to the trade south from the Deccan.[23]

[23] Madurai Collectorate Records, 1819, vol. 1168, pp. 77–82, TNA; Madurai Collectorate Records, 1812, vol. 1156, pp. 145–50, TNA; Tinnevelly Collectorate Records, 1811, vol. 3572, pp. 239–62, TNA; South Arcot Collectorate Records, 1795, vol. 100, pp. 129–31, TNA.

APPENDIX 2.3

1. With the exceptions of Masulipatnam and Coimbatore, the cotton output figures were obtained from English East India Company, *Reports and Documents Connected with the Proceedings in Regard to the Culture and Manufacture of Cotton-wool, Raw Silk and Indigo in India* (London, 1836), pp. 398–415.
2. The output figures for Ganjam, Vizagapatnam and Trichinopoly were given in terms of raw cotton. These have been converted to figures for cleaned cotton upon the assumption that the seed accounted for three-fourths of the weight of the raw cotton.
3. For Cuddalore, Madurai/Ramnad/Dindigul and Tinnevelly only acreage figures were given. For Tinnevelly, output was calculated using a yield of 17 pounds per acre. This figure was given in Tinnevelly Collectorate Records, 1811, vol. 3572, pp. 239–62, TNA. No similar yield figures are available for Cuddalore or Madurai/Ramnad/Dindigul. For these districts, I have made use of late nineteenth-century yield information for red and black soils for Coimbatore. This was obtained from F. A. Nicholson, *The Coimbatore District Manual* (Madras, 1898), p. 235 and are $22\frac{1}{2}$ pounds per acre for nadam or red and $62\frac{1}{2}$ pounds per acre for uppam or black. Using these yield data will if anything overestimate cotton output, and not affect the conclusion that before the nineteenth century these districts grew only a small fraction of the cotton cultivated in South India. In Cuddalore, extensive cultivation predominated so output has been estimated using the yield figure for nadam, $22\frac{1}{2}$ pounds per acre. For Madurai/Ramnad/Dindigul I have assumed that the cotton acreage was evenly divided between extensive and intensive cultivation and used an average yield of $42\frac{1}{2}$ pounds per acre to calculate total output.
4. The figure for Masulipatnam is from (1) Masulipatnam District Records, Revenue Consultations, 1789, vol 2794, pp. 3–8, APSA; and (2) Letter from G. E. Russell, Collector Masulipatnam District, to Board of Revenue, 20 March 1819, para. 19, Board Miscellaneous, Coimbatore District, TNA.
5. For Coimbatore a figure for acreage under cotton was obtained from Coimbatore Collectorate Records, 1813, vol. 606, pp. 88–90, TNA. To calculate cotton output, I used the late nineteenth-century yield figures from Nicholson and assumed that acreage was divided equally between extensive and intensive cultivation.
6. For the Raichur Doab see Bellary District Records, 1806, vol. 401, pp. 164–71, TNA; Bellary District Records, 1813, vol. 426, pp. 9–20, TNA; English East India Company, *Reports and Documents Connected with the Proceedings in Regard to the Culture and Manufacture of Cotton-wool, Raw Silk and Indigo in India* (London, 1836), p. 414. For other Deccan sources see Guntur Collectorate Records, 1797, vol. 979, pp. 662–7, APSA; Godavari District Records, 1798, vol. 847, pp. 156–65, APSA.

APPENDIX 2.4

NOTES ON THE CLOTH TRADE

The cloth trade in the seventeenth and early eighteenth centuries is one of the most extensively investigated areas in the economic history of early modern South Asia.[1] This discussion consists merely of notes and additions to this voluminous literature. Previous discussions of the cloth trade have focused almost exclusively on the export trade of the European Companies. This is perhaps not surprising given that abundant information is available on the trade of these Companies and very little on local and Asian trade. The attention given to the European Company trade may not be misplaced, however. This is suggested by a calculation of the share of total South Indian cloth production purchased by the Dutch and English East India Companies. Similar calculations have been made for Bengal and Northern Coromandel. These, however, are flawed in crucial respects.

Om Prakash has estimated that Dutch and English East India Companies' cloth purchases in Bengal accounted for between 8.69 and 11.11 percent of total employment in the textile trades. He has also estimated that this export trade resulted in an annual addition of 34 million rupees to the income of Bengal.[2] Similar calculations have not been done for the whole of South India. However, Joseph Brennig has estimated in the case of Northern Coromandel that less than half of the total cloth produced in the late seventeenth century was destined for the Dutch and English Companies' export trade.[3]

According to my calculations, between 1700 and 1725 the exports of the English and Dutch Companies, which were by a very wide margin the largest European buyers at this time, accounted for 22 percent of total South Indian cloth production. This figure is in terms of quantity, but would be much higher in value terms since the Companies' cloth purchases were on the whole of higher than average quality. Their cloths therefore fetched a higher than average price.[4] The details of my calculation are given at the end of this appendix.

---

[1] See Chaudhuri, *The Trading World*; John Irwin and P. R. Schwartz, *Studies in Indo-European Textile History* (Ahmedabad, 1966); Subrahmanyam, *Political Economy of Commerce*; Kristoff Glamann, *Dutch-Asiatic Trade 1620–1740*, (Copenhagen, 1958; repr. 'S-Gravenhage, 1981); Tapan Raychaudhuri, *Jan Company in Coromandel 1605–1690* ('S-Gravenhage, 1962); W. H. Moreland, "Indian Exports of Cotton Goods in the Seventeenth Century," *Indian Journal of Economics*, 5 (1925), pp. 225–45; S. P. Sen, "The Role of Indian Textiles in Southeast Asian Trade in the Seventeenth Century," *Journal of Southeast Asian History*, 3 (1962), pp. 92–110; Arasaratnam, *Merchants, Companies and Commerce*; Om Prakash, "Bullion for Goods: International Trade and the Economy of Early Eighteenth Century Bengal," *IESHR*, 8 (1976), pp. 159–87; Om Prakash, *The Dutch East India Company and the Economy of Bengal 1630–1720* (Princeton, 1985).

[2] Prakash, "Bullion for Goods," p. 161.   [3] Brennig, "Textile Producers," pp. 343–4.

[4] The coming of the Europeans not only increased demand, but also changed the type of cloth demanded. Southeast Asian markets largely sought patterned cloths, either patterned in the loom, painted or printed. The demand for plain cloths was very small in these markets. The European market demanded plain goods, mostly calicoes. And after 1700 the demand was almost exclusively for plain cloths. A more important difference between the two markets, however, was that Europeans demanded much higher quality cloths than Southeast Asians. These cloths required greater technical sophistication to produce: the spinning, weaving and finishing were all more technically demanding. Concomitantly, the value added in these cloths was much greater.

73

I believe my estimate is superior to the earlier calculations of Om Prakash and Joseph Brennig. A major weakness in their estimates is that data from contemporary India are crucial to both calculations. Om Prakash uses contemporary cloth consumption figures to estimate the size of the textile industry in eighteenth-century Bengal. Brennig uses contemporary figures for the number of annual work days for a South Indian weaver in order to estimate total output per loom. I do not rely upon proxies drawn from contemporary India as these in all likelihood very poorly describe the conditions of work and consumption in the seventeenth and eighteenth centuries. In addition, Brennig's estimates are exclusively for Northern Coromandel where an unusually large proportion of production may have been oriented for export. My estimate is for the whole of South India.

It is now widely accepted that the entry of European Companies into the Indian Ocean led to an expansion of textile production in South India.[5] This was also the case in the other major textile manufacturing centers in South Asia: Gujarat, Punjab and Bengal. The mechanisms by which textile production expanded for any of these regions remain unclear, however.

Om Prakash has presented a comprehensive statement on the process by which output was increased. In an analysis of Bengal he has attributed the growth in textile output to the operation of the market, and in particular to increases in the prices of export goods. The higher prices had two effects. First, they induced producers to shift resources to the production of export goods. According to Prakash: "This overall increase in the prices of textiles and raw silk would have constituted a clear signal for reallocating resources to increase the output of these goods."[6] However, he has supported this assertion with only two pieces of evidence. The first is drawn from mulberry cultivation and illustrates the responsiveness of the Bengal peasant to demand conditions. The second is from silk reeling and demonstrates that there was no labor supply constraint limiting output expansion. No evidence is provided from the cotton textile industry, the largest sector in which output expanded.

Second, in response to higher prices, producers made fuller utilization of existing capacity for production – looms, spinning equipment, etc. – and also purchased more of these tools in order to add to capacity. Prakash argues that this posed no insuperable hurdles. Land was abundant and only moderate quantities of capital were needed to produce new spindles, wheels, looms and other tools. In addition, there was no labor constraint, according to Om Prakash. Artisans who worked part-time may have severed their ties to the land and become full-time artisans. He argues that there must have also been a demographic response to supply greater quantities of labor to meet the growing export demand. However, Om Prakash provides no evidence to support these assertions.

One thing that is clear, however, is that the expansion of output was not met by significant technological innovations. Several writers, Om Prakash and K. N. Chaudhuri among them, have concluded that this may be explained by the abundance of labor and the scarcity of capital which characterized the subcontinent. Such a situation was not conducive for labor-saving (historically the most

[5] Brennig, "Textiles Producers," p. 344; Subrahmanyam, *Political Economy of Commerce*, p. 98.
[6] Prakash, "Bullion for Goods," p. 168.

important) technological innovations.[7] However, as this work argues, there is much reason to doubt this belief in surplus labor, which appears to be a rather facile projection of contemporary conditions into the South Asian past. Rather the seventeenth and eighteenth centuries were characterized by labor shortages.

Although there is substantial evidence that the relative prices of textiles as well as of cotton and yarn increased in seventeenth- and eighteenth-century South India,[8] my findings suggest that this was not the key to the expansion of textile production. In other words, the growth in output was not simply driven by the market mechanisms described by Om Prakash. Rather, the South Indian evidence indicates that the crucial factors were the supply of credit and peasant strategies to cope with uncertainty, especially in rainfall. These factors explain the expansion in output in the three steps which accounted for the bulk of value added in textile production: cotton growing, spinning and weaving.

Let us begin with the cultivation of cotton. In this case, there appears to be no simple relation between the price and extent of cultivation. Cotton prices in the seventeenth and eighteenth centuries were on a steady upward trend. However, there is a substantial body of evidence which indicates that at the end of the eighteenth century – after 150 years of steady increases in cotton prices – South Indian peasants did not find the returns from cotton to be particularly remunerative. Company servants in many parts of South India found that the price of cotton was still low relative to other crops and that earnings from cotton were not greater than those from grain. For these reasons, the cultivation of cotton was not particularly attractive to many cultivators. Nevertheless, cotton cultivation must have expanded in the eighteenth century to meet growing cloth production. Thus decisions to increase the cultivation of cotton, either extensively or intensively, were not based solely on the price.

In the case of intensive cultivation, which was the chief source of cotton surpluses, the supply of credit acted as a constraint. However, the availability of credit was not a function of cotton prices. Rather, it was determined by political processes, in particular by the formation and expansion of political authority. The expansion of intensive cotton cultivation in the Deccan had its origins in the late medieval (Vijayanagar) period, long before the textile export boom.[9] Cotton formed an essential part of crop rotation and cultivators grew cotton on as much land as they could obtain the capital to clear. And states and rulers were willing to provide this capital in order to attract agrarian producers and thereby create a more secure revenue base. Extensive cultivation of cotton was also not motivated simply by the price of cotton. This form of cultivation was integral to peasant strategies to minimize uncertainties associated with the timing and extent of the monsoon.

Spinning too was motivated not by the price of yarn, but by uncertainties in rainfall and the seasonality of agricultural work. In fact, at times the supply of

---

[7] Chaudhuri, *Trading World*, p. 274.

[8] For some seventeenth-century prices see Joseph Brennig, "The Textile Trade of Seventeenth Century Coromandel: A Study of a Pre-Modern Asian Export Industry," Ph.D. Dissertation, University of Wisconsin-Madison (1975), pp. 210, 238. For some eighteenth-century prices see chapter 2 of this work and Tsukasa Mizushima, *Nattar and Socio-economic Change*, pp. 284–99.

[9] Stein, *Vijayanagar*, chap. 4.

spinners was inversely related to the price of yarn. Spinning was pursued as it was both an excellent source of supplementary incomes for peasant households during the agricultural off-seasons and a source of insurance.[10] Therefore, the growth in spinning accompanied the expansion of agrarian settlement into the dry areas of South India. This agrarian expansion may have been driven by increases in population, but it was also a product of the shifting of the political center in South India from the valleys to the plains and the consequent growth in settled agriculture in the dry areas. This was a long-term process and began in the late medieval period with the rise of the Vijayanagar Empire.[11]

In weaving as well, increases in cloth prices may have acted as an inducement to weavers to devote more time and effort to weaving. But even given weaver desires, higher prices could not automatically lead to more cloth output. The majority of weavers relied upon credit from merchants and the supply of this credit was the most important constraint on the quantity of cloth produced. Therefore, an increase in the price of cloth was not a sufficient condition for the expansion of weaving. Rather the growth in European Company demand increased the credit available to weavers. Certainly part of this was from the bullion brought to South India by the European Companies, but the South Indian merchant intermediaries themselves had to supply a large proportion of the advances to weavers. The merchants obtained these funds from local credit markets, and, in some years, the merchants themselves raised the whole of the capital for the English Company's cloth investment. The creditworthiness of South Indian cloth merchants was increased by their connections to the European Companies, which enabled them to command more funds from the local banking system. This more privileged access was new for these cloth traders and it is likely that more capital entered the textile industry. Merchants maintained their relations with the English Company, even in the face of heavy losses, because of the access it gave them to South Indian credit markets.

Given the lack of data on local consumption as well as on the trade under the control of Asian merchants, it is enormously difficult to measure the size of regional textile industries in early modern South Asia. In fact, the methods that have been used to estimate total textile output are often the weakest links in estimates of the proportion purchased by European Companies. Om Prakash relied upon an estimate of Bengal's population in 1700 and contemporary figures for cloth consumption to derive an estimate for total local consumption. His population estimate is essentially a guess, and is quite possibly very far off the mark. Given the enormous changes in the level and distribution of income, there is nothing to suggest that levels of cloth consumption in early eighteenth-century Bengal were identical to those in post-independence India. Joseph Brennig used contemporary figures for the number of days weavers work in the year to estimate total cloth production in late seventeenth-century Northern Coromandel. However, we have no reason to assume that weavers at that time worked either the

---

[10] For a similar argument on the expansion of rural industry in England see Joan Thirsk, "Industries in the Countryside," in F. J. Fisher (ed.), *Essays in the Economic and Social History of Tudor England* (Cambridge, 1961).

[11] Stein, *Vijayanagar*, chap. 4; Ludden, *Peasant History*, chap. 3.

same number of days or with the same intensity or as many hours as weavers today.

In my calculation I have used the total output of raw cotton in South India as a proxy for total cloth output. This figure of 10,894 tons is given in table 2.1. Although it is from the early nineteenth century, it is the earliest I have been able to assemble. It is likely that cotton cultivation expanded in the eighteenth century. Thus my calculation of the proportion of output purchased by the European Companies, which is for the period from 1700 to 1725, will understate the importance of this source of demand.

Figures for the purchases of the English East India Company have been obtained from K. N. Chaudhuri.[12] To calculate the weight of these cloth purchases (for comparability with the cotton output figure) I drew upon information which gives the weight of an English bale of cloth as 0.18 tons[13] and the fact that there were typically thirty pieces of cloth per bale.[14] Thus between 1700 and 1725 the average weight of English cloth purchases was 982.6 tons.

Dutch cloth purchases are given in terms of bales by S. Arasaratnam.[15] I have taken the weight of a bale to be 300 pounds. According to Kristoff Glamann, a Dutch bale in the seventeenth century contained twenty pieces of guinee cloth (or longcloth) of 30 to 40 yards in length.[16] Glamann does not give the weight of the guinee cloth, but in the early eighteenth century a piece of English longcloth weighed 14 to 15 pounds.[17] Thus a Dutch bale of twenty pieces weighed between 280 and 300 pounds. On this basis, between 1700 and 1725 the average weight of Dutch cloth purchases was 798.5 tons.

The quantity of raw cotton required to produce these quantities of cloth was calculated by adding in the cotton that would have been wasted in cleaning, spinning, and other preparatory steps. Taking the cotton wastage figure as 27 percent,[18] the English cloth purchases would have required 1,339.9 tons of cotton and the Dutch 1,088.9 tons. To sum up, between 1700 and 1725 English and Dutch cloth purchases together represented 22 percent of cotton production in South India. Of course, this figure would be higher in value terms since the quality of the cloth purchased by the Companies was on average superior to the cloth consumed locally.

[12] See his *Trading World*, pp. 542–3.   [13] MPP, 1793, vol. P/241/39, p. 1894, OIOC.
[14] MPP, 1792, vol. P/241/30, p. 183, OIOC.
[15] See his "The Dutch East India Company and its Coromandel Trade," p. 337.
[16] See his *Dutch-Asiatic Trade*, p. 135.   [17] *FSGDC*, 1736, p. 77.
[18] This figure was given in MPP, 1790, vol. P/241/16, p. 338, OIOC.

3   Weaver distress 1765–1800

During the economic crisis of the late 1720s and early 1730s the prices of cotton, rice and cotton cloth rose sharply. By the end of the 1730s, however, the prices of cotton and rice had returned nearly to their pre-crisis levels, but the price of cloth continued to remain high. These prices were to last for nearly three decades and during this time weavers in South India may have enjoyed a "Golden Age" as they benefitted from low costs for food and materials and high prices for their manufactures. From the late 1760s, however, the weavers' situation began to deteriorate sharply and their incomes began to decline precipitously.[1] Reports of weaver distress came from several parts of South India. In 1779, weavers in Cuddalore reported that since 1768 their incomes had fallen by 35 percent.[2] This decline in earnings, however, was not due to harvest shortfalls or crises in agriculture; prices for grain, cotton and yarn were stable at Cuddalore through the decade of weaver troubles. In the 1790s, the incomes of weavers in the Baramahal and the Northern Sarkars also fell dramatically, but weavers could not formulate the response which came to them so easily earlier in the century: weavers were unable to push up cloth prices or to reduce the quality of the cloth.[3]

The loss of the methods by which weavers had maintained their earn-

---

[1] The massive scale of weaver distress in this period has not been previously identified by earlier scholars. However, S. Arasaratnam has described a change in relations between the Company and the weavers, which he has characterized as a shift from an independent craft-based mode of production to wage labor. As I shall show below, this characterization misconstrues the nature of the profound changes which did occur. See his "Trade and Political Dominion in South India," and "Weavers, Merchants and Company."

[2] Earnings per piece of nine-call longcloth fell from 0,37,5 to 0,23,1 (pagodas, fanams, cash). The figure for 1768 is calculated from South Arcot Collectorate Records, Cuddalore Consultations, 1768, vol. 66, pp. 28–36 and 54–5, TNA. The figure for 1779 is from South Arcot Collectorate Records, Cuddalore Consultations, 1779, vol. 81, pp. 206–7, TNA.

[3] English East India Company, *The Baramahal Records*, Section VII: *Imposts* (Madras, 1920), pp. 26–7. In 1796 the Commercial Resident at Vizagapatnam observed that yarn for a piece of fourteen-punjam longcloth cost 8 rupees, but the price paid to the weaver was only $7\frac{1}{2}$ rupees. Costs exceeded the price for eighteen-punjam cloth as well. English East India Company, *The Baramahal Records*, Section IV: *Products*, p. 59.

ings suggests that the cloth market had turned against weavers and that weavers had lost the market power which they had possessed in such great abundance. However, this does not appear to have been the result of a collapse in the cloth market itself. Only from the early nineteenth century, with disruptions in trade caused by the Napoleonic Wars and the take-off in British cloth production, did the demand for South Indian cloth enter the severe slump from which it was never really to recover. The weakening of weaver power, however, began from the late 1760s.

To make sense of this timing of events we must turn away from the market and examine the political transformations of the late eighteenth century. The decline in weaver market power was merely a symptom of a broader decline in the position of weavers in South India. And what the weavers lost was gained by the English East India Company, which was expanding its political authority at this time. Before turning to the Company and the implications of its political expansion, however, we must first be satisfied that the weakening of weavers and the fall in their incomes were not due to a decline in demand for cloth. In other words, that the weavers' plight was not simply the outcome of the operation of "impersonal" market forces.[4]

The cloth trade, 1770–1800

Only from the early nineteenth century, with the onset of the Napoleonic Wars and the great expansion in British cotton textile production, did South Indian cloth begin to lose its prominent place in world markets.[5] Certainly the servants of the English East India Company were not of the opinion that the demand for cloth declined before then.[6] In the final decades of the eighteenth century the Company records are peppered with bitter complaints about the severe competition for cloth and the proliferation of buyers who paid little heed to quality. The English blamed in particular their European competitors who in their keenness for cloth paid exorbitant prices for poorly manufactured stuff. The actions and attitudes of weavers are consistent with such a picture of the

[4] At this time weavers in Bengal also came under pressure with the expansion of English power. This is documented in Mitra, *Cotton Weavers of Bengal* and Hossain, *Company Weavers of Bengal*. Both of these works show that the sufferings of the Bengal weavers were closely linked to the rise of English power. Unfortunately, it is difficult to gauge the extent to which the Company represented a novel political force as neither work investigates in any detail the pre-Company conditions and status of weavers.

[5] For some areas of South India, Tinnevelly being an outstanding example, there was buoyant demand for cloth well into the nineteenth century. See Ludden, "Agrarian Commercialism in Eighteenth Century South India," pp. 496–8.

[6] The market for muslins in Europe went into a slump in the final decade of the eighteenth century, but demand as a whole for cloth was strong until the early nineteenth century.

cloth market. In 1768 weavers in Northern Coromandel refused advances from Company merchants because they had already taken on more than enough work.[7] In the 1770s and 1780s Vizagapatnam and Cuddalore weavers found ready sale for their manufactures as there were many buyers and intense competition for cloth.[8]

The activities of the major cloth purchasers also support such an impressionistic picture of the market.[9] Demand for South Indian cloth in Europe remained strong between 1770 and 1800 and European Companies and private traders were keen buyers of cloth.[10] With the exception of a dip in the 1780s, when there was a shortage of funds, the cloth purchases of the English East India Company remained largely stable between 1725 and 1800 and there is no suggestion of a decline at the end of the century.[11] After the Treaty of Paris in 1783 the French Company rapidly expanded its operations in South India from its factories in Northern Coromandel and Pondicherry. In some years French cloth purchases exceeded those of the English. In 1784, for instance, the French collected 2,500 bales of cloth at Ingeram while the English figure was around 1,000 bales.[12] The Dutch continued to be active in the cloth market and made large advances to weavers in Northern Coromandel, Sadras and Tinnevelly. The Dutch also purchased fine quality muslins from Arni and other weaving villages in the Company's jagir.[13] Also indicative of the continued and serious Dutch interest in the cloth trade, officials of the Dutch East India Company lodged many protests over English interference in the cloth market. The Danish, Portuguese and Ostender Companies also purchased cloth in South India, although more intermittently.[14] And as late as 1794, the French, Dutch, Danes,

[7] Masulipatnam District Records, 1768, vol. 2871, pp. 217–29, APSA.
[8] Vizagapatnam District Records, Commercial Consultations, 1783, vol. 3686, pp. 238–40, APSA.
[9] The largest market for South Indian cloth was domestic, but as discussed in Appendix 2.4, there is little information on this market. However, the economic expansion and growth of the eighteenth century make it likely that local demand remained buoyant. The weakening of local demand, as a consequence of the dismantling of Indian courts and armies, was felt in the nineteenth century. For a discussion of these developments for North India see Bayly, *Rulers, Townsmen and Bazaars*, pp. 280–3.
[10] See S. Arasaratnam, *Maritime Commerce and English Power: Southeast India 1750–1800* (Brookfield, Vt. 1996), pp. 78, 101, 119, 169, 173–4, 193, 212–13.
[11] For pre-1760 purchases see Chaudhuri, *Trading World*, pp. 542–3. For post-1770 see I. Durga Parshad, *Some Aspects of Indian Foreign Trade* (London, 1932), p. 211.
[12] MPP, 1785, vol. P/240/60, pp. 153–5, OIOC. Also see Arasaratnam, *Maritime Commerce*, pp. 101, 171.
[13] Godavari District Records, 1792, vol. 830, p. 16, APSA.
[14] South Arcot Collectorate Records, Cuddalore Consultations, 1786, vol. 86, pp. 5–8, TNA. Ole Feldbaek, *India Trade under the Danish Flag 1772–1808* (Copenhagen, 1969), pp. 21–2, 49–51, 81–8.

Americans and Portuguese were said to purchase cloth and at high prices.[15]

Private traders were also major buyers of cloth in the final decades of the eighteenth century. Holden Furber and others have documented the activities of European traders well.[16] Far less is known about the trade of Asian merchants who continued to control a major share of cloth exports from South India. Asian merchants were active all along the southeastern coast, but they operated from a network of ports and ships that was distinct from the networks of the European Companies. In 1768 the Cuddalore Council estimated that private Asian traders annually exported substantial quantities of cloth (2 to $2\frac{1}{2}$ *lakhs* of pagodas was its estimate) from Porto Novo to Acheh and Kedah.[17] Into the early nineteenth century "Mogul" merchants were major buyers of painted cloth in Masulipatnam for export to the Persian Gulf.[18] The continued importance and large scale of Asian traders' operations are reflected in their opposition to the expansion of the English Company's commercial system. By 1800 the Company's commercial arm reached almost everywhere in South India and several new factories had been recently established to tap additional centers of cloth production. In 1795 merchants in Tanjore complained that the creation of the Nagore factory would make it difficult for them to procure cloth for their trade to Southeast Asia.[19] Similarly, the "Mogul" merchants around Masulipatnam were alarmed by Company expansion as it interfered with their purchases for the Persian Gulf.[20]

The strong demand for cloth in South India in the late eighteenth century suggests that the weakened position of weavers did not stem simply from a downturn in the market. Nor was the weakened position of weavers a product of the military conflicts of the period, which were certainly on the increase and created uncertain and unsettled conditions in many parts of South India. Although the economic effects of warfare in early modern South Asia are poorly understood,[21] it is clear that warfare

---

[15] MPP, 1794, vol. P/241/47, p. 1646.

[16] Holden Furber, *John Company at Work* (Cambridge, Mass., 1948); Arasaratnam, *Maritime Commerce*, pp. 107, 173–4, 184, 214–15.

[17] South Arcot Collectorate Records, Cuddalore, Consultations, 1768, vol. 66, p. 24, TNA.

[18] P. Sudhir and P. Swarnalatha, "Textile Traders and Territorial Imperatives: Masulipatnam, 1750–1850," *IESHR*, 29 (1992), pp. 158–69.

[19] Tanjore Collectorate Records, Nagore Factory Records, 1795, vol. 3325, pp. 65–9, TNA.

[20] Sudhir and Swarnalatha, "Textile Traders and Territorial Imperatives," pp. 163–4.

[21] An important contribution is Stewart Gordon, *Marathas, Marauders, and State Formation in Eighteenth Century India* (Delhi, 1994).

was capable of both stimulating and disrupting economic activity. In 1700, for example, sea customs collections fell in Madras for the "want of a Moors Army in this Country, which for many years past, has taken off vast Quantitys of all sorts of foreigne Comoditys."[22] In 1734 and 1743, however, warfare disrupted trade routes, which interfered with commercial life.[23]

The impact of warfare on weavers was equally unpredictable. At times armies could represent an important source of demand. In 1743 the English East India Company was unable to procure cloth at Fort St. David because the weavers were working their looms to supply an army encamped at Trichinopoly.[24] However, the approach of armies also raised the specter of plunder, and forced weavers to flee to safer zones.[25] Cloth, because of its high value and ease of transport, was a favorite target for marauding armies. And weavers themselves could be the targets of armies. In the early 1780s, inhabitants of weaving villages around Masulipatnam were pressed into service as coolies and one contingent was forced to accompany an army on the march from Masulipatnam to Pondicherry, a distance of 400 miles.[26] In the late eighteenth century, to escape plundering troops weavers often sought protection at European settlements.[27] Although warfare certainly created unsettled conditions at the end of the eighteenth century, it cannot alone account for the loss of weaver market power and the decline in weaver incomes.[28] As these examples suggest, warfare was capable of creating temporary hardship, but the problems weavers faced in the final quarter of the century were not transitory but permanent. In addition, they began in the late 1760s, several years before the major Mysore wars, and they were sustained at a time when the market for South Indian cloth was thriving.

The problems weavers faced at the end of the century did not have their origins in the market or in military conflicts. Rather, they may be traced to the profound reordering of political relations which began from the middle of the eighteenth century. Although politics were in flux at the

---

[22] *FSGDC*, 1700, p. 16.
[23] *FSGDC*, 1734, p. 3; *FSDC*, 1743, p. 22.
[24] *FSDC*, 1743, pp. 22–3.
[25] In the 1780s roving armies plundered many weavers in Guntur and the northern Tamil country. See MPP, 1781, vol. P/240/52, pp. 139–40, OIOC; Masulipatnam District Records, Commercial Consultations, 1787, vol. 2838, pp. 72–8, APSA.
[26] MPP, 1781, vol. P/240/52, pp. 139–40, OIOC.
[27] South Arcot Collectorate Records, 1766, vol. 162, p. 18, TNA; MPP, 1778, vol. P/240/45, pp. 346–7, OIOC.
[28] The extent to which warfare affected South India as a whole in the late eighteenth century is in need of careful evaluation. There is much to suggest that the devastation of the northern Tamil country may have been matched by a shift of production and resources, both agricultural and industrial, to Mysore.

time and changing in myriad ways, for weavers the key development was the growing power of the English East India Company. The location of weaver distress and crisis further points to the importance of the English. These began in territories which were under the political control of the English East India Company and closely followed the expansion of English power.

Relations between weavers and the Company

By the mid-1760s cloth prices in South India had been stable for more than twenty years, but quality had deteriorated considerably. In 1764 the Cuddalore Council reported that much of the cloth produced in the area was coarse and loosely woven.[29] In 1768, upon conducting a more detailed investigation, the English learned that the staple longcloths of the Cuddalore region typically contained only 80 percent of the required quantity of yarn. This shortfall represented substantial, additional income for weavers. Weavers also added to their earnings by using less expensive, inferior counts of yarn, which further diminished quality.[30] Similar problems were identified in the Northern Sarkars.[31]

In Cuddalore, Company servants raised these findings with weavers and demanded an immediate improvement in quality. The weavers in response demanded higher prices for their cloth on the grounds that only that would enable them to purchase the proper quantity and quality of yarn.[32] The Company was strongly opposed to raising prices, or any other scheme for that matter, which threatened to reduce its profits. The Company's servants were also reluctant to raise cloth prices for fear that they could never be brought down again. The servants, therefore, explored measures which would leave cloth prices unchanged but would force weavers to increase their expenditures on yarn. In other words, the Company sought to implement schemes that would force weavers to spend a larger fraction of their advance on yarn. This would lead to improvements in cloth quality, but at the price of lower weaver earnings, not lower Company profits.

As its first step, in what was to turn into a protracted struggle with weavers, the Company eliminated the South Indian merchant intermediaries and took over their functions, most importantly making advances to weavers. The English had long wanted to eliminate these merchants, but

---

[29] MPP, 1764, vol. P/240/22, p. 488, OIOC.
[30] South Arcot Collectorate Records, Cuddalore Consultations, 1768, vol. 66, pp. 28–36, TNA.
[31] For Vizagapatnam and other northern factories, see MPP, 1770, vol. P/240/29, pp. 243–7, OIOC.
[32] For the weavers in the Andhra districts see MPP, 1768, vol. P/240/27, pp. 665–6, OIOC.

it had been reluctant to shoulder the enormous risks associated with advancing large sums of money to thousands of weavers. From the 1760s, after achieving political power in South India the Company believed that it could use that power to reduce these risks.[33] Therefore, from the beginning these efforts were closely linked to the political expansion of the Company.

After bringing weavers under its direct employ, the Company set out to systematically undermine the market power, the mobility and the contractual advantages of weavers. First, the Company eliminated competitors for cloth from its territories and created a monopoly in the cloth trade. The artificial decline in cloth demand which followed reduced the bargaining power of weavers. Second, the Company restructured the traditional contract between weavers and merchants. The asymmetries of contract were reversed and contracts began to be enforced far more strictly than had been customary under South Indian merchants. Debt recovery systems were also created and implemented. Finally, the Company transformed the conditions under which cloth was produced. It used its political power to intervene in the work process itself, which had been traditionally under the absolute control of weavers. With these changes in the market, contract and production, the Company was able to bring about an improvement in cloth quality, but these gains were achieved at the expense of weavers. By the end of the century weaver incomes were both lower and far less secure.

By the 1760s the English had established a half dozen factories in South India, but the bulk of its cloth was provided at three centers. The most valuable parts of the Company's investment, muslins and other fine cloths, were manufactured in weaving villages near Madras. Ordinary cloths, mostly calicoes, were produced at Cuddalore. Calicoes were also manufactured to the north of Madras in weaving villages in the Northern Sarkars. Coarse and fine calicoes were produced in these villages and delivered to the factories at Ingeram and Madapollam. The Company focused its energies to transform its relations with weavers at these three centers.

---

[33] This chapter details the direct effects of Company political rule. The political power of the Company also affected weavers indirectly. These indirect effects of Company political power, which are described in chapter 5, followed from the incorporation of indigenous merchants into the Company state. Merchants were largely excluded from state power within the indigenous political order and they had their first taste of that power with the rise of the Company state. The Company's political power – which merchants brought to bear in their conflicts with weavers – put merchants in an unprecedented position of advantage over weavers.

Direct advances to weavers

The Company's first measure was to replace its merchant intermediaries
with a system of direct advances to weavers. Initially the only change for
weavers was higher prices for their cloth as they were given the prices that
the Company had formerly given to its merchants. With higher prices,
and therefore higher incomes, the Company expected that weavers would
have less reason to debase the quality of their cloth. In addition, the
Company was dissatisfied with the performance of these merchants,
which was an added reason for creating a system of direct advances. In the
1760s the Company's factories in South India came under pressure from
London to increase cloth procurement, but the South Indian merchants,
far from responding to these demands, failed repeatedly to keep to
contracts. In 1764, for instance, the Cuddalore merchants fell short of
their contract by 20,000 pieces and the Company's servants saw little
reason for the merchants to mend their ways. As the Fort St. George
Council put it: "[the merchants] derive their principal advantage from
the privileges and influence which they acquire in the country through the
Company's protection and which could receive no addition from an
increase of their contracts."[34]

The Company also suspected the merchants of misappropriating the
funds they received from the Company. Since the crisis of the 1720s and
1730s the Company had been advancing money to merchants for the
procurement of cloth. Although initially the merchants used these funds
for the intended purpose, by the 1760s many merchants were neglecting
the Company's business and using its capital for their own trade. To
conceal this, merchants brought in cloth which was clearly below the
Company's quality standards, knowing full well that the Company's
sorters would refuse the cloth. The merchants were then free to sell this
cloth to private European traders whose prices were often higher than
those given by the Company.

In 1768 the Company inaugurated the system of direct advances in the
villages around Cuddalore where there were approximately a thousand
looms. A large administrative network was established to make advances
and supervise weavers on this scale. At its apex was an English servant of
the Company, the Commercial Resident, who was stationed permanently
at these villages. The Resident was assisted by several categories of Indian
servants. His immediate subordinates were *gumastahs*, who, in turn, were
assisted by brokers. The brokers with the aid of three or four servants
made advances, received and sorted the cloth, and were responsible for

[34] MPP, 1771, vol. 105B, pp. 278–81, TNA.

the weavers' debts. In some villages the head weavers agreed to serve as brokers.[35]

The Company's servants anticipated strong opposition from the Cuddalore weavers to the new system, but to their great surprise the weavers accepted it without protest. They had only one demand and that was for the Company always to make advances available and in this way provide guaranteed employment for the whole year.[36] The Company's servants believed this to be reasonable and they prepared funds to meet the obligation.[37] To make its employ even more attractive, the Company reduced the loom tax in the weaving villages around Cuddalore and protected weavers who received its advances from the debt claims of South Indian merchants.[38]

In 1771 direct advances were extended to the 2,000 looms in the jagir near Madras. The weavers in the northern half of the jagir agreed to the new system with little hesitation, but in the southern half weavers stridently opposed direct advances from the Company. This difference may be attributed to the fact that in the northern part of the jagir the Company continued to advance money, as was traditionally done, and simply substituted itself for the merchants. In the southern part, however, the Company wanted to make permanent a system of advances in both yarn and money. Some South Indian merchants had included yarn in the advance, but only on occasion and it was understood to be temporary. In addition, under South Indian merchants the yarn had never accounted for more than half the value of the advance, but the Company sought to raise that proportion to two-thirds.[39] The weavers vehemently opposed both changes and they argued that the small sums of money which the Company proposed to advance were not sufficient for them to support themselves and their families. However, after lengthy negotiations, the Company prevailed upon the weavers to accept the increase in the proportion of yarn.[40] Also as in Cuddalore Company employ allowed the weavers to escape their debts to merchants.

In 1774 direct advances were expanded to the Northern Coromandel factories of Ingeram and Madapollam. The Company was satisfied with

[35] MPP, 1771, vol. 106B, p. 855, TNA.
[36] A century earlier some weavers themselves perceived that their returns would increase if the merchant middlemen were eliminated. They proposed to the Dutch East India Company that advances be made directly to them, but the Dutch were unwilling to hazard money in the weavers' hands. See Raychaudhuri, *Jan Company in Coromandel*, p. 64.
[37] South Arcot Collectorate Records, Cuddalore Consultations, 1768, vol. 66, pp. 72–5, TNA.
[38] South Arcot Collectorate Records, Cuddalore Consultations, 1768, vol. 66, pp. 50–1, 72–5, 174–80, TNA.
[39] MPP, 1771, vol. 106B, p. 857, TNA.
[40] MPP, 1771, vol. 106B, pp. 1019–20, 1028, TNA.

Table 3.1. *Change in longcloth prices at Ingeram, 1775*

Punjams	Old price	New price	Change	% change
24	70,14,32	66,26,21	− 3,24,11	− 5.3
22	67,3,48	63,32,62	− 3,8,66	− 4.8
20	63,28,64	61,3,25	− 2,25,39	− 4.2
18	53,32,32	48,14,54	− 5,17,58	− 10.2
17	51,25,16	45,21,16	− 6,4,0	− 11.8
16	47,10,64	42,27,58	− 4,19,6	− 9.6
15	44,0,0	39,34,20	− 4,1,60	− 9.2
14	40,25,16	37,4,62	− 3,20,34	− 8.8
$13\frac{1}{2}$	39,1,64	34,11,34	− 4,26,30	− 12.1

Note: Prices are per corge and are given in pagodas, fanams, cash.
    1 pagoda = 36 fanams = 2,880 cash.
Source: MPP, 1775, vol. 113A, p. 117, TNA.

the quality of the cloth manufactured at these centers, but it wanted to institute direct advances in order to eliminate the merchant intermediaries who on several occasions had disrupted the investment. In 1772 the merchants at Ingeram, in alliance with weavers, protested the Company's sorting of the cloth and the investment was at a standstill for two months.[41] These merchant protests continued intermittently for another year.[42] In addition, the Company came to believe that its funds were not secure in the hands of these merchants. The cloth merchants at Ingeram and Madapollam were not of high standing within the local commercial community and had limited access to credit from local sources.[43]

Unlike Cuddalore and Madras, however, there was very strong resistance in the Northern Sarkars to direct advances. In February 1775, several months after the system was introduced, a protest erupted among the Ingeram weavers. Many weavers abandoned their looms and, in the words of a Company servant, prevented the "contented and peacable" weavers from working. The Commercial Resident appealed to the local *zamindars* to quell the uproar, but received no support from them.[44] Although the weavers never systematically set out the reasons for their protest in petitions or letters, the discussions of the English Company servants centered on three weaver grievances. The first was the Company's reductions in cloth prices. In table 3.1 I have compiled data which

[41] MPP, 1772, vol. 108B, pp. 825–6, 850, 944–5, TNA.
[42] MPP, 1773, vol. 110A, pp. 411–13, TNA.
[43] Masulipatnam District Records, General Consultations, 1770, vol. 2751, pp. 22–8, APSA.
[44] MPP, 1775, vol. 113A, p. 163 and vol. 113B, pp. 196–9, TNA.

suggest a steep decline in prices which accompanied the system of direct advances: longcloth prices were reduced by 4.2 percent to 12.1 percent and the reductions were greatest for the lower counts of cloth.[45] The weavers themselves were concerned about the price cuts and in December 1775 they presented accounts to the Company to support their arguments that the prices were unremunerative.[46] The second weaver grievance was that the Company demanded two pieces of longcloth every month from each loom. The weavers said such a level of demand was "impossible and oppressive."[47] The final grievance was that the Company was attempting to monopolize the cloth trade and, thereby, the weavers. The weavers saw such interference in the market as a grave threat to their livelihood.

The weavers supported themselves during the protest with the advances they had previously received from the Company. These were exhausted quickly and after a few tumultuous months the weavers accepted direct advances and returned to their looms. Within a year, however, major problems had arisen with cloth production in the Northern Sarkars. First, during their protest the weavers had accumulated sizable debts to the Company and these, rather than shrinking, had grown even larger after the weavers had returned to work. Second, the Company achieved reductions in cloth prices, but these came at the expense of cloth quality. For decades the calicoes produced at Ingeram and Madapollam were considered to be the finest in South India, but direct advances destroyed that reputation in one short year. In July 1775 the Commercial Resident at Ingeram reported that he had rejected one-third of the cloth the weavers had delivered. As a result, in September 1776 the Company gave up on direct advances to weavers in Ingeram and Madapollam and brought back the merchant intermediaries.[48]

The cloth market

As we have seen the weavers' freedom to cancel their contracts with merchants was crucial to their power. As has already been elaborated, weavers could cancel a contract by simply selling their cloth on the open market and returning the advance to the merchant. To exercise this privilege weavers depended upon the availability of many sources of advances and many buyers for their cloth. The Company was well aware of the importance of these market conditions and its second major intervention into the cloth business consisted of measures to create a monop-

[45] MPP, 1775, vol. 113A, p. 117, TNA.   [46] MPP, 1776, vol. 115B, pp. 393–9, TNA.
[47] MPP, 1775, vol. 114A, pp. 652–8, TNA.
[48] MPP, 1776, vol. 115B, pp. 388–92; vol. 116A, pp. 512–16, TNA.

oly in cloth within its territories in South India. By eliminating competitors the Company expected that the bargaining position of weavers would
be significantly weakened.

The Company's attempts to monopolize the cloth trade began in
Cuddalore where since 1766 the Company had assumed an exclusive
right to employ weavers. In that year the Company ordered the weavers
residing in villages around Cuddalore to receive advances only from
Company merchants. The Company was forced to revoke this order after
the French East India Company, which also made advances to these
weavers from its factory in Pondicherry, lodged several protests. As a
compromise, the French were permitted to employ the weavers after the
Company's demand for cloth had been satisfied, but such limits were
difficult to enforce.[49] After this failure, the Company contemplated fiscal
measures to induce weavers to work exclusively for the Company. In
1768, for example, the Cuddalore Council debated the institution of a
loom tax in its weaving villages, but with the proviso that weavers who
supplied cloth only to the Company would be exempt.[50] Such a tax was
never implemented, however, as weavers began to work exclusively for
the English from 1768 when direct advances were established. At this
time weavers were guaranteed plentiful advances, which meant that they
had no need to seek credit from other sources. However, to ensure that
weavers did in fact deliver their cloth to the Company and not to other
buyers, the Company closely monitored the movement of cloth in these
villages.[51]

Although fiscal measures to monopolize weavers were never attempted
at Cuddalore, they were instituted at Ingeram where in 1768 the Company instituted a 4 percent tax, paid by the weaver, on all cloth manufactured at the factory. Cloth produced for the Company, however, was
exempt from the tax. In addition, as an inducement to weavers to maintain quality, cloth that fell below the Company's quality standards was
taxed at a higher rate of 8 percent. Private traders, but not the French and
Dutch Companies, were also banned from trading in the varieties of
longcloth demanded by the Company. These cloths comprised the bulk
of the Company's purchases at these weaving centers.

The taxes on cloth as well as limitations on trade were met with
vehement weaver opposition. The weavers tied up their looms and refused to work for the Company until the measures were repealed. The
protest lasted several weeks and during that period it was reported that

---

[49] MPP, 1766, vol. P/240/24, pp. 175–8, 203, 358–9, OIOC.
[50] South Arcot Collectorate Records, Cuddalore Consultations, 1768, vol. 66, pp. 4–6,
TNA.
[51] MPP, 1772, vol. 107A, p. 168, TNA.

not a single loom was at work in the weaving villages surrounding the Ingeram factory. Local rulers also opposed these measures as they were fearful that the Company was seeking to usurp their authority to tax and they prevented Company officials from collecting the taxes on cloth. The combined opposition from weavers and states forced the Company to back down and the taxes, as well as the restrictions on trade, were removed.[52]

The Company remained undiscouraged and in the 1770s was more successful with its attempts to monopolize the Ingeram weavers. These greater successes were due in large part to the fact that the Company gave up on persuasion and resorted instead to force and compulsion. In 1772 the Company issued an order prohibiting weavers who produced cloth for the Company from receiving advances from any other merchant and this directive was strictly enforced with the backing of the Company's growing political power. If a "Company weaver" was caught with funds from other merchants, he was dealt with quickly and harshly: the weaver was immediately forced to return the Company's advance and was barred from future Company employment.[53] A few years later, weavers were treated even more summarily. If a weaver was suspected of producing cloth for the French, Dutch or other buyers, Company servants, with the assistance of Company *sepoys*, cut the cloth out of the loom and forced Company advances upon the weaver. In addition, at Ingeram, weavers were forced to take new Company advances when they brought their completed cloth to the factory.[54]

Similar strong-arm tactics were used in the 1770s against weavers in the Company's jagir. In 1771, when direct advances were introduced, the Company also sought to introduce a plan to divide weaving villages among the Dutch, French and English Companies. Under the plan, each Company was to have the exclusive right to employ weavers in its villages. The weavers saw the scheme as a serious threat to their livelihood and they immediately voiced their opposition to it. To earn even a minimum income weavers in the jagir required several sources of advances. For example, weavers found it attractive to work for the Dutch Company since it paid high prices. However, the Dutch were able to provide advances, and thus work, for only six to eight months of the year. For the other four to six months, weavers relied upon advances from other sources. Similarly, no jagir weaver was willing to work exclusively for the

[52] MPP, 1768, vol. P/240/27, pp. 665–6, 683–4, 686–7, OIOC; Masulipatnam District Records, 1768, vol. 2871, pp. 125–8, APSA.
[53] MPP, 1772, vol. 108A, pp. 640–2, TNA.
[54] MPP, 1773, vol. 110A, p. 517, TNA; MPP, 1774, vol. 111, p. 335, TNA; MPP, 1775, vol. 113B, pp. 227–9, vol. 114A, pp. 486–8, 550, TNA; etc.

English Company because its prices were very low, but they were willing to work for it when no other advances were available. In 1771 the opposition of the weavers persuaded the Company to drop its plan to allocate villages among the Europeans.[55] However, later in the decade, the Company renewed its attempts to limit the employment of the jagir weavers, but this time it turned to coercion and force. Company servants and sepoys harassed weavers who manufactured cloth for other buyers, especially for the Dutch. The English Company justified these actions on the grounds that weavers in the jagir were exempt from Company duties and that they abused this privilege when they worked for other merchants.[56]

With these measures, the Company increasingly became the dominant buyer for cloth, and thus employer for weavers, within its territories, but much of its success came through the deployment of force and coercion. Through strong-arm tactics, the Company eliminated alternative sources of advances and prevented weavers from selling their cloth to other buyers. The weavers protested the Company's attempts to restrict the free exercise of their rights of work, trade and contract, and the Dutch and French Companies complained repeatedly, although with little success, about the English policies as they interfered with their attempts to procure cloth.

Reversing the asymmetries of contract

The English Company's growing monopoly of the cloth trade reduced the bargaining power of weavers and in essence nullified their freedoms of contract as alternative sources of advances and outlets for cloth were closed. The Company went even further, however, and reversed the asymmetries of contract and appropriated for itself the rights weavers had possessed. The Company, in the process of monopolizing weavers, created for itself the right to break contracts with weavers, which it did in Ingeram upon its declaration that weavers who did not supply cloth exclusively to the Company were to return their advances. South Indian merchants did not possess such a right to break a contract and demand the return of an advance.

The Company also reversed the merchant obligation to accept all cloth from weavers. In particular, the Company persuaded weavers to take back cloth that did not meet its quality standards, which radically transformed its relationship with weavers. Both the Company and its South

---

[55] MPP, 1771, vol. 106B, pp. 870–1, 1010–11, 1028–9, 1039, 1041–2, TNA.
[56] MPP, 1773, vol. 110A, p. 517, TNA; MPP, 1777, vol. 117A, pp. 167–9, TNA.

Indian brokers viewed this as a major victory: "Subramania [a broker] says that he turned out about eighty pieces and prevailed on the weavers to receive them back again and looked upon that as very great point gained as it is no easy matter to beat them out of their old customs."[57] The weavers found the rejection of cloth to be a great hardship and they mounted several major protests against the practice. In 1778 a Commercial Resident at Cuddalore remarked that turning cloth out always occasions "noise and confusion" from the weavers and this was a great point of contention between weavers and the Company at the close of the century.[58] Further compounding the weavers' difficulties, the Company's cloth monopoly made outlets where the rejected cloth could be sold less accessible.

The Company was also more stringent than South Indian merchants in holding weavers to the conditions of their contracts which had the effect of reducing weaver incomes. The contractual conditions the Company was most concerned to enforce were those pertaining to cloth quality and delivery schedules. In order to improve cloth quality, in addition to rejecting cloth, the Company sorted cloth more carefully and took price abatements more strictly. The Company also raised quality standards and interpreted them more inflexibly: deductions for poor workmanship and quality were taken without exception. For example, in 1771 weavers in Cuddalore complained that the Company made large deductions on cloth which the merchants would have taken at full price.[59] Similar complaints were expressed at other weaving centers and the Company's sorting policies led to numerous weaver protests in the final quarter of the eighteenth century.

In the jagir, to improve cloth quality the Company instituted a policy of sorting each piece of cloth twice. The brokers performed the first sorting in the weaving villages and abatements were taken at that time. The commercial servants of the Company undertook a second sorting at Fort St. George and the weavers were held responsible for any additional price deductions that were made at that time. From its introduction, the weavers opposed the second sorting.[60] To press this demand, in 1776 weavers in the southern division of the jagir formed a "combination" and called a halt to all work. As a compromise, the Company made the

---

[57] MPP, 1771, vol. 106B, p. 1006, TNA. There is no information on why the weavers agreed to this change.
[58] South Arcot Collectorate Records, Cuddalore Consultations, 1777, vol. 77, p. 130, TNA; 1778, vol. 79, pp. 11–15, TNA.
[59] South Arcot Collectorate Records, Cuddalore Consultations, 1771, vol. 70, pp. 104–6, TNA.
[60] MPP, 1771, vol. 106B, p. 1006, TNA.

brokers, rather than the weavers, accountable for any price deductions taken in the second sorting.[61]

A second condition of contracts enforced more strictly by the Company was adherence to production and delivery schedules. The Company pressured weavers to meet deadlines and demanded prompt delivery of cloth. Finished cloth was collected monthly.[62] As was mentioned previously, weavers in Ingeram complained that the Company expected two pieces of longcloth every month, which they found excessive.[63] The Company also reduced the size of each advance in order to keep weaver balances small.[64] These changes minimized the amount of money in the hands of the weavers, which reduced the risks of weaver debts. In addition, they hastened the turnover of working capital, which increased the Company's profits. The weavers resisted these changes on the grounds that they could not support themselves and their families with the much smaller advances. South Indian cloth merchants made larger advances and received cloth and settled accounts three or four months after the contract. This gave the weavers a sizable supply of money with which they stocked up on paddy and materials in the cheap seasons.[65] With great patience and persistence, however, the Company prevailed upon the weavers to accept smaller advances.

The Company also compelled weavers to respect their debt obligations. The Company used its political power to tie down weavers and reduce their mobility. Debt recovery systems were created to prevent weavers from running off with advances. On occasion, the Company deployed sepoys to prevent weavers from deserting with its money.[66] The Company also noted that weavers who ran away with advances could be recalled as "Company debtors."[67] The Company was so successful that in 1776 weavers in the jagir demanded the return of the merchants because they were "not so hard upon them in collecting debts."[68] And in 1789, weavers in Arni flogged Company brokers who, in violation of custom, demanded balances which had been lost to plundering armies.[69]

[61] MPP, 1776, vol. 115B, pp. 327–42, TNA.
[62] MPP, 1771, vol. 106B, p. 857, TNA.   [63] MPP, 1775, vol. 114A, pp. 654–5, TNA.
[64] See for example, MPP, 1771, vol. 106B, pp. 1001, 1014, 1020, 1022, TNA; MPP, 1774, vol. 111, pp. 352–4, TNA. This is a recurring theme in the Company records for the 1770s.
[65] MPP, 1771, vol. 106B, pp. 1019–20, 1028, TNA.
[66] See for example, South Arcot Collectorate Records, Cuddalore Consultations, 1772, vol. 71, p. 171, TNA.
[67] South Arcot Collectorate Records, Cuddalore Consultations, 1768, vol. 66, pp. 28–36, TNA.
[68] MPP, 1776, vol. 115B, pp. 331–40, TNA.
[69] MPP, 1789, vol. P/241/14, pp. 2420–1, OIOC.

Production conditions

The Company instituted direct advances to the weavers, increasingly monopolized the cloth trade and enforced contracts more rigorously, yet it continued to remain dissatisfied with the quality of its cloth. In order to make further improvements, the Company embarked upon a series of ambitious efforts to regulate the production process itself. Customarily, production decisions had been under the absolute control of weavers.[70] Merchants had simply advanced money and collected the completed cloth. All else was left to the weavers. Weavers had autonomy when purchasing materials and judicious buying of yarn could substantially increase their incomes. Tools and other instruments of production were also under their control. Weavers obtained their own looms and they took responsibility for their maintenance. In its desire to improve cloth quality, and thus its profits, the Company intruded upon these weaver prerogatives.

The Company's first forays into the production lives of weavers took place in Cuddalore in 1772, four years after direct advances had been instituted. The Company believed that in this period there had been little improvement in the cloth because weavers did not purchase yarn of the proper quality. To ensure that the weavers used good yarn, the Company appointed sorters who were to inspect the yarn before the weavers fitted it to their looms. Such inspection proved to be time-consuming and difficult, however, which led the Company to take responsibility for the purchase of the yarn itself. Instead of advancing money to weavers, the Company began to advance yarn along with a small amount of cash; three-fourths of the value of the advance was yarn and one-fourth money.[71] *Kanakkapillais* (accountants in Tamil) were appointed to distribute the yarn and oversee the looms.

The announcement of the scheme caused an immediate uproar among the weavers, who abandoned their looms in protest. The head weavers reported to the Company that they preferred to reduce cloth prices rather than receive advances of yarn, which is indicative of the control weavers sought to maintain over the production process. The Company imprisoned the head weavers – fearing their influence – and tried to persuade the remaining weavers to accept yarn advances. It had little immediate success, but after a month the head weavers capitulated and

---

[70] This appears to have been true in other areas of production also, most importantly agriculture. See chapter 5 and also David Ludden, "Archaic Formations of Agricultural Knowledge in South India," in Peter Robb (ed.), *Meanings of Agriculture* (Delhi, 1996), pp. 35–70.

[71] South Arcot Collectorate Records, Cuddalore Consultations, 1772, vol. 71, pp. 40–9, 92–3, TNA.

agreed to the advances of yarn. They persuaded the other weavers to return to their looms, and by September peace had been restored and yarn distributed.[72]

The opposition of the Cuddalore weavers to yarn advances does not reflect an unqualified preference for advances of money over those of materials. In the jagir, in some villages it was customary for yarn to constitute a part of the advance. In Cuddalore as well, yarn and other materials had been advanced on occasion. In 1734 a group of weavers recently settled at Fort St. David accepted advances of yarn and grain.[73] In 1768, when cotton prices were very high, weavers in Cuddalore accepted advances of cotton which the Company had imported from Surat, but by the following year cotton prices had fallen and the weavers refused the cotton.[74]

In 1778, the Company inserted itself even more deeply into the production process with the financing and overseeing of loom repairs by the Cuddalore Council. These interventions were set in motion early in the year when a Commercial Resident discovered that much of the cloth manufactured in the Cuddalore area did not contain the proper number of warp yarns. In the course of his inquiry, he found that many of the loom combs were worn and in need of replacement. The head weavers agreed to replace the combs if they were advanced money for the purchase of new ones and repayment was to be demanded slowly. Having the approval of the head weavers, the Commercial Resident was confident that the remaining weavers would also agree to the repairs, but, to his dismay, the general body of weavers refused and called a halt to their work.[75]

In a meeting with the Resident the weavers claimed that the poor quality of the cloth was due not to the combs, but to the fact that they did not receive sufficient quantities of yarn in the advance. In addition, the weavers reported that the yarn they received was frequently of poor quality. As an alternative to fixing new combs, the weavers demanded an increase in cloth prices, an end to the rejection of their cloth, and the dismissal of the kanakkapillais who, they said, cheated them when making advances.[76] The Cuddalore Council was unwilling to meet these demands and the weavers responded by migrating from the Company's

[72] South Arcot Collectorate Records, Cuddalore Consultations, 1772, vol. 71, pp. 93–6, 114–16, 124, TNA.
[73] FSDC, 1734, p. 19.
[74] South Arcot Collectorate Records, Cuddalore Consultations, 1768, vol. 66, p. 123, TNA; 1769, vol. 68, pp. 37–8, TNA.
[75] South Arcot Collectorate Records, Cuddalore Consultations, 1778, vol. 79, pp. 11–15, TNA.
[76] South Arcot Collectorate Records, Cuddalore Consultations, 1778, vol. 79, pp. 11–15, TNA.

territories.[77] Several Company servants feared that the weavers would never return, but by May 200 looms were back at work in Cuddalore. By July the majority of weavers had returned and agreed to the installation of new combs.[78]

The Company state

The Company's efforts to improve quality and reduce prices met with opposition from weavers. However, the Company, in contrast to South Indian merchants, was able to overcome weaver resistance and power. It was able to sort cloth more rigorously, eliminate weaver privileges of contract and regulate the production process itself. As a consequence, the power of weavers to set cloth prices and determine cloth quality was broken. South Indian merchants were incapable of achieving such hegemony and dominance over weavers and in the 1720s and 1730s this failure led to disastrous merchant losses. Why was the Company able to succeed where South Indian merchants had failed?

The answer to this question lies in the Company's political power. The Company, unlike local merchants, was able to call upon state power to defeat weaver opposition and resistance. Two aspects of the Company state, in particular, were novel to South India and were crucial to the Company's successes. First, the English East India Company brought to the region a conception of state power and authority which was unlike anything known in late pre-colonial South India. These novel features of the Company state are addressed in chapter 5. Second, the Company state brought together two forms of power, political and economic, which had existed in some tension in pre-colonial South India. This second aspect of the Company state is explored in the remainder of this chapter.

The English East India Company had been a trading presence in South India from the early seventeenth century. From even its earliest days, the Company's commercial importance made it a significant political force, but its formal political authority in South India dates only from the mid-eighteenth century. In 1763 the Company received revenue collection rights (jagir) in a very sizable piece of territory north, south and east of Madras which came to form the present-day Chingleput district. Over the next forty years the Company steadily added more territory.[79] The

[77] South Arcot Collectorate Records, Cuddalore Consultations, 1778, vol. 79, pp. 45–7, 78–81, TNA.

[78] South Arcot Collectorate Records, Cuddalore Consultations, 1778, vol. 79, pp. 45–7, 112–13, TNA. This major weaver protest is described in greater detail in the following chapter. In Masulipatnam the Company also became involved in replacing the loom combs, but there is little information on the response of weavers. See Masulipatnam District Records, 1787, vol. 2900, pp. 261–6, APSA.

[79] See map in Bayly, *Indian Society*, p. 88.

reasons for the Company's transition from commercial to political power are complex and still continue to be debated.[80]

In pre-colonial South India, weavers were subject to two forms of power. The first was the power of merchants, which was chiefly economic. Merchants exerted their power through their control of credit and in their positions as purchasers of cloth. They received a share of the weavers' product in the form of profits. The structure of contracts, the absence of debt collection institutions and the mobility of weavers limited the power merchants could wield against weavers. The second form of power was political, or the king, who lay claim to a share of the weavers' product in the form of taxes on looms, yarn and cloth.

Political authorities and merchants existed in an uneasy relationship in pre-colonial South India. In particular, kings in South India frequently checked the power of merchants and protected producers. There are several instances of such kingly action in the closing decades of the eighteenth century, especially from the Northern Sarkars. In 1768, according to a Company account, weavers in Ingeram "if much pressed by the merchants either for their ballances or to fulfill their agreement they fly to the villages belonging to the Company's Braminy [presumably also a local holder of political power] at Masulipatnam and there find protection."[81] In 1787, a zamindar in Ingeram prohibited merchants from carrying weavers away from their villages or placing peons over the weavers to extract debt repayment. The zamindar sent instructions to the merchants to submit their claims against weavers to him and he would take responsibility for settling accounts in a just manner.[82] Zamindars in Madapollam were similarly reluctant to assist merchants as were political authorities in the jagir who protected weavers in conflicts with mercantile power.[83] Weavers were well aware of the tensions which existed between merchants and kings, and exploited them to their own advantage.

The Company state merged merchant and kingly power, with devastating consequences for weavers. In its dealings with weavers, the Company was no longer limited to its economic power, but was also able to call upon political power. The Company's ability to deploy force in its conflicts with weavers, an important prerogative of political authority, was

[80] See Bayly, *Indian Society*, chap. 2 for a summary.

[81] Masulipatnam District Records, 1768, vol. 2871, pp. 217–29, APSA.

[82] MPP, 1787, vol. P/241/3, p. 3187, OIOC. Also see MPP, 1768, vol. P/240/26, pp. 391–2, OIOC and MPP, 1792, vol. P/241/30, pp. 78–81, OIOC. Also see Prasannan Parthasarathi, "Merchants and the Rise of Colonialism," in Burton Stein and Sanjay Subrahmanyam (eds.), *Institutions and Economic Change in South Asia* (Delhi, 1996), pp. 85–104. This is not to deny the possibility of cooperation between merchants and kings in other respects. See Sanjay Subrahmanyam and C. A. Bayly, "Portfolio Capitalists and the Political Economy of Early Modern India," *IESHR*, 25 (1988), pp. 401–24.

[83] MPP, 1789, vol P/241/14, pp. 2422, 2470, OIOC. Also see MPP, 1784, vol. P/240/58, p. 311, OIOC.

critical to its successes. This ability to command political and coercive power sharply distinguished it from South Indian merchants. The Company was well aware that these powers were essential to its victories against weavers. In the early decades of the eighteenth century, the Company had experimented with direct advances to weavers in villages around Madras and Fort St. David. These trials had been on a small scale and involved only fifty to a hundred weavers. Several times during the century the Company had contemplated expanding the system of direct advances, but was reluctant to distribute its money to large numbers of weavers. In the 1760s the Company reasoned that it could use its newly won political power to reduce such risks. Similar political calculations were made in Masulipatnam, where in 1787 the Council decided that it was better to obtain *chay* goods using the intermediation of merchants rather than direct advances to the weavers since chay goods were made in Guntur, where the Company had "no influence or authority."[84] The Company was also aware that its political authority made its relations with weavers very different from those of private traders with whom weavers seldom abided by their contracts. Weavers also typically kept a portion of the advance from a private trader as an addition to their incomes. According to the Company, weavers took these contracts lightly because private traders had "no authority in the country."[85]

A comparison of the weavers' situations at different Company factories illustrates the important role that political power played in the Company's conflicts with weavers. The Company had greater success defeating the opposition of weavers in Cuddalore and Madras than in Ingeram and Madapollam. This was because the Company's political power, and therefore its power over weavers, was greater in Madras and Cuddalore. At these places the Company could exercise direct political authority over weavers, but at Ingeram and Madapollam the Company could only exercise indirect authority. In the latter two factories, zamindars stood between the Company and weavers and constrained the Company's exercise of political power. The Company was aware of these limits to its authority, which also embroiled its servants in complex negotiations with zamindars. The following extract from the Company's proceedings makes these points apparent:

For Sadleir [a Commercial Resident] to successfully make [direct] advances to the weavers he must be invested with the proper degree of authority in weaving villages. This authority should extend to the entire direction and control of weavers employed by the Company as far as respects their conduct in investment

[84] Masulipatnam District Records, Commercial Consultations, 1787, vol. 2838, pp. 72–8, APSA.
[85] Godavari District Records, 1803, vol. 832, p. 429, APSA.

but no further. He should not interfere with other inhabitants or possess any other influence which may weaken the authority of Zamindars.[86]

The same limits on Company political power in Ganjam convinced the Commercial Resident there to contract with weavers who resided in *havelly* land, which was under direct Company control, rather than with weavers belonging to zamindar lands. The Commercial Resident said that weavers residing in zamindar territories had not done as well in past contracts with the Company because they were "less under our [Company] inspection."[87] At the end of the century, in order to exercise more fully its political power, the Company stepped up its efforts to attract weavers to its territories.[88]

Conclusion

Weavers were a powerful group in eighteenth-century South India. Nevertheless, they were vulnerable to the integration of political and economic power. This chapter has described the consequences of one form of this integration in late eighteenth-century South India: the English East India Company's rise to political power. The Company, however, was only one of many integrations of politics and economics in the late eighteenth century. These others, which emerged from within South Indian society itself, formed when states in South India entered the arena of commerce. Tipu Sultan's Mysore is perhaps the best known of these, but there were many others. And many rulers were not content simply to trade, but began to create monopolies in products. Some of the most important of these monopolies were in cloth. As did the Company, South Indian rulers also began to bypass merchants and sought to establish direct relations with weavers: negotiating prices, making advances and collecting cloth.

The South Indian state monopolies, however, did not have the same devastating impact on weavers. Thus the integration of political and economic power alone does not fully account for the effects of the Company's political authority on weavers.[89] As we will see later in this book, the Company's conceptions of statecraft and legitimate authority

[86] MPP, 1774, vol. 112, pp. 427–8, TNA.
[87] MPP, 1774, vol. 112, pp. 536–7, TNA.
[88] South Arcot Collectorate Records, Cuddalore Consultations, 1772, vol. 71, pp. 172–3, TNA.
[89] Another integration of economic and political power came about when merchants entered the state as revenue farmers, but this also did not have the same consequences as the Company's rise to power. In the late eighteenth century a Company servant noted that weavers in the Northern Sarkars were often treated best in areas where the "subrenter" was a cloth merchant. MPP, 1789, vol. P/241/15, p. 3137, OIOC.

were far different from what existed in South India. The Company brought with it ideas on the relationship between the state and laborers which prevailed in Britain and these ideas were contrary to long-standing traditions in South India. This may explain why the Company, far more than South Indian merchants and states, was able to do as it wanted with weavers. And in this novel form of the state also lies the secret of the colonial economy. But before turning to these matters, we will first undertake a more detailed investigation of the weavers' protests which have been alluded to on several occasions in this chapter.

4   Weaver protest

Weavers hotly contested the Company's attempts to regulate the cloth market, transform the customs of contract and control the cloth production process. They orchestrated work stoppages, desertions and even riots in order to derail the Company's schemes. Many of these actions were local affairs in which a few dozen weavers participated, but there were also large-scale protests that drew upon several hundred weavers from a score or more towns and villages. In 1768, for example, weavers in the Northern Sarkars declared a work stoppage in which 900 participated. Merchants touring the area "found every loom tied up . . . and were told they would find it the same at every town."[1] In 1775, again in the Sarkars, weavers organized a work stoppage which was comparable in size and scope and sustained it for nearly four months. In 1778 Cuddalore weavers mobilized more than a thousand of their number and paralyzed the Company's investment for seven months. In 1798 300 weavers in Madapollam abandoned their looms in protest of their deteriorating conditions. They roamed the countryside, recruited 200 more to their cause, and disrupted yarn markets and cloth deliveries to the Company. Eventually the weavers assembled at the Madapollam factory where they demanded higher prices for their cloth.[2]

Despite the number and scale of these protests they have received little scholarly attention.[3] Indeed, very little is known about the nature and forms of resistance or protest in eighteenth-century South India, or South Asia for that matter.[4] The energies of the Subaltern Studies group, for instance, have been devoted to the nineteenth and twentieth centuries, and particularly to the period after 1850. Nevertheless, although largely

---

[1] Masulipatnam District Records, 1768, vol. 2871, pp. 25–8, APSA.
[2] Godavari District Records, 1798, vol. 830, pp. 24–46, APSA.
[3] S. Arasaratnam has noted the existence of widespread weaver discontent, but made little analysis of these protests. See his "Trade and Political Dominion in South India," "Weavers, Merchants and Company," and *Maritime Commerce and English Power.*
[4] For Southeast Asia there is the fine work of Michael Adas, "From Avoidance to Confrontation: Peasant Protest in Precolonial and Colonial Southeast Asia," *Comparative Studies in Society and History*, 23 (1981), pp. 217–47.

unexplored, an earlier tradition of resistance haunts these writings, as it is often invoked to explain the peculiarities, and especially the failures, of protest in the colonial period. There are frequent references to the persistence of pre-colonial, semi-feudal or pre-capitalist traditions or modes of behavior and to the "primordialism" of subaltern groups, be they peasants, workers or tribals.[5]

What emerges from a study of late eighteenth-century protests is not the rigidity of the weavers' social world, as primordialism implies, but its plasticity.[6] As we have seen previously, the ties of solidarity that weavers created were not fixed, but continually made and remade. In their protests of the late eighteenth century weavers built upon these experiences, and the mutual solidarities which emerged in this period demonstrate extraordinary inventiveness, resourcefulness and creativity. Weavers did not take social relations or solidarities as given and ties of caste, kinship or other "primordialisms" did not in some simple or automatic way determine or limit their actions. In fact, as we shall see, the act of protest itself and the demands of mobilizing for protest led weavers to explore and create new forms of solidarity. Thus in myriad ways, weavers defined their social worlds through these acts of protest and resistance. In addition, the weavers' vision of the world was broad: they understood and operated upon a large South Indian canvas. Of course, as we shall also see, the weavers may be criticized for not recognizing the novelty of the Company and the economic and political conceptions which were the basis for its rule. As a consequence they fought too defensive a battle as they strove to restore a world which had been lost, a world which had existed before the Company. Perhaps, perceiving the novelty of the Company, they should have struggled for a new vision, but this is often an imposition of political ideas developed in later times, most importantly in the nineteenth century, upon the actors of the past.[7] The weavers fought with the weapons they had and that had long served them so well and in the following pages we will inquire further into why these pre-Company techniques of protest failed weavers in the Company order.

Before entering the world of the weavers, a few words are necessary on the sources. The following analysis is based on letters and reports contained in the records of the English East India Company. These accounts are often fragmentary and for many protests we possess a description of no

---

[5] See especially Ranajit Guha, *Elementary Aspects of Peasant Insurgency in Colonial India* (Delhi, 1983); Ranajit Guha, *Dominance without Hegemony* (Cambridge, Mass., 1997); and Dipesh Chakrabarty, *Rethinking Working Class History* (Princeton, 1989).

[6] Thus the political failures of workers and peasants in colonial India cannot simply be attributed to an inherited "Indian culture."

[7] This point has been made trenchantly by Ranajit Guha himself. See his *Elementary Aspects*, chap. 1.

more than a few sentences. In addition, the Company's servants took a very narrow interest in these protests. They were motivated by a need to put a quick stop to them in order to minimize the disruption to the Company's cloth supplies and their accounts are fine examples of the "prose of counter-insurgency."[8] Only in rare instances were Company officials driven to understand the process of protest in its depth and complexity. As a result of this narrow interest, we often catch only glimpses of the weavers and their activities. And for much we have not even glimpses. Critical elements such as the contributions of the weaver family to protest and relations between men and women during the process of protest are inaccessible. Finally, Company servants were often reluctant to assign weavers agency. In their opinion, the weavers were incited to protest by merchants, who were manipulating the weavers for their own ends. This is not atypical for these sorts of observers, but weavers were not pawns of others, but sophisticated actors in their own rights.

The Cuddalore protest of 1778

I begin my discussion with an account of the Cuddalore protest of 1778, which not only was one of the largest protests in this period, but is also very well documented. The protest began in two large weaving villages which were known as the Pollams villages. By 1778 the merchant inter-mediaries had been eliminated from the Pollams and the weavers were receiving advances of money and yarn from the Company itself. These operations were supervised by a Commercial Resident who was posted permanently at the villages. In February 1778, while carrying out a routine inquiry into a recent decline in cloth quality, the Resident found that the loom combs (reeds) were defective, which permitted the weavers to decrease the number of warp threads. As a consequence, the cloth was "thin and flimsy."[9]

The Resident summoned the "principal weavers" and informed them that the combs would have to be replaced. In the words of the Resident: "At first they hesitated at my proposal, but on my promising to demand the price of new combs by degrees and to advance the first cost myself, they seemingly came into the measure. As I thought these secured, I little doubted but that I should carry my point with the rest." However, when the Resident began to replace the combs, "the whole body of weavers stopt work." Upon making inquiries, he discovered that the combs were

[8] Ranajit Guha, "The Prose of Counter-Insurgency," in Ranajit Guha (ed.), *Subaltern Studies II* (Delhi, 1983).
[9] Unless otherwise specified all quotations in this section are from South Arcot Collectorate Records, Cuddalore Consultations, 1778, vol. 79, TNA.

not the sole reason for the stoppage and that the weavers had numerous grievances. As the Resident described them:

on enquiring the cause (which I knew before, the dislike of proper looms) they told me the thread was insufficient to make the several assortments true. That it was not good. That their cooley was not enough. That they could not afford to have their cloth turned out. That being obliged from their poverty to employ their children, the cloth could not be expected to prove all good, and a variety of other silly arguments, some saying one thing, some another.

This passage suggests that there was a vast reservoir of weaver discontent in Cuddalore. This discontent had not erupted in protest, but was like tinder ready to catch fire. The Company's proposal to replace the loom combs provided the necessary spark. It is likely that the Company's interference in cloth production had produced similar deep discontent in other weaving centers in South India.

After lengthy negotiations, the Resident persuaded the weavers to continue working with the old combs "till further orders." He believed that the matter was concluded, but the next morning he discovered that the weavers were not at their looms. The Company sources contain little information on the weavers' activities at this time, but it is likely that they were meeting as a body, which they had done during a dispute with the Company in 1768. We possess a description of that meeting from a Company spy:

[The head weavers] assembled all the weavers of both [Pollams] villages in a Tope [grove of trees] and there held a consultation and in the meanwhile sent some of their people to watch and hinder any others from interfering in their cabals. They then one and all came [to] a positive determination that unless the merchants and brokers advance them the money, they would not work for the Company at all.[10]

Before embarking upon a protest weavers assembled, agreed upon their grievances, settled upon a plan of action and proclaimed their unity. It was also not uncommon at these assemblies for weavers to record their grievances in writing. In 1771 weavers from Cuddalore recorded their "complaints in a cadjan."[11] In 1778, one of the first acts of the Cuddalore weavers was to write their complaints on "four or five cadjans" which were promptly delivered to the Commercial Resident.[12]

Why did weavers enumerate their grievances in writing? One reason may have been the practical need to present them to the Company in a form its servants found acceptable and legitimate, but a more interesting reason derives from the contribution of the act to weaver solidarity. The

---

[10] South Arcot Collectorate Records, 1768, vol. 66, pp. 28–36, TNA.
[11] South Arcot Collectorate Records, Cuddalore Consultations, 1771, vol. 70, pp. 120–2, TNA.
[12] South Arcot Collectorate Records, Cuddalore Consultations, 1778, vol. 79, pp. 11–15, TNA.

act of assembling, agreeing upon their grievances and putting them in writing both forged weaver unity and served to represent it. This interpretation is suggested by an account of a meeting between several head weavers and the Cuddalore Council which took place in the early days of the protest in 1778. The Council summoned the head weavers and asked them why the weavers had abandoned their looms. The only response of the weavers was to call for their *cadjans*, which they knew were in the possession of the Company, to be brought into the room.[13] With their refusal to speak, the head weavers deferred to the greater authority of the cadjans. The cadjans derived this authority from the fact that they represented the weavers as a whole. They were the crystallization of the demands of the weaver collectivity.[14]

Other evidence conveys the powerful sense of solidarity which gripped the Cuddalore weavers. After their meeting with the head weavers, the Cuddalore Council informed their superiors in Madras that the weavers were emphatic that they "were all *equally* aggrieved."[15] The Commercial Resident at the Pollams villages concurred with this assessment and wrote that the weavers were "combined like a liberty mob *and are determined staunchly to adhere together.*"[16] These may have been the powerful collective feelings which the cadjans both embodied and helped to create.

The weaver cadjans have not survived, but Company discussions suggest that they made no mention of the Resident's proposal to replace the loom combs. Nor does it appear that the cadjans complained of the inadequacy of yarn and cooly, which were the grievances the weavers had voiced to the Resident immediately upon halting work. Rather the cadjans contained a third set of grievances relating to the "conicoplies" (kanakkapillais), the generic title for the South Indians the Company employed as brokers in the cloth procurement machinery. These servants advanced yarn and money to the weavers, supervised the looms, and collected and sorted the cloth. The weavers accused the kanakkapillais of systematically cheating them of yarn and cooly and demanded their immediate dismissal.

The shifts in grievances – from the replacement of the combs, to inadequacies in the advance system, to oppression by kanakkapillais – perplexed the Company's servants.[17] To make sense of these shifts, the

[13] South Arcot Collectorate Records, Cuddalore Consultations, 1778, vol. 79, pp. 20–1, TNA.
[14] A respect for the written word may have led to its adoption as a vehicle for weaver unity.
[15] South Arcot Collectorate Records, Cuddalore Consultations, 1778, vol. 79, pp. 24–6, TNA.   [16] Emphasis added.
[17] In subsequent discussions with Company servants, the weavers continued to emphasize the removal of the kanakkapillais, but a list of demands the weavers submitted in mid-April 1778 included not only the grievances already enumerated but also the freeing up of the grain trade in the Company's villages, the elimination of the resident's prerogative to reject cloth and a return to money advances instead of advances in cotton yarn.

Cuddalore Council and other Company officials labeled some of the grievances as true, and these they were willing to address, and others false, and these they chose to ignore. From our perspective, we may see all the weaver complaints as valid. The decision to focus in the cadjans on the replacement of the kanakkapillais may have been based on practical and strategic considerations. With a new set of kanakkapillais, weavers may have believed that they would be able to redefine the relationship with these intermediaries and thereby put an end to the practices they found oppressive and irritating. The Commercial Resident himself perceived this possibility. "Its reported," the Resident wrote, "they even say among themselves if they can get the better of these [kanakkapillais], others will be cautious in what manner they act towards them." However, the source of the weavers' difficulties was not simply wayward or corrupt kanakkapillais, but the Company state itself, in which kanakkapillais were merely functionaries, and the Company's political innovations. The magnitude and novelty of the Company's power may not have been evident to the weavers in the midst of the 1778 protest, but it appears to have become more apparent in its aftermath. In 1786, in an attempt to minimize their contact with that power, the Cuddalore weavers demanded a return to the pre-Company advance system and the intermediation of the South Indian merchants. As we will learn shortly, however, these merchants themselves were being invested with new authority under the aegis of the Company state.

The weaver cadjans were brought into the room, but the head weavers and the Cuddalore Council were unable to resolve their differences. Nothing is known of the weavers' activities later that day or that night, but by the next morning, they and their families had packed up their belongings and left the Pollams villages. The weavers did not go far – according to one report, they were "dispersed in bodies at some little distance from their places of abode." But what was of great importance to the weavers was that they were outside the jurisdiction of the Company, which allowed them to work their looms for other buyers without harassment from Company sepoys. This made it possible for the weavers to sustain a long struggle.

The weavers' subsequent actions indicate that they possessed a sophisticated knowledge of the Company and of the South Indian political and economic order. As one of their first acts, the weavers broke off discussions with the Cuddalore Council and sent representatives to Madras to meet with superior Company authorities. The Cuddalore Council attempted to resume its negotiations with the weavers, who refused to do so until "they heard from their agents at the Presidency [Madras] whether their complaints would be attended to." A relay of forty weavers was set up between Madras and Cuddalore to maintain a rapid line of communication between the protesting weavers and their emissaries. In 1786 aggrieved weavers in Cuddalore also sent representatives to appeal to the council in Madras.[18] Weavers in the Northern Sarkars displayed a similar knowledge of the structure and policies of the Company. In 1768 weavers at Ingeram found it puzzling that they were subject to restrictions on the cloth trade while weavers in Vizagapatnam were not.[19] In 1794 during a dispute at Madapollam, the weavers circumvented the local Commercial Resident and sent representatives to petition the recently formed Board of Trade in Madras.[20]

The weavers' understanding of the Company and South India is revealed in yet another way. After deserting the Pollams, the weavers sent representatives to the nearby villages of Bandipollam and Trivendiporam (which were known as the Bounds villages) and persuaded the weavers residing in these places to pack up their looms and leave the Company's territories. At its peak, a thousand weavers from Cuddalore participated in the work stoppage. However, the Pollams' weavers did not remain content with these successes, but were tireless in their efforts to widen the scope of the protest. The Cuddalore Council learned of these and wrote: "We are likewise acquainted that they are exerting every expedient to prevail on the Company's weavers about Conjeeveram, etc. villages dependent on Madras to unite with them the more effectually to carry their wished for end of subverting the investment."[21] Kanchipuram and its surroundings were the main centers for muslins and other fine cloth, which were some of the most valuable parts of the Company's investment. Recruiting these weavers to the protest would have greatly strengthened the Cuddalore weavers' hand. In 1786 also weavers from Cuddalore attempted to expand a work stoppage to these areas. The Company records do not report the outcome of these efforts, and quite possibly they were unsuccessful, but they indicate that the vision of weavers was not narrowly focused only upon the local. Rather weavers, as did merchants, rulers and the European Companies, operated on a broad South Indian canvas.

Upon leaving Cuddalore, many of the weavers settled in the territories of the Nawab of Arcot and, preparing for a protracted struggle, turned their looms to manufacturing cloth for private merchants. Several contin-

---

[18] South Arcot Collectorate Records, Cuddalore Consultations, 1778, vol. 79, pp. 35–7, TNA; 1786, vol. 86, pp. 30–1, TNA.
[19] Masulipatnam District Records, 1768, vol. 2871, pp. 25–8, APSA.
[20] MPP 1794, vol. P/241/48, p. 2154, OIOC.
[21] South Arcot Collectorate Records, Cuddalore Consultations, 1778, vol. 79, pp. 35–7, TNA.

gents of weavers travelled to Pondicherry, where they supplied cloth to the French East India Company. This state of affairs continued for several months with desultory attempts at negotiation and only passing mention of the weavers in the Cuddalore and Madras Consultations. Neither side, however, was willing to concede defeat. In the opinion of the Company during this interlude the weavers were if anything becoming more intransigent.

After several months the Nawab of Arcot intervened on behalf of the Company and broke the stalemate. Although he had refused several Company requests for assistance, in late May the Nawab ordered his *amildars* to seize any weavers who had recently migrated from the Company's villages. The amildar in the Trivady country, which bordered Cuddalore, obliged and rounded up 200 weavers and returned them to Company territory. However, there were signs that the protest was beginning to weaken even before the intercession of the Nawab. In May 200 weavers returned of their own accord to the Bounds of Fort St. David and resumed cloth production for the Company. These weavers manufactured the lowest priced and poorest quality cloth in Cuddalore, the kerchiefs which entered the African trade, which may explain why they were the first to give up the protest. They probably possessed the fewest financial resources, both as individuals and as a community, and were unable to keep up the struggle.

After returning to the Company's territories, the Cuddalore weavers quietly resumed the production of cloth for the Company. They allowed their loom combs to be replaced and little was heard from them until September 1779, when they sent the Cuddalore Council a long and detailed petition requesting higher cloth prices. In support of this request, the weavers cited their acceptance of the new combs, since which time they had "heartily exerted themselves to make the investment good and to gain your approbation by a quiet and proper behavior." The Cuddalore Council concurred with this assessment and granted higher prices.

The Cuddalore protest of 1778 shared many features with other weaver protests of the late eighteenth century.[22] These protests were defensive affairs in which weavers sought to maintain the privileges which they had possessed in the pre-colonial political and economic order. To do this, however, they had to take on the Company behemoth, which forced them to construct new solidarities and deploy novel techniques of resistance

---

[22] It also appears that weaver protests shared features with the protests of other laboring groups in the late eighteenth century. For a treatment of a protest by adimai in Chingleput in the 1790s, although brief, see Sivakumar and Sivakumar, *Peasants and Nabobs*, chap. 4 and Irschick, *Dialogue and History*, chap. 1.

and political alliances. These themes are examined in greater detail in the remainder of this chapter, but with our lens widened to South India as a whole.

The sources of discontent

Much of the weaver discontent in the late eighteenth century may be traced to the English East India Company's reorganization of cloth procurement and production. Through acts of protest and resistance weavers fought to defend and restore the prerogatives which they had possessed in the late pre-colonial order. Not surprisingly, weavers associated these rights with South Indian merchants and many early protests sought to preserve the role of these merchants. This remained an undercurrent in protests until the 1790s, when a new Company–merchant order began to take shape in South India. However, with time weavers came to accept the Company's appropriation of the merchant role and weaver protests sought to soften the more onerous features of its advance system, especially the low prices for cloth, the stringent and inflexible cloth sorting and the rejection of cloth. The last, in particular, created great hardship for weavers as the English were at the same time eliminating alternative buyers for the weavers' cloth.

The Company's actions caught weavers in price scissors. With one blade, the Company exerted enormous pressure on weavers to reduce cloth prices. With the other, it demanded improvements in cloth quality, which translated into higher costs in weaving. The result was sharp declines in weaver incomes. Weavers in South India were keenly aware of their costs and prices. This knowledge is most evident from their petitions to the Company which consistently display an impeccable economic logic. In these petitions, weavers backed up their demands for higher prices, increased cooly or larger advances with a detailed accounting of costs and prices.[23] K. N. Chaudhuri has previously remarked upon the sophisticated economic thinking found among the ordinary people of South India. He has singled out for praise a 1736 petition from the washermen of Madras to the English Company which enumerated costs in superb detail, breaking them down into nine categories, including beating, two forms of cooly hire, fuel and materials such as goat dung, *chunam*, soap and indigo.[24]

[23] An outstanding example is contained in South Arcot Collectorate Records, Cuddalore Consultations, 1779, vol. 81, pp. 206–7, TNA.
[24] To show that their situation in Madras was very unfavorable, the washermen compared the conditions for washing at Madras, Fort St. David, Porto Novo and Vizagapatnam. Outside Madras, they argued, washers "have larger privileges and larger benefits to support themselves out of their allowances by reason of their having rivers of good and

It is possible that this form of economic thinking was alien to weavers and washermen in South India, but was adopted by them to communicate more effectively with the Company. They may have seen it as a discourse understood by the English, so to speak. Recent research, however, has found that accounting and numeracy skills in South Asia were extremely advanced in the late pre-colonial and early colonial periods. Merchants in particular had developed sophisticated systems of accounts which were not simply emulations of European methods, but developed independently to meet the demands of early modern South Asian economic life.[25] Weavers, who were extremely active in the commercial economy of the time, possessed the knowledge to keep track of their market activities. In the words of an English Company servant, "every weaver is known to keep [a record] of all his transactions" on "Cajans" or palm leaves.[26]

Of course, the English East India Company was not responsible for all expressions of weaver discontent in these decades. Several protests were directed against local revenue authorities and, as we shall see shortly, the lines of conflict became extremely complicated at the end of the century and South Indian merchants and even other weavers became the targets of weaver protest. Nevertheless, the majority of protests as well as the largest ones were directed at the English East India Company, which is reflected in their spatial distribution. The most active sites, as well as the settings for the most spectacular uprisings, were Cuddalore and Northern Sarkars. The Company's interventions in cloth production were the most sustained and far-reaching in these two areas.

Solidarity

The account of the Cuddalore protest of 1778 showed that discontent had existed among weavers for some time, but had not expressed itself in the form of a protest. To make this leap, from an initial cacophony of wrongs, violations and injustices, to an organized movement of protest, required powerful ties of solidarity. In the Cuddalore protest, which began in the Pollams villages, it is likely that the initial rumblings of

fresh water proper for washing of Cloths and their places being near to the woods, whereby they are likewise gainers in purchasing the several Ingredients required in washing, as soap, Chinam, Choud, Goat's dung, Fuel etc." The petition is contained in English East India Company, *Fort St. George Diary and Consultation Book, 1736* (Madras, 1930), p. 78. Also see Chaudhuri, *Trading World*, p. 270.

[25] C. A. Bayly, "Pre-Colonial Indian Merchants and Rationality," in Mushirul Hasan and Narayani Gupta (eds.), *India's Colonial Encounter: Essays in Memory of Eric Stokes* (Delhi, 1993); David West Rudner, *Caste and Capitalism in Colonial India* (Berkeley, Calif., 1994).

[26] South Arcot Collectorate Records, 1803, vol. 111, pp. 24–5, TNA.

solidarity drew upon pre-existing connections between the weavers of these villages. These links derived from the political and territorial organization of weavers, marriage and kinship alliances, ritual activities and cooperation in the work of weaving, and they were not fixed, immutable or primordial. Weaver solidarity was made and remade continuously through work, worship, marriage and politics. Conflicts between weavers could lead very quickly to redefinitions of these weaver links. Perhaps it was the fluid and tenuous nature of these sources of solidarity which led weavers to assemble, record their grievances on cadjans and decide as a body to embark upon protest. These acts may have reinforced and strengthened the pre-existing ties between weavers.

The Cuddalore protest of 1778, in common with the other large protests in this period, was not a local affair, but recruited to it weavers from both near and far. In this case, the locally bound weaver solidarities, largely formed from everyday connections and circuits, would have been far weaker or altogether nonexistent. To organize these large protests, which encompassed several hundred weavers dispersed over a large territory, weavers had to construct new forms of solidarity which could unify and unite. A sign that the ties of solidarity in large-scale protests were of recent origin was their fragility, which is evident from the way these protests came to an end. Their denouement was often a slow and protracted process as contingents of weavers gradually abandoned protest and returned to the business of making cloth. If the protest was still vibrant, there was no guarantee that these weavers would remain at their looms. This was a frequent Company concern: "[The Company Warehouse-keeper] is now very apprehensive that weavers of about 200 looms which have within these few days settled themselves in their places of abode and are now employed in Company's investment may again desert, If others established in Nabob's country almost within our view are permitted to remain there with impunity." And at Arni in 1795, the majority of weavers had ended a work stoppage, but they were harassed by "weavers desirous of continuing disturbances."[27]

How were these ties of solidarity, which were the basis of large-scale protests, constructed? In the opinion of many Company servants, they were the products of intimidation, coercion and violence. There is no doubt that violence often accompanied weaver protests, particularly in the Northern Sarkars.[28] In the Sarkars weavers used violence against

---

[27] MPP, 1795, vol. P/241/58, pp. 3543–4, OIOC.
[28] The reasons for the greater use of violence by weavers in the Northern Sarkars remain a mystery. Perhaps it was because the Cuddalore weavers were concentrated in a few very large weaving villages around the town of Cuddalore, which made the mobilization for protest far easier. In the Sarkars, by contrast, weavers were spread in many villages located over a large area. It may also have to do with the structure of the Company's

Company servants who in one incident were severely beaten with sticks.[29] The Sarkars weavers also used violence to disrupt thread markets, which prevented working weavers from obtaining materials, thus paralyzing the Company's investment.[30] The weavers achieved enormous success with this tactic and in 1778 the Commercial Resident at Madapollam appealed to Madras for assistance to ensure that "thread markets be permitted to receive no obstruction."[31]

Weavers in the Northern Sarkars also used violence, or its threat, to expand the scale of protests. In 1795, several weavers halted work and "invited those of the neighboring mootahs to join them (threatening to cut from the loom the cloths of such as refuse to do so)."[32] Similar threats had been issued in 1775.[33] In Cuddalore threats of violent reprisal were also used to maintain weaver solidarity. In 1768 several head weavers confronted one of their fellows who had consented to a Company proposal and "threatened to turn him out from being any longer a head weaver if he made a single piece."[34]

Undoubtedly threats passed between weaver and weaver, but they alone can account for neither the scale of these protests nor the mutual solidarity they display. The following passage, penned in 1775 by the Commercial Resident at Madapollam, reveals that far more was involved:

Weavers under this factory are satisfied with my treatment of them of which they give me assurances via their head weavers. Consequently for one month after the Ingeram weavers had quit work and [begun] strolling the country those of this place continued at their looms; at length yielding to *threats and solicitations* of the former, they joined in the general uproar.[35]

As this passage makes apparent, threats were accompanied by solicitations, perhaps requests or arguments, which aimed to persuade. The feverish activity which this demanded of weavers is well conveyed in the Company records:

About twenty days ago two of the Head Weavers went to a village called Pattampaukum in the District of Trevady under pretence of a wedding and departed to Pondicherry instead where they had a meeting with the Weavers who had lately deserted from the Company's bound at Bandipollam and persuaded some to

operations and the rather freer hand that its servants appeared to wield in the Northern Sarkars, which resulted in greater oppression of the weavers.
29 MPP, 1775, vol. 113B, pp. 196–9, 366–7, TNA.
30 Masulipatnam District Records, 1795, vol. 2944, pp. 43–4, APSA.
31 Godavari District Records, 1798, vol. 887, pp. 321–4, APSA.
32 Masulipatnam District Records, 1795, vol. 2944, pp. 43–4, APSA.
33 MPP, 1775, vol. 113B, pp. 196–9, 352–3, TNA.
34 South Arcot Collectorate Records, 1768, vol. 66, pp. 28–36, TNA.
35 MPP, 1775, vol. 114B, pp. 828–9, TNA. Emphasis added.

proceed with them to Madras and about ten days after their arrival there, it is asserted that they wrote to the Weavers of Pattampoakum [*sic*] to contrive means to seduce the Weavers of Chinnamanaickpollam and Naideput in the like manner as those that had quitted Bandipollam where upon four of the Head Weavers of the pollams went to Pattampaukum under pretense of accommodating some disputes which those of that place had to settle. They remained two days in Pattampaukum and returned back to the pollams after they confered together and it appeared by their motions as if they had concerted some scheme to leave the place in a few days, accordingly seventy weavers have deserted from the pollams.[36]

It is difficult to recover the solicitations and arguments weavers used to exhort others to join with them. However, the records of the Company do yield several insights. Of particular importance are weaver petitions, which regrettably are found only in translation. In these weavers communicated their grievances and demands to the Company, local political authorities and revenue officials.[37]

The idiom in which grievances were presented in these documents typically centered upon the notion of *mamool* or custom. Cuddalore weavers, for instance, complained of a Company servant on the grounds that he had "acted contrary to the Custom,"[38] and weavers in Masulipatnam demanded that higher taxes on dyeing pots be removed on the grounds that they were "contrary to mamool."[39] And in a petition to the Nawab of Arcot, weavers in Udaiyarpolliam reported that his amildar had raised the loom tax in violation of "mamool."[40] The use of custom to comprehend the world and to express a wrong suggests that the defence of customary practices, or tradition, may have served as a rallying point for weavers. In the process, weavers also constructed a normative tradition with which they evaluated the present and struggled to shape the future.

An appeal to custom implies that weavers possessed an awareness of their shared situation in the South Indian political and economic order. These common interests, particularly those deriving from an opposition to the Company, were the basis for a *samayam*, or association, formed in 1775 by the four main weaving jatis in the Northern Sarkars. The creation of this alliance indicates that weavers perceived a mutual solidarity which transcended kinship, lineage and caste considerations. These four main

[36] South Arcot Collectorate Records, Cuddalore Consultations, 1786, vol. 86, pp. 35–8, TNA.
[37] I have been informed that the English East India Company records for Bengal contain similar weaver petitions, but in the original Bengali.
[38] South Arcot Collectorate Records, Cuddalore Consultations, 1771, vol. 70, pp. 120–2, TNA.
[39] Masulipatnam District Records, 1799, vol 3075, pp. 282–8, APSA.
[40] South Arcot Collectorate Records, 1796, vol. 102, pp. 121–4, TNA.

weaving castes in the Northern Sarkars also united during a protest in 1798.[41]

In 1775 the weaver samayam received the support of agriculturalists, specifically from the Mahanadu of Jagganadaporam, whose inhabitants sent a letter to the Mahanadu of Mundapettah soliciting their support for the weavers' cause. The letter, which is available only in translation, reads as follows:

As the four different casts of the weavers namely Salavar, Davanguloo, Carnevar and Kackullavar have formed a Samayem (or a Company of people gathered to enforce the execution of some particular business) Regarding Mr. Sadleir [the Company's Commercial Resident at Ingeram] it becomes you to cause one man out of each house of the weavers to join the said Samayem, you will therefore advise the weavers to do so. We must remark that ever since the Samayem hath been formed at Golconda we both (meaning our people and those of the weavers) lived in perfect union as the milk and water wherefore you will exert yourself at this time to support the said Samayam by all means which will gain us a good name and reputation. This is not to be regarded like other Business. As you are ingenious I need not enlarge much to you upon the subject. Take the aforegoing information into consideration and give the Bearer a seer of rice and a Dubb.[42]

This letter itself suggests that the weaver samayam was not part of the everyday social landscape of the Northern Sarkars. It was an extraordinary undertaking and demanded extraordinary participation and support from weavers. It was for this reason that one weaver was to join from every household. The letter also indicates that support from agrarian classes for a weaver cause was an unusual occurrence. There may have been a history of conflict between these groups, perhaps rooted in the right-hand and left-hand divide in South India.[43] To encourage agriculturalists to support the weaver cause, the authors of the letter found it necessary to state that since the formation of samayam, agriculturalists and weavers have "lived in perfect union as the milk and water." The reasons for this cooperation remain unclear, but it may have developed in opposition to the growing political power of the English East India Company. This opposition may also have been territorially rooted which is suggested by the reference to Golconda.

Language and words, whether written or spoken, were not the only material with which weavers constructed ties of solidarity. In 1792, a Company servant in the Northern Sarkars wrote: "I learned for the first

[41] Godavari District Records, 1798, vol 830, pp. 24–46, APSA.
[42] MPP, 1775, vol 113B, pp. 365–6, TNA.
[43] For further details on this great divide see Appadurai, "Right and Left Hand Castes."

time utmost dissatisfaction prevailed among weavers and two head weavers in village of Dagloroo in Mootah of Chintapurroo having assembled a body of approximately three hundred weavers entertained them with supper and then prevailed on them to swear they would never weave for the Company."[44] In South India, and in South Asia more widely, the giving of food creates a powerful bond between the giver and receiver and "can serve to indicate and construct social relations," as Arjun Appadurai has put it.[45] In this instance, weavers used the social power of food to construct solidarity. The giving of the food was the first act and served to deepen and strengthen the relationship. Only after establishing this more profound connection, and with it a sense of obligation, did the givers of food broach the topic of boycotting the Company. After taking food, the recipients of this gift would have been under its charisma and under greater pressure, both social and psychological, to reciprocate.[46]

Weavers and writing

Letters, petitions, and other forms of the written word were integral to weaver protests.[47] Weavers used writing to create and represent ties of solidarity, to communicate with the Company, and to expand the scale of protest. The circular letter from the Mahanadu of Jagganadaporam is a particularly impressive example of the last, but on many other occasions writing was used for the same purpose. In 1798 weavers in the Northern Sarkars issued "letters inviting all weavers of the casts to join them." In this way, according to a Company servant, weavers "too well succeeded" in widening the protest.[48] In 1786 weavers in Cuddalore called a halt to work when a letter from their representatives in Madras instructed them "to leave the place as they cannot carry their point unless they do so."[49]

Protesting weavers, who were often spread over a large area, relied

---

[44] Godavari District Records, 1798, vol. 830, pp. 24–46, APSA.
[45] Arjun Appadurai, "Gastro-Politics in Hindu South Asia," *American Ethnologist*, 8 (1981), pp. 494–511.
[46] I am grateful to Chitra Sivakumar for this insight.
[47] It is very difficult to gauge the extent of literacy among weavers. The English translations of petitions to the Company typically give the names of the head weavers who signed the petition. In some translations, the names of the weavers who were signatories are written in both English and Tamil or Telugu. On occasion, a head weaver was not able to sign and instead made his mark, which was duly noted in the translated version contained in the Company records. Further evidence for weaver literacy comes from the early nineteenth-century account of Elijah Hoole, who encountered two weavers in Kanchipuram reading a Tamil translation of a Christian tract. See Hoole, *Mission*, p. 344.
[48] Godavari District Records, 1798, vol. 830, pp. 24–46, APSA.
[49] South Arcot Collectorate Records, Cuddalore Consultations, 1778, vol. 79, pp. 35–7, TNA; 1786, vol. 86, pp. 32–3, TNA.

upon letters to maintain the bonds of solidarity and to sustain the momentum of protest. This was the purpose of an anonymous letter from weavers in Pondicherry to their compatriots in Cuddalore, which the Company intercepted:

> We are in good health at Pondicherry and hope to have the pleasure of hearing of your welfare. We are certain of receiving good news in a short time and therefore we advise you to be [of] courage and to refuse to give your consent though twenty fanams offered to you for every piece of cloth. Should anyone of you consent relating to this affair of thread we will set his house on flame. If he kills four or ten of you to induce you to obedience you must not yield but attribute their death to their bad destiny.[50]

Contrary to widespread images of India, fatalism did not lead weavers to be resigned to their destiny.[51] In this example, the conventional wisdom is turned upside down as weavers used a belief in fate to sustain a struggle and actively shape their future.

English East India Company servants were aware of the importance of the written word for weavers and they themselves used cadjans and letters to communicate with them. In one instance, the Company even sought to take advantage of the weavers' reliance upon this mode of communication.[52] In 1786 the Cuddalore Council summoned several head weavers, whom they had taken into custody, and pressured them to "write a letter under the inspection of Vencatarangia, the Company's interpreter, directing the absent weavers to return to their looms and another to the weavers remaining at the pollams to proceed without difficulty or delay upon the Company's investment, under pain of severe punishment." The head weavers refused to write such a letter and they reiterated their refusal to work for the Company until their demands were met. Nor would such a letter, according to the head weavers, persuade the protesting weavers to return to their looms.[53] There is no evidence that the Company asked its interpreter to write the letter himself and to sign it with the names of the head weavers. Perhaps the interpreter, who was not a weaver himself, was fully capable of translating the weavers' letters, but unable to capture the idiom of their writing, which would have immediately revealed such a letter as inauthentic. Or the letter may have possessed no value without the handwriting, signatures, marks or seals of the head weavers, which

[50] MPP, 1785, vol. P/240/61, p. 761, OIOC.
[51] For an analysis which relies upon South Asian fatalism, see Paul R. Greenough, "Indulgence and Abundance as Asian Peasant Values: A Bengali Case in Point," *Journal of Asian Studies*, 42 (1983), p. 833.
[52] South Arcot Collectorate Records, Cuddalore Consultations, 1778, vol. 79, pp. 35–7, TNA.
[53] South Arcot Collectorate Records, Cuddalore Consultations, 1786, vol. 86, pp. 35–8, TNA.

suggests that these signs were known widely within a community of weavers.

In the closing years of the eighteenth century, the Company continued to bear the brunt of weaver discontent. However, South Indian merchants and head weavers, who came to be associated increasingly with the English East India Company, were also the targets of weaver protests. This marked a significant departure from earlier weaver protests and resistance. In 1768, for instance, weavers in Cuddalore, closely allied with South Indian merchants, rejected a Company proposal to eliminate these merchants and for the weavers to receive advances directly from the Company. And as should be apparent from the discussion thus far, head weavers played crucial roles in the organization and execution of protests. In particular, they used their authority and prestige to mobilize weavers and maintain ties of solidarity.

The rupture between ordinary weavers and merchants and headmen was a product of the Company's attempts to control and regulate the cloth market and production process. The Company came to utilize the power and knowledge of these intermediaries to gain access to the ordinary weaver. Merchants were relied upon for their knowledge of weaving villages, the details of production organization and their networks of brokers who operated the cloth procurement process. By rendering these services, these merchants were invested with the authority and coercive powers of the Company state, which they used for their own purposes. Head weavers also became linchpins in Company efforts to reach the weaver directly. Head weavers served as Company brokers, supervised the weaving villages and monitored the looms of the ordinary weavers. The result was growing conflict between ordinary weavers and their heads and merchants. In 1800 in the Northern Sarkars, "About 1000 weavers together with their arms proceeded against Maudapettah and seized the head weavers thereof who are minding the Company's business without joining with them."[54] Similar protests were mounted against merchants. In 1798, a large protest developed after a South Indian merchant grabbed a weaver by the ear and pushed another weaver down to the ground. The merchant was also accused of paying unfair prices for cloth and of cutting cloth out of a loom.[55]

The most dramatic of these protests took place in 1795 when four weavers constructed a straw figure of Davie Veerapah Chetty, the "principal headman of several payekets under Arnee."[56] In an open act of

---

[54] Godavari District Records, 1800, vol. 858, pp. 102–3, APSA.
[55] Godavari District Records, 1798, vol. 830, pp. 24–46, APSA.
[56] MPP, 1795, P/241/58, pp. 3555–61, OIOC.

defiance, the weavers staged a "mock funeral" for the straw representation. Such a ceremony has a ring of familiarity. Burning an effigy has formed a part of protests on several continents for many centuries and from its widespread use we may derive some common-sense meaning of the act. It is a death threat; it is a great act of rejection and humiliation. In the cultural context of South Asia, however, we may go beyond general statements and give the act more precise meaning.

The death ritual for an effigy, or *putla vidhan*, is part of the repertoire of funerary rites in South Asia and is performed in cases of "bad" death.[57] Although there are several types of bad death, the most common is the death of an individual who lived a sinful life. By performing the putla vidhan, the weavers may have been communicating to their headman that the wrongs that they had suffered at his hands (and these are not specified in the Company's accounts) were grave and sinful acts. The putla vidhan ritual was also carried out in cases of untimely death, which included deaths by violence. In such cases the body of the victim was considered to be unfit for cremation. However, an effigy was burned so the deceased did not continue an indefinite existence as a marginal ghost (*preta*). With the putla vidhan ritual, the protesting weavers also conveyed to the headman that his actions could invite violent retribution: the performance of the ritual was simultaneously a threat and a prophecy of his future. And in fact, the weavers shortly thereafter launched a violent attack upon the headman.[58]

Conclusion

The weaver protests of the late eighteenth century were spectacular affairs. They reflect a formidable organizational capability and are a testimony to the creativity and resourcefulness of weavers in late pre-colonial South India. The extraordinary scale of these protests is also a sign of the strong position of weavers in the late pre-colonial order. However, their appearance at the end of the eighteenth century is a sign not of weaver strength but rather of a deterioration in their position, which made earlier and less dramatic forms of protest less effective.[59]

---

[57] Veena Das, *Structure and Cognition* (Delhi, 1977), p. 123 and Jonathan Parry, "Sacrificial Death and the Necrophagous Ascetic," in Maurice Bloch and Jonathan Parry (eds.), *Death and the Regeneration of Life* (Cambridge, 1982), pp. 79, 83.

[58] MPP, 1795, P/241/58, pp. 3555–61, OIOC.

[59] Michael Adas has argued that in Southeast Asia the form of protest changed with the coming of colonial rule. In pre-colonial times, the canonical form of protest was avoidance: "flight, sectarian withdrawal, or other activities that minimize challenges to or clashes with those whom they view as their oppressors." Colonialism, according to Adas, for myriad reasons made avoidance increasingly difficult, which led to confrontation, riot and outright rebellion. The weaver protests at the end of the eighteenth century in South

"When the merchant reduces the money, the weaver reduces the thread."[60] So ran a proverb reported by Edgar Thurston in his ethnographic survey of Southern India. Although Thurston encountered the proverb more than a century after the events described in this book, I suspect it has a long history in South India. In the eighteenth century, long before the rise of English power, reducing the thread was one method by which weavers could register their displeasure with merchants. Perhaps more importantly, by reducing the thread, weavers had the power to maintain a fair distribution of earnings between themselves and merchants. The effectiveness of such a protest was dependent upon the existence of a particular political and economic order in South India, which from 1768 the English East India Company set out systematically to undermine. As we have seen, the English attacked the long-standing customs of the contracting system, restricted the cloth trade within its territories and with great determination encroached upon the prerogatives of weavers.

Weaver desertion and perhaps more importantly its threat were other less spectacular forms of protest, but these also became less effective with the rise of English power. For weavers desertion and its threat were crucial for bargaining and negotiating with merchants. But for much of the eighteenth century it was a card merchants and rulers as well as the Company were unwise to ignore as weavers were eminently capable of picking up and moving, an ability which was demonstrated many times. As a Commercial Resident in Cuddalore remarked in the midst of a protest: "[The weavers] know how necessary they are to the Company and think if they become turbulent they need fear no severe treatment for their insolence lest they should desert, which they are ever ready to threaten if not dealt with according to their pleasures."[61] In the final decades of the eighteenth century desertion as a form of protest became increasingly less effective. The English Company used its political power to fix weavers and to prevent them from deserting. Furthermore, the

India were some of the earliest protests directed against the emerging colonial state. As such, and given their confrontational nature, they would appear to conform to the pattern of protest Adas identified for Southeast Asia. However, we know too little about pre-colonial protests to draw such a conclusion. In the first decades of the eighteenth century there is no evidence of weaver protests on a comparable scale, although there is a terse entry in Ananda Ranga Pillai's diary on 31 March 1747 that weavers in Kanchipuram were rioting. See *The Private Diary of Ananda Ranga Pillai*, vol. IV, p. 45. In addition, Adas' emphasis on avoidance as characteristic of pre-colonial protest underestimates the important role played by the *threat* of flight or desertion, which suggests the aim was not so much avoidance but the fulfillment of complex rights and obligations. See Adas, "From Avoidance to Confrontation."

[60] Edgar Thurston, *Castes and Tribes*, vol. III, p. 41.
[61] South Arcot Collectorate Records, Cuddalore Consultations, 1778, vol. 79, pp. 11–15, TNA.

growing territorial reach of the Company made it increasingly difficult for weavers to relocate. And the Company's successful elimination of competitors in the cloth trade made weavers more dependent upon the Company for their livelihood.

As a consequence, weavers were forced to abandon long-standing and highly effective everyday forms of protest in favor of large-scale work stoppages. It is striking that between 1672 and 1768 the correspondence and proceedings of the English East India Company contain no mention of weaver protests or work stoppages comparable to those of the final decades of the eighteenth century. Perhaps this is the single greatest testimony to the magnitude and unprecedented nature of the changes introduced by the English. The fact of these protests, and the existence of accounts chock-a-block with insights into the lives of the participants, may be a cause for celebration by the historian. For the weavers, however, there would appear to have been far less to celebrate. From our vantage point, it is apparent that the changes which fomented weaver protest were simply the first wave in the colonial transformation of the South Indian economy and polity. Although the weavers caught in this maelstrom could not have interpreted it in this way, the scale of their actions suggests that they knew that change was in the air and much was at stake. It is perhaps this which explains the almost desperate violence of the Northern Sarkars weavers.

5 Laborers, kings and colonialism

The Company defeated fierce weaver resistance, reorganized cloth production, and drove down the earnings of weavers. Kings in South India, by contrast, did not exercise such disciplinary authority. They did not enforce weaver contracts with merchants. Nor did they assist merchants in collecting debts or limit migration by weavers. Rather, kings were more likely to do the opposite, checking merchant power and protecting weavers from the claims of merchants. Similarly, in agriculture kings in South India were not in a position to limit the mobility of agrarian producers, which created a powerful incentive for agricultural improvement. What accounts for the profound differences between South Indian kings and the Company state, both in the power they wielded and in the ways state power was deployed?

The answer to this question lies in the very different conceptions of authority that guided the Company and South Indian kings. To put it simply, the coercion and disciplinary authority exercised by the Company were not seen as a legitimate use of the powers of kingship in South India. Therefore, these powers were not available to South Indian kings. Conceptions of proper rule, which checked South Indian political authority, did not limit the Company as it operated, in part, according to a vision of the state as it had developed in England. For several centuries the English state had been intervening actively in the lives of laborers and in the operation of the labor "market." Certainly some of these interventions were intended to protect laborers from the abuses of employers, but more often their purpose was to discipline and weaken producers. In South India, by contrast, there was no such tradition of state interference in or regulation of labor or the labor "market."

The state and labor in England

State regulation of labor in England dates from at least the late fourteenth century. In the aftermath of the Black Death, and the labor shortages which followed, several local and kingdom-wide ordinances were implemented

121

to counteract the increase in wages and the growing power of laborers. These measures set maximum wages for a variety of occupations, regulated the prices that craftsmen received for their goods, and restricted the occupational and geographical mobility of workers. Under these ordinances landlords had priority as regards the labor of their tenants; workers risked imprisonment if they left their employer in the middle of a contract; and servants were prohibited from working by the day and forced to enter into long-term contracts, usually for one year. Historians have debated the effectiveness of these regulations, but for our purposes, their enactment is in itself of extreme importance as they reflect the ideas of statecraft and uses of political authority which prevailed in England.[1] Similar ordinances were passed on the continent, but England was unique in the geographical scope and comprehensiveness of its measures.[2]

These fourteenth-century measures were the models for the Statute of Artificers of 1563, which was a far more comprehensive regulation of laborers and the labor market. As with the medieval ordinances, the Statute reduced the mobility of labor: in a wide range of occupations all hiring was to be for periods of at least one year and a person seeking work had to provide a certificate of termination from his or her previous employer. The act also stipulated methods of engagement, hours of work and means of giving notice. Also along the lines of the fourteenth-century measures, the Statute enacted wage regulations. Wage rates were to be set at the local level, either by justices of the peace in the countryside or by mayors and bailiffs in cities. In addition, the Statute of Artificers contained clauses which sought to ensure a sufficient supply of labor for agriculture and imposed a uniform apprenticeship of at least seven years throughout the kingdom.[3]

Portions of the Statute of Artificers remained on English legal books until the early nineteenth century, but in the eighteenth century state regulation of the labor market became less common.[4] However, this was due not to a change in conceptions of legitimate state activity, but to the fact that such interference by political authorities came to be less necessary. From the early eighteenth century conditions in the labor market had

[1] According to M. M. Postan the regulations had little effect on the labor market, but Dyer and Penn remark that regulation "for all its patchy enforcement, may have inhibited the demands of workers." M. M. Postan, *The Medieval Economy and Society* (London, 1972), p. 170 and Christopher Dyer and Simon A. C. Penn, "Wages and Earnings in Late Medieval England: Evidence from the Enforcement of the Labor Laws," in Christopher Dyer, *Everyday Life in Medieval England* (London and Rio Grande, Ohio, 1994), p. 188.

[2] Dyer and Penn, "Wages and Earnings," pp. 168–9.

[3] W. E. Minchinton (ed.), *Wage Regulation in Pre-Industrial England* (New York, 1972).

[4] John Rule, *The Experience of Labor in Eighteenth-Century English Industry* (New York, 1981), p. 95.

swung very much in favor of employers and the upward pressures on wages of earlier centuries were no longer a pressing concern.[5] In addition, laborers in eighteenth-century Britain were strongly fixed geographically. The early modern English, and later British, state had a long legacy of statutes against vagrancy which made movement, especially for the poor, difficult and sometimes dangerous. In the early eighteenth century vagrants could be whipped, branded and/or made to suffer transportation.[6] The operation of the poor laws further limited mobility in the English countryside. Only by residing in the parish in which he or she was eligible for poor relief could an individual receive such assistance, which discouraged migration.[7]

Nevertheless, the eighteenth century witnessed several new forms of state interference in the lives of laborers. The most important of these were redefinitions of property and criminality, which eroded the power and customary rights of workers.[8] In the eighteenth century the laborer also held a key place in political and economic thinking. Wages and, in particular, the need to keep them low were topics of great importance. This was in part a product of mercantile thinking which sought to increase the competitiveness of British manufactures both at home and abroad. Competition against the much cheaper cottons of India may have also contributed to this line of reasoning. However, a number of writers advocated low wages not only on grounds of competitiveness, but also to spur industriousness among laborers. High wages, it was believed, produced indolence. As workers could satisfy their needs with less effort, according to this view, they would reduce working hours and increase the time devoted to debauchery and slothfulness.[9]

The reports and correspondence of the English East India Company indicate that its servants were steeped in these attitudes towards labor.

[5] In the opinion of R. Keith Kelsall wage regulation decayed in the eighteenth century because "wage-earners both agricultural and otherwise found themselves in a weaker bargaining position, and the danger of excessive exactions was materially lessened." See Kelsall, "Wage Regulation under the Statute of Artificers," in Minchinton (ed.), *Wage Regulation*, p. 193.

[6] Peter Clark, "Migration in England during the Late Seventeenth and Early Eighteenth Centuries," *Past and Present*, no. 83 (1979), pp. 84–5. For a discussion of an earlier period, see Paul A. Slack, "Vagrants and Vagrancy in England, 1598–1664," *Economic History Review*, 27 (1974), pp. 360–79.

[7] Edgar S. Furniss, *The Position of the Laborer in a System of Nationalism* (Boston and New York, 1920; repr. New York, 1965), p. 146.

[8] For a brilliant exposition of these themes see Peter Linebaugh, *The London Hanged: Crime and Civil Society in the Eighteenth Century* (Cambridge, 1992).

[9] See the classic works of Furniss, *Position of the Laborer*, chap. 6 and Thompson, "Time, Work-Discipline and Industrial Capitalism." Of course, a minority of writers for a variety of reasons advocated high wages. See A. W. Coats, "Changing Attitudes to Labour in the Mid-Eighteenth Century," *Economic History Review*, 11 (1958), pp. 35–51.

Lionel Place, for example, in his famous report on the jagir, wrote: "If a man, in three or five days, can earn sufficient to subsist him for a week he will be idle the rest of it. It is always an object to give this class of people a natural or compulsive incitement to employ themselves."[10] The views of these servants may have been attenuated because of their commercial and gentry backgrounds. Nevertheless, attenuated or not, these attitudes influenced Company policy-making in South India. Tax policies, for instance, were evaluated according to their effects on industriousness: "By the abolition of the tax on looms they [weavers] were so much relieved from the necessity of working and what was intended to give a spur to their industry had I imagine a contrary effect."[11] As we shall see shortly, along with these discourses on labor, the Company's servants brought English practices on labor to South India.

Kings and laborers in South India

Until recently it has been assumed that states in pre-colonial South Asia were quintessential examples of the oriental despot. Conventional wisdom has held that there was no limit or check on the scope of state authority, which also was believed to be exercised in a capricious and arbitrary manner. W. H. Moreland has given a canonical statement:

> The Indian governments with which we are concerned were in all cases despotic ... everything that was done was in theory done by order of the Ruler, though it might in fact be the work of a subordinate acting in his master's name ... apart from religious obligations, the Ruler was untrammelled, and an order given one day might be reversed the next.[12]

In more recent times, several historians have promulgated this view of the state. Perhaps the most forceful and influential has been Irfan Habib, who has described the Mughal Empire in strikingly similar terms.[13] More recently, John McLane has portrayed kingship in eighteenth-century Bengal as essentially despotic and resting on great coercion.[14] The despotic view has been applied also to states in eighteenth-century South India, especially Mysore under the rulership of Hyder Ali and Tipu Sultan.[15]

---

[10] Board of Revenue Proceedings, 1796, vol. 144, TNA. Another Company servant said that weavers "being naturally of so Knavish and indolent disposition that few of them will devote a larger time to labor, than will barely suffice, to earn the common necessaries of Life." MPP, 1790, vol. P/241/16, pp. 335–6, OIOC.

[11] Chingleput Collectorate Records, 1799, vol. 493, paras. 356 and 358, TNA.

[12] W. H. Moreland, *From Akar to Aurangzeb* (London, 1923; repr. Delhi, 1990), pp. 233–4.

[13] Habib, *Agrarian System of Mughal India*.

[14] John R. McLane, *Land and Local Kingship in Eighteenth-Century Bengal* (Cambridge, 1993), chap. 4.

[15] Kate Teltscher, *India Inscribed* (Delhi, 1995), chap. 7.

Laborers were believed to be some of the chief victims of despots, who reduced them to an impoverished and insecure existence. In an influential account, Bernier described despotism in India as "a tyranny often so excessive as to deprive the peasant and artisan of the necessaries of life, and leave them to die of misery and exhaustion."[16] Bernier himself may have been influenced by earlier travellers, such as Francisco Pelsaert, who wrote:

> For the workman there are two scourges, the first of which is low wages ... The second is [the oppression of] the Governor, the nobles, the Diwan, the Kotwal, the Bakhshi, and other royal officers. If any of these wants a workman, the man is not asked if he is willing to come, but is seized in the house or in the street, well beaten if he should dare to raise any objection, and in the evening paid half his wages, or nothing at all.[17]

In the wake of reinterpretations of the eighteenth century, oriental despotism has been subjected to severe criticism and new characterizations of the state have emerged. In these, local political power and the agrarian community, as well as other territorial and political groupings, are seen to have limited the power of sovereigns.[18] The enormous contributions of this literature have derived in part from the close attention that has been devoted to the cultural context in which authority and statecraft operated in South Asia.[19] Nevertheless, alongside this careful contextualization of politics and authority there are other writings which have adopted a more instrumental view of the state. State actions and policies are assumed to follow directly from a need to maximize state interests, chiefly having to do with revenue, the military and administration. Such instrumentalism has also led to the interpretation of South Asian phenomena on the basis of European models.[20] Military fiscalism, mercantilism and capitalism, for instance, have been invoked to characterize the policies and political economy of late pre-colonial South Asia.[21] However,

---

[16] François Bernier, *Travels in the Mogul Empire, 1656–68* (London, 1891), pp. 205, 226–7, cited in Tapan Raychaudhuri, "The State and the Economy: The Mughal Empire," in Tapan Raychaudhuri and Irfan Habib (eds.), *CEHI*, vol. I, p. 175.

[17] Francisco Pelsaert, *Jahangir's India*, trans. W. H. Moreland and P. Geyl (Cambridge, 1925), p. 60.

[18] See in particular Muzaffar Alam, "Aspects of Agrarian Uprisings in North India in the Early Eighteenth Century," in Sabyasachi Bhattacharya and Romila Thapar (eds.), *Situating Indian History for Sarvepalli Gopal* (Delhi, 1986); Perlin, "State Formation Reconsidered"; Stein, "State Formation"; André Wink, *Land and Sovereignty in India* (Cambridge, 1986).

[19] See in particular Wink, *Land and Sovereignty*; Perlin, "State Formation Reconsidered"; Frank Perlin, "Concepts of Order and Comparison, with a Diversion on Counter Ideologies and Corporate Institutions in Late Pre-Colonial India," *Journal of Peasant Studies*, 12 (1985), pp. 87–165.

[20] For examples, see Stein, "State Formation"; Bayly, *Indian Society*, chap. 1.

[21] For instance, Burton Stein has written: "the political economy of much of India during the seventeenth and eighteenth centuries was based on an advanced level of mercantile

to force South Asian states into European frameworks, no matter the surface similarities, is to shear them of the meanings attached to these actions and the principles which guided them. As Quentin Skinner has observed: "What it is possible to do in politics is generally limited by what it is possible to legitimise. What you can hope to legitimise, however, depends on what courses of action you can plausibly range under existing normative principles."[22] These were far different in South Asia.

Questions of legitimacy and conceptions of authority are absolutely central for an understanding of the relationship between state power and labor in late pre-colonial South Asia. Although recent examinations of the eighteenth-century state have failed to examine this relationship, there is much to suggest that the laborers and the labor market were not seen as legitimate sites for the exercise of state coercive powers. The illegitimacy of such actions emerges clearly in a letter from the Nawab of Arcot to the English East India Company during the Cuddalore weaver protest of 1778. The Nawab, in response to English requests that weavers who had fled to his territories be rounded up and returned, wrote:

When you desired me to send an order to my aumil to seize and send back the weavers to Cuddalore my intention was that some of the Company's people should in concert with my aumil endeavour by soothing and encouraging methods to carry them back; *for to seize them and take them by force from the country belonging to the Circar is contrary to custom and it was never done before.*[23]

The Nawab recommended an alternative method:

These weavers came to this place to complain of the treatment they had suffered from the people at Cuddalore. If the people there will still endeavour by fair words and good treatment to bring them back, these weavers will be satisfied and it must tend to the good of the Company's affairs. If on the contrary I send an order as you desire to seize and send them by force to Cuddalore, the weavers will as others have done before fly to Pondicherry and seek for protection in an enemy's settlement or go to distant countries and this will occasion a loss to me and the Company.[24]

These views may be found in other South Indian contexts, ranging from works on statecraft, to policy directives issued by Tipu Sultan.

According to the *Rayavacamaku*, *dharma* and *artha*, virtue and prosperity, increase only when "favour is shown to the poor cultivators in the

capitalism" and "capitalist class relations had made their appearance in pre-colonial times." Burton Stein (ed.), *The Making of Agrarian Policy in British India 1770–1900* (Delhi, 1992), pp. 21, 22. Also see Washbrook, "Progress and Problems," pp. 61–4.

[22] Quentin Skinner, *Liberty before Liberalism* (Cambridge, 1998), p. 105. The existence of normative principles which limited state actions should certainly not be confused with benevolence.

[23] MPP, 1778, vol. P/240/75, pp. 556–9, OIOC. Emphasis added.

[24] MPP, 1778, vol. P/240/75, pp. 556–9, OIOC.

matter of taxation and services."[25] Furthermore, "collecting money by oppressing the subjects" was only to be found in the territories of the sovereign's enemies. However, the duty of the sovereign was far more than not oppressing his subjects. He was also to protect them during times of hardship. Those who acted in his name were to be so instructed: "That king is never prosperous even though he conquers all the seven *Dwipas*, who has an officer who does not call back the subjects when they leave the state on account of suffering, who would sell away their cattle and stores of corn and would consider their houses as fit for using for fuel and who thus resemble [*sic*] the jackal in the battlefield."[26]

Although the economic context had changed considerably, this vision of the state and laborers persisted into the eighteenth century and is reflected in the policies of the Mysore state under Hyder Ali and Tipu Sultan. According to revenue regulations issued by Tipu Sultan, "*Reyuts* who have fled the country are to be encouraged to return and the balances due from them are to be recovered by gentle means."[27] In addition, in keeping with earlier works on statecraft, Tipu Sultan's regulations gave great importance to protecting cultivators from oppression:

If a [tax] farmer, neglecting the cultivation of his farm, and suffering the lands to lie waste, shall impose fines upon the *Reyuts*, and make undue exactions from them to enable him to fulfil his own engagements, he shall be made to pay to Government the amount of such undue exactions... Measures must also in future be adopted to prevent any person from levying oppressives, &c. from the *Reyuts*.[28]

After the *Aumil* shall have arrived in the district, if, owing to his oppression, any of the *Reyuts* who were in the country upon his arrival shall abscond, the *Aumil* shall be made to pay twenty pagodas for every plough of a respectable *Reyut* who has fled, and ten pagodas for every plough of the poor *Reyut*.[29]

Tipu Sultan's concern for the status of the peasantry stemmed from the political imperative to retain producers within his territories. To further ensure this, an officer of government was required to take an oath, in which he placed a Koran on his head and swore that "he would not allow the poor or the peasantry to be oppressed in word or deed."[30] Evidence suggests that this was not a mere formality. In the opinion of a British Officer

[25] Wagoner (trans.), *Tidings of the King*, pp. 94–5.
[26] Rangasvami Sarasvati, "Political Maxims of Krishnadeva Raya," p. 69.
[27] Crisp, *Mysorean Revenue Regulations*, article 50.
[28] Crisp, *Mysorean Revenue Regulations*, article 8. For similar sentiments, see Home Miscellaneous Series, vol. H/251, Regulation 8, OIOC.
[29] Crisp, *Mysorean Revenue Regulations*, article 49.
[30] Mir Hussein Ali Kirmani, *The History of the Reign of Tipu Sultan*, trans. Col. W. Miles (London, 1864; repr. New Delhi, 1980), p. 154.

named Mackenzie, "Checking the frauds of intermediate agents by severe and exemplary punishments, the Sultan protected the raiyats, who were chiefly of Hindu religion, from the enormities of black collectors."[31]

The organization of state monopolies in South India further reveals that coercion was not the basis for relations between states and producers. The motivations for these monopolies and their impact will be discussed in greater detail shortly, but of relevance at the moment is that in many instances states sought to establish, much as did the English East India Company, an exclusive relation with the producer. The force and violence the English brought to this problem have been described, but the approach of South Indian rulers stands in sharp contrast. In the cloth trade, for instance, a common method by which weavers were employed exclusively was to obtain their signatures on bonds. In 1792, several Company cloth merchants complained of this practice:

provision of the cloth at present is entirely and totally prevented by the Amuldar, who was appointed to the Management of the district of Warriarpollam by his Highness the Nabob Wallajah, the said Amuldar having lately on the 29th of September summoned all the weavers and brokers at the said district including those that wove cloth for the Company's investment and obliged them to sign a Mutcheleca [bond] to forfeit Pagodas 1200 if [it] should be detected that any of them in future weave at least a single piece of cloth on account of any of the merchants whatsoever, but directed and bind them to weave cloth on account of his Highnesses Circar.[32]

The following letter from Tipu Sultan further suggests that it was neither typical nor routine for violence to be used against weavers:

What you write, respecting the excuses made by the manufacturers of the district [under you] for declining to weave the stuffs we require, has excited our astonishment; we therefore direct, that they be compelled, by menaces, to prepare the number of pieces required, with the utmost expedition, and agreeably to the pattern [heretofore] sent. If, notwithstanding your injunctions and menaces, they persist in their false pretexts and disobedience, they must be well flogged.[33]

The order to use violence appears to be extraordinary and we have no evidence that it was ever executed. It is very possible that it was simply bluster on Tipu's part, of which there are many examples in his letters.[34]

---

[31] R. Mackenzie, *A Sketch of the War with Tippoo Sultaun* (2 vols., Calcutta, 1793–4), II, pp. 72–3, cited in Mohibbul Hasan Khan, *History of Tipu Sultan* (Calcutta, 1951), p. 330.

[32] MPP, 1792, vol. P/241/34, pp. 2863–5, OIOC. It should be noted that in 1794 the Nawab, it appears in emulation of the Company, placed sepoys over weavers. MPP, 1794, vol. P/242/45, pp. 534–5, OIOC.

[33] William Kirkpatrick, *Select Letters of Tipu Sultan to Various Public Functionaries* (London, 1811), letter xxxv.

[34] Kirkpatrick, in his preface, declared that Tipu in these letters showed himself to be "the cruel and relentless enemy; the intolerant bigot or furious fanatic; the oppressive and

Mysorean policies under Tipu Sultan were far less oppressive than British portrayals of them. Lionel Place himself remarked that cultivators in Mysore had "no cause of complaint in injustice or an arbitrary deprivation of the due share of the fruits of their labour; on the contrary that they enjoyed abundance."[35] In addition, Mysore, as with other states in South India, did not penetrate into the realm of production to increase its revenues. Rather these states sought to eliminate intermediaries who stood between the state and the producer.[36]

The labor market was off-limits not only to state coercive powers, but also to state regulations. South Indian texts on statecraft contain no discussion of measures to reduce the power of producers such as those implemented in England. Nor is there any evidence that states limited mobility, set wages, determined the terms of contract or in other ways interfered in the operation of the labor market. In Tanjore, Charles Harris, the first English collector, found:

As the Mahrattas had no written rule for the controul [sic] of the Puttuckdars and Cawlgars, I found when the former were removed and the latter awed by the introduction of English government that there was no original standard by which I could form my management and that *there did not exist so much as a single rate of pay for labour.*[37]

Why was coercion not used against laborers in South India? And more generally, why was the labor market off-limits to the sovereign and not an object for state intervention and regulation?

Frank Perlin, in a different context, has argued that the power of the sovereign reached its limits at the community. As Perlin has put it in the case of the Maratha territories: "'Sovereignty', as it were, stopped at the frontiers of another's *vatan* property right, at the edge of the category over which another, in short, was already proprietor (*khavand*) or sovereign."[38] The inviolability of the vatan, according to Perlin, arose from the fact that it was a property right granted by the community, not by the sovereign.

As we have seen on several occasions, laborers in South India possessed strong community organizations and, in many respects, the laborer was actualized as a laborer through membership in a community. In weaving, skill and knowledge were contained in communities and were transmitted

unjust ruler; the harsh and rigid master; the sanguinary tyrant." See Kirkpatrick, *Select Letters*, p. x.
[35] Board of Revenue Proceedings, 1796, vol. 144, p. 525, TNA.
[36] In Mysore, this was the strategy of eliminating poligars. See Stein, "State Formation."
[37] Madras Board of Revenue Proceedings, 1802, P/286/80, p. 2183, OIOC. Emphasis added.
[38] Perlin, "Concepts of Order and Comparison," p. 132.

to successive generations through membership and participation in community life. In this way, skill and knowledge became inheritable, which is an essential quality of property. However, they were community, not individual, forms of property.[39] The rights possessed by adimai also had their origins in communities, in this case the agrarian community, and the adimai right to a share of the agricultural product, as it was transmitted from one generation to the next, was a form of property right.[40] Kingly interference in weaving, in the distribution of the agricultural product or in the agricultural production process itself would have violated community-sanctioned property rights and privileges. For this reason such interference may have been deemed illegitimate and outside the purview of sovereignty in South India.[41]

A just and moral king in South India respected the integrity of community-based rights and the limits they imposed upon state power. However, the Company, as it did not operate within this political framework, did not have to abide by such precepts and used its power to enter into community matters. In early nineteenth-century Tinnevelly, for example, Company courts did not recognize the property rights of adimai as they sought to "free" the labor market.[42] The Company's failure to conform to South Indian norms may account for the intensity of weaver protests. Weavers may have been responding not only to material deprivation, but also to the Company's violations of deeply held notions of just rulership and a moral polity. Far from upholding justice, a chief responsibility of kingship in South India, the Company engaged in egregious abuses of it.[43]

---

[39] For a discussion of the links between skill, property and community in England see John Rule, "The Property of Skill in the Period of Manufacture," in Patrick Joyce (ed.), *The Historical Meanings of Work* (Cambridge, 1987), pp. 91–118, and Margaret R. Somers, "The 'Misteries' of Property. Relationality, Rural-Industrialization, and Community in Chartist Narratives of Political Rights," in John Brewer and Susan Staves (eds.), *Early Modern Conceptions of Property* (London, 1996), pp. 62–92.

[40] F. W. Ellis also noted that adimai claim *miras* (rights of inheritance) to their "villeinage." See Parliamentary Papers, 1841 (I), vol. XXVIII, p. 122.

[41] The community and property nature of knowledge may explain why elites and states in late pre-colonial South India did not produce the manuals on agricultural techniques which were common in Europe and China at this time. These groups could not penetrate into the details of the agrarian production process. See David Ludden, "Archaic Formations of Agricultural Knowledge."

[42] Ludden, *Peasant History*, p. 175. Of course, this ruling may have had the support of elites in agriculture, who also shared an interest in "freeing" the labor market.

[43] Entwined with notions of the moral polity were the geographical limits on states in South India. As the Nawab himself noted in the passages above, it was impractical to use force against weavers as they would simply run away. The Company eliminated the frontier, in some sense, as its political reach slowly expanded to cover the whole of South India. It created a state whose geographical scope and authority were far greater than those of any South Indian predecessor. Although the spatial reach of the Company state must be recognized, its innovativeness cannot be reduced to this feature alone. It should be borne in mind that the Company's attempts to limit labor mobility long preceded its closing of the frontier. Sovereigns in South India accepted the mobility of the laboring classes, but

And the consequence was the breakdown of the power of producer communities.

The fact that South Indian kings did not use coercion to limit the power of laborers does not mean that they never used force. However, state violence was not exercised arbitrarily but followed principles which were seen as just and legitimate. The use of force also was not unlimited, but rather was restricted in its aims and functions. Force, for example, was recognized as legitimate when utilized for the collection of revenue. The king's right to tax was one of the prerogatives of sovereignty and was enforceable by state coercive powers.[44] Sovereigns were also permitted to use force to punish criminals, and, in fact, this was their responsibility.[45]

Another legitimate use of kingly coercive power was for the commandeering of labor services. In late eighteenth-century South India such actions ranged from those of a *tahsildar* in Tanjore who forced weavers to water his plants to those of the Raja of Ramnad who requisitioned weavers for agricultural work. However, the rarity of commandeering suggests that such actions were not central to the organization of productive activity. The English East India Company records for the final quarter of the eighteenth century contain only about a dozen references to such coercion of weavers.[46] The Company servants made much of these incidents, chiefly to draw favorable comparisons between their rule and

the Company did not. In addition, geographical limits on individual states do not mean that attempts to limit mobility could not be made through cooperation between political authorities. Although there is no evidence for such cooperation in South India, it did occur in early modern Germany where princes and urban authorities coordinated policies to limit the mobility of journeymen. See Kristina Winzen, "The Perception of Guildsmen by the City Representatives in the Imperial Diet of the Late Seventeenth Century," paper presented at the ESTER Seminar on Guilds and Guildsmen in European Towns 16th to 19th Centuries, International Institute of Social History, Amsterdam, November 1996.

[44] Wink, *Land and Sovereignty*, pp. 251–5; Ludden, *Peasant History*, pp. 71–2.

[45] I am drawing this conclusion from research on Western India and Bengal where the question of crime and punishment has been investigated. For Western India, see V. T. Gune, *The Judicial System of the Marathas* (Pune, 1953) and, more recently, Sumit Guha, "An Indian Penal Regime: Maharashtra in the Eighteenth Century," *Past and Present*, no. 147 (1995), pp. 101–26. For Bengal, J. Fisch, *Cheap Lives and Dear Limbs: The British Transformation of the Bengal Criminal Law* (Wiesbaden, 1983).

[46] Harbans Mukhia found only a few incidents of *begar* or forced labor in eighteenth-century Rajasthan and concluded that it was not central to production: Harbans Mukhia, "Illegal Extortions from Peasants, Artisans and Menials in Eighteenth Century Eastern Rajasthan," in his *Perspectives on Medieval History* (New Delhi, 1993). For eighteenth-century Western India, Hiroshi Fukazawa has found fifty records on begar. He has remarked that "the principle, as it were, of the central government was not to exact as much corvee from the people as possible but to impose it upon them 'properly' (*shist*), namely 'according to custom' (*shirastpramanen*) and to the extent that the central government demanded or sanctioned." See his "A Note on the Corvee System (Vethbegar)," in his *The Medieval Deccan: Peasants, Social Systems and States Sixteenth to Eighteenth Centuries* (Delhi, 1991), p. 138.

the despotism which prevailed in South India, and with such arguments they urged weavers to settle in Company territories. However, an English servant also remarked that the Company saw relief from these practices as more pressing than the weavers themselves did.[47] Weavers may have accepted these actions, although certainly not uncomplainingly, as legitimate in times of emergency or duress. Commandeering of services may have increased in the late eighteenth century, but it was often associated with warfare. In particular, armies outside their home territories used it to obtain labor services, but this, of course, operated according to different principles.

The rise of Company rule in South India produced a break with South Indian political practices. The consequences of this new state, however, have thus far been examined from the perspective of weavers. To more fully understand the implications of British rule in South India, and its rise and impact, we must consider two other vantage points. The first is that of producers in agriculture who like weavers were subjected to the new forms of disciplinary authority embodied in the Company state. The weakening and fixing of these producers were to have profound consequences for the dynamism of agriculture in South India. The second is that of Indian elites, in particular merchants and dominant classes in agriculture. These groups were attracted to the forms of power exercised by the Company state and represented an important indigenous source of support for British rule in South India.

Merchants and kings in South India

In recent years earlier water-tight distinctions between merchants and kings, and their respective spheres of influence and power, which dominated the historiography of early modern South Asia have been subjected to trenchant critiques. Increasingly mercantile power is seen to have penetrated the state in the seventeenth and eighteenth centuries through mechanisms such as revenue farming, political office and financial support for regimes.[48] These re-evaluations have in part emerged as a consequence of revisionist scholarship on the eighteenth century, and the work of Christopher Bayly has played an influential role. However, moving from revenue and commerce to the world of the producers sheds different light on the relations between merchants and kings, and shows that significant tensions characterized this relationship.[49] In the case of

[47] MPP, 1777, vol. 117A, p. 206–9, TNA.
[48] Subrahmanyam and Bayly, "Portfolio Capitalists."
[49] For an extended discussion, see my "Merchants and the Rise of Colonialism."

cloth merchants, who have been examined in some detail, rulers were more likely to support weavers, rather than merchants, at times of conflict between the two groups. These tensions were to worsen in the second half of the eighteenth century as fiscal pressures led many rulers to encroach upon the commercial world of merchants.

The revenues collected from taxing trade were of utmost importance to kings in late pre-colonial South India. Towards this end, kings in early modern South India focused much energy on the promotion of commerce within their territories. However, the fiscal pressures of the eighteenth century, which may be traced in part to changes in the form of warfare, including the rise of permanent, standing armies and a shift from cavalry forces to infantries, led rulers not simply to promote commerce but also to enter directly into commercial activities. No longer satisfied with the revenues received from taxing trade, kings sought to enrich their treasuries further by trading on their own account. By appropriating merchant functions, kings sought to appropriate merchant profits.[50]

Several kings in eighteenth-century South India established monopolies in lucrative commodities as a means to increase their profits from trade even further. One of the earliest and most successful of these state monopolies was the Travancore pepper monopoly of the early eighteenth century. Travancore's success, along with the monopolies created by European trading companies, may have served as inspiration for rulers in South India and in the final decades of the century monopolies in a variety of commodities mushroomed. The Nawab of Arcot attempted to form a monopoly in cloth and one of his amildars tried to corner the grain market.[51] The Raja of Ramnad was an active monopolizer and grain was only the most prominent of the many goods he sought to bring under his control.[52] However, the most ambitious commercial system was that of Tipu Sultan in Mysore whose goal was to create a far-reaching system of monopolies in a number of Mysore's most valuable export goods, including sandalwood, areca nuts, pepper and cardamom. Perhaps in imitation of the European trading companies, he also established factories in Southern India and the Persian Gulf to conduct this trade.[53]

---

[50] Of course, there are pre-eighteenth-century precedents for kingly participation in commerce.

[51] South Arcot Collectorate Records, Cuddalore Consultations, 1788, vol. 94, pp. 3–5, TNA; MPP, 1794, vol. P/241/46, pp. 1152–4, OIOC.

[52] Tanjore Collectorate Records, Nagore Factory Records, 1793, vol. 3323, pp. 5–10, TNA.

[53] See Ashok Sen, "A Pre-British Economic Formation in India of the Late Eighteenth Century: Tipu Sultan's Mysore," in Barun De (ed.), *Perspectives in Social Sciences I* (Calcutta, 1977).

With these expanding commercial activities rulers increasingly en-croached upon merchant terrain. In Travancore, the pepper monopoly pushed merchants out of the trade and their duties were taken over by a state commercial department. According to Ashin Das Gupta, the trans-formation took place slowly, but the outcome was unmistakable:

The merchants became suddenly of little significance. It was "the Government's contract" that now supplied the English at Anjengo. It was the king with whom they were now to haggle from year to year about the quantity that could be procured. The king's officials had to be bribed. The new order was there to stay. Merchants within the kingdom of Travancore would never be permitted the freedom they had known before.[54]

Similar limits on merchants were instituted in Mysore as state commer-cial departments began to take over their functions.[55]

Even if merchants were not made entirely redundant, state commercial systems created unwelcome competition and interference. This was cer-tainly the case with the Nawab's entry into the cloth trade, which led the cloth merchants of Cuddalore to seek the Company's assistance and support:

The principal cloth dealers expressed an anxiety to know how far they might depend upon the protection and assistance of government in case such proposals as they meant to offer should be accepted. That the assistance alluded to would be wanted in the Nabobs country where large quantities of cloth were now contract-ing for under His Highness' immediate patronage and direction and where the Company's contractors must consequently meet with difficulties which nothing but the most effectual support from government could enable them to overcome that unless they could be assured of receiving such support it would be not only fruitless but even ruinous to themselves to engage in such undertaking.

The Company officials informed the merchants that "Persons engaging to furnish the Company's investment might always rely upon meeting with every proper encouragement."[56]

This configuration of political forces in the late eighteenth century, in which merchants found themselves squeezed on one side by the en-croachment of state commercial systems and on the other by the strong claims and powerful demands of weavers and other producers, set the stage for merchant support for the political expansion of the Company in South India.

---

[54] Ashin Das Gupta, *Malabar in Asian Trade* (Cambridge, 1967), p. 39.
[55] Sen, "Pre-British Economic Formation," pp. 87–95.
[56] South Arcot Collectorate Records, Cuddalore Consultations, 1788, vol. 94, pp. 3–5, TNA.

Merchants and the Company state

To South Indians, who operated in a very different world of politics, the Company state must have been remarkable. While weavers fought this new power, merchants were drawn to it. The first group of merchants to enter the Company's sphere were cloth merchants who from the 1780s, after the Company's experiments in cloth provision of the previous two decades came to a close, were brought back to supply the Company's investment. With their long history of conflicts with weavers and their lack of disciplinary authority, cloth merchants were easily attracted to a state which assumed, as well as exercised, enormous power over laborers.

Cloth merchants began to use the power of the Company state against weavers at much the same time that the English themselves commenced their own attacks on the prerogatives of this group. In 1768, Gundareddy Mannar Chitty, who provided muslins at Madras, in emulation of Company policies, asked the Madras Council to issue an order prohibiting weavers from supplying cloth to private merchants until his quota, which he was purchasing for the Company, was met. In 1770 the Madras merchants requested that private traders be prevented from buying the Company's assortments and that the merchants be empowered to deal with weavers who did not bring in good cloth. Although the merchants did not reveal how they intended to "deal" with weavers, in 1774 George Paterson, while travelling near Kanchipuram, witnessed merchants with an accompaniment of Company sepoys announcing that all weavers were forbidden to work for the French and any weaver who disobeyed this order was to be *Chabucked*, or whipped.[57]

In the final decade of the century merchants began to make more liberal use of the coercive powers of the Company state. In 1791, a merchant in Madras declared that without the authority to "compell the weaver to give a preference to the Company over the private merchant that it would be extremely difficult for him to fulfill the conditions of the contract." The same merchant went on to cite Company precedent to justify the use of force against weavers:

The contractor being called before us said he had used every reasonable endeavour to engage the services of the weavers, that he had proposed to erect sheds (there being no topes) for their accommodation, but that they had declined working for him. That in consequence he had adopted the mode always customary of using a little coercion, which if it met with our displeasure, he could not fulfill his engagements, he added that *every export warehouse keeper had used the*

---

[57] MPP, 1768, vol. P/240/27, pp. 660–1, OIOC; MPP, 1770, vol. P/240/29, p. 338; The Paterson Diaries, vol. 8, pp. 87–8.

same means for securing the labor of the weavers for the Company, and that there had been instances even of destroying the looms if they continued refractory.[58]

Merchant coercion was also found in the Northern Sarkars, where in 1788 merchants with the support of Company peons moved weavers to new villages and then forced advances upon them.[59] In 1792, Company servants remarked that weavers in Godavari were working for merchants only because of the extreme compulsion that had been brought to bear against them.[60]

With their access to the disciplinary forces of the Company state, merchants dramatically reduced the power of weavers and transformed the conditions of contract and production. As their first step, merchants weakened the bargaining position of weavers. In Ingeram this was done with a new system of merchant monopolies. Weaving villages were allocated among the cloth merchants in the area and each merchant confined his advances to designated villages. Initially the weavers welcomed the scheme, believing that an exclusive relationship with a single merchant would reduce harassment by numerous merchants and brokers, but they discovered that their bargaining and price-setting powers were reduced sharply and they sought to have the monopolies removed. Just as with their opposition to the Company's monopolization of the cloth market, however, their efforts ended in failure.[61]

By 1798, the growing power of merchants manifested itself in a steep decline in the earnings of weavers. At Madapollam weavers set forth their troubles in a petition to the Company's revenue collector:

The merchants do not pay us the just price for all pieces of cloth we supplied according to their quality and patterns of the punjums, but at a very lesser rate, as is payable for such as being more inferior . . . the merchants buying bad pagodas in cutting a certain batta on a purpose of advancing them to us instead of good ones for their own advantage and when they do it in Dubbs we suffer a small deficiency in every pagoda . . . The above act of the merchants in addition to our depriving of the practice of weaving the country cloth and the other sufferings . . . are too injurious being remained unable to provide cloth for another merchant even by which cause *we have been reduced to very poor condition in different means of distress to procure maintenance at this very cheap time.*[62]

The situation of the Madapollam weavers turned even more desperate

---

[58] MPP, 1791, vol. P/241/26, pp. 2491–5, OIOC. Emphasis added. It is significant that this merchant used the example of the Company, and not local practice, to justify his use of coercion.
[59] MPP, 1788, vol. P/241/9, pp. 3100–1, OIOC.
[60] MPP, 1788, vol. P/241/9, pp. 3100–1, OIOC; Godavari District Records, 1792, vol. 830, p. 13, APSA.
[61] Godavari District Records, 1798, vol. 830, pp. 24–46, APSA.
[62] MPP, 1798, vol. P/242/3, pp. 642–8, OIOC. Emphasis added.

later in the year as escalating prices for cotton and copper coins further slashed their earnings. Weavers attempted to push up cloth prices as compensation for their higher costs, which they had done with great success earlier in the century, but merchants, with their newly gained power, were able to hold fast on prices. In desperation, 500 weavers assembled at the Madapollam factory and demanded that the Company support them in their struggle to raise cloth prices, but received little sympathy and no assistance.[63]

Merchants also used their strengthened position to transform their contracts with weavers. The Company had already reversed the asymmetry in the weaver–merchant contract. South Indian merchants followed that lead and refused to accept any cloth from weavers which they deemed to be of inferior or inadequate quality. In 1799 Lionel Place reported that in the jagir a "merchant is at liberty to reject such cloths as are not of the texture engaged for and if he cannot dispose of them, it is probable that the weaver cannot."[64] Weavers not only lost the enormous leverage which they possessed when merchants had no choice but to accept the weavers' cloth, but they now faced the specter of not finding a market for their product, which must have greatly magnified their distress.

Merchants also exploited the power of the Company state to enforce weaver debt obligations more rigorously. At Ingeram merchants began to place peons over weavers to prevent weavers from absconding with advances.[65] In Madapollam, the Company pressured local zamindars to assist merchants in collecting weaver debts.[66] In Vizagapatnam, Company merchants systematically lowered the prices paid to weavers in order to liquidate weaver debt obligations.[67] And in Madras, the Company pledged to give all possible assistance to merchants in recovering balances from weavers.[68] Merchants also devolved the responsibility for debts on to head weavers. On several occasions weavers voiced complaints to the Company about the coercive methods by which merchants forced the repayment of debts and appealed for English assistance, but received none.[69]

The creation of these merchant measures to recover weaver debts dealt a sharp blow to what was, in the final analysis, the weavers' most

[63] Godavari District Records, 1798, vol. 830, pp. 24–46, APSA.
[64] Chingleput Collectorate Records, 1799, vol. 493, p. 365, TNA.
[65] MPP, 1788, vol. P/241/4, pp. 26–7, OIOC.
[66] MPP, 1789, vol. P/241/14, p. 2470, OIOC.
[67] MPP, 1791, vol. P/241/25, pp. 2263–7, OIOC.
[68] MPP, 1793, vol. P/241/37, pp. 689–96, OIOC.
[69] Godavari District Records, 1798, vol. 847, pp. 141–2, APSA; Godavari District Records, 1798, vol. 830, pp. 24–46, APSA.

important source of power: their mobility. Weavers became less free to pick up and move as coercive methods were used to fix them or to drag them back when they did migrate. Company support to merchants was crucial for this process of fixing. In 1791, for instance, a Company merchant turned to the Board of Trade to help him bring back forty weavers who had left Arni with his advances and settled in Madras.[70] Once immobilized, weavers became even more subject to the heightened powers of merchants.

The crucial role of the Company state in the forging of these new relations between merchants and weavers is made evident by the stark contrast, in the final years of the eighteenth century, between the position of merchants in areas under Company control and that of those under South Indian kings. In Tanjore, which the Company annexed only in 1799, merchants continued to face well-organized weaver power. In particular, merchants received poor-quality cloth and had great difficulties recovering weaver debts. As a consequence, they were often at the brink of enormous losses.[71] Merchants encountered similar problems in Ramnad where weavers took their contractual obligations lightly. In the minds of many merchants, the risks associated with advancing money to weavers in that kingdom was not worth the meager and uncertain profits.[72]

Weavers came to recognize the interests which were bringing South Indian merchants and the Company together. As early as 1770, a Company servant in Masulipatnam observed that one of the reasons merchants were eager to supply cloth to the Company was that "weavers from fear of punishment more readily serve them than they otherwise would."[73] In 1768, during a work stoppage by Ingeram weavers in protest of Company taxes on cloth, the weavers "treated the merchants with a great deal of insolence" and told them that they "would not give themselves any concern about their ballances."[74] Similarly, in 1800 weavers in Salem launched a "riot" in response to the mistreatment of several weavers by Company peons. The weavers quickly expanded their targets of protest, however, to include the chitty who the weavers "sent for" and "threatened him never to be paid 400 rupees which he had advanced to

[70] MPP, 1791, vol. P/241/26, pp. 2866–7, OIOC. As late as 1829 the Company used its revenue collection machinery to track down weavers who were indebted to its Nagore factory. See Trichinopoly District Records, Trichy Board of Revenue Correspondence, 1829, vol. 4400, p. 85, TNA. Also see Trichinopoly District Records, Trichy Board of Revenue Correspondence, 1805, vol. 3646, pp. 188–9 and vol. 3664, p. 102, TNA.
[71] Tanjore Collectorate Records, 1795, vol. 3325, pp. 29–30, TNA.
[72] Tanjore Collectorate Records, Nagore Factory Records, 1793, vol. 3323, pp. 5–10, TNA.
[73] Masulipatnam District Records, 1770, vol. 2751, pp. 22–8, APSA.
[74] Masulipatnam District Records, 1768, vol. 2871, pp. 25–8, APSA.

the weavers."[75] Ranajit Guha has analyzed the broadening of protest, or "transference" as he has labeled it, by peasants in colonial India: "By directing his violence against all three members of this trinity [*sarkar*, *sahukar* and zamindar] irrespective of which one provoked him to revolt in the first place, the peasant displayed a certain understanding of the mutuality of their interests and the power on which this was predicated."[76] By simultaneously targeting both the Company and merchants, the Ingeram and Salem weavers revealed that they were well aware of the connection which had formed between the two groups. It was, in their minds, a tight interlocking of power which had to be addressed as a single block.

Despite weaver resistance and opposition, by the early nineteenth century, in sharp contrast to only thirty or forty years earlier, the position and power of weavers in much of South India had declined. This is conveyed in a description from 1802 of the cloth sorting process in Cuddalore: "The system adopted when the cloth is received is exactly upon the same principle at Salem. Whatever is inferior to number three is rejected and returned to the weavers, stamping every fold with a rejected mark to prevent it being again brought to the factory on account of the Company."[77]

Only a decade earlier, the rejection of cloth was often the spark that set weavers off in protest. And the bargaining power of weavers had been so severely eroded that merchants in Trichinopoly encountered little resistance when they forced weavers to accept lower cloth prices.[78] Therefore, by the early nineteenth century, powerful merchants came to be arrayed against weak producers:

The proposed reduction in duty [on cloth] may perhaps give the manufacturer a little more employment or it might cause the employment of more hands but the actual gain would go to the merchant. *The weavers here are mostly in the situation of labourers for hire*; the merchant who wants cloths advances to a weaver just so much as will maintain him in addition to the purchase of materials and he would not give better terms if the duties were reduced.[79]

These relations of power should sound familiar as they are characteristic of colonial and post-colonial India. However, as I have shown in this work, the enormous power merchants came to wield over producers was

[75] Coimbatore Collectorate Records, 1800, vol. 592, pp. 74–6, TNA.
[76] Guha, *Elementary Aspects of Peasant Insurgency*, pp. 26–7.
[77] South Arcot Collectorate Records, 1802, vol. 110, p. 21, TNA.
[78] Trichinopoly District Records, Board of Revenue Correspondence, 1820, vol. 3678, pp. 203–4, TNA. Of course, by 1820 demand for South Indian cloth had also slumped.
[79] Tinnevelly Collectorate Records, 1826, vol. 4700, Letter from J. Monra to Board of Revenue, TNA. Emphasis added.

not a timeless feature of India, but emerged from the late eighteenth century with the rise of English rule. Nor was it simply a product of deindustrialization or competition against British textile manufacturers. In South India, the position of weavers began to deteriorate long before the impact of European industrialization was felt. The decline in weaver power and their subordination to merchants were products of the political transformations wrought by English East India Company rule. In turn, merchants who were empowered by the rise of Company rule were drawn to its political authority and may have provided crucial support for it.

The perspective of the producer given in this work permits us to broaden our understanding of the indigenous roots of colonialism. Alongside the limits the indigenous political economy placed on British rule, and the crucial role Indian financiers played in the political expansion of the Company, we must add the perspective of the producer. Merchants and, as we shall see shortly, agrarian elites were trapped in bitter conflicts with producers in late pre-colonial South India. The Company state resolved these conflicts to the great benefit of these groups.[80] In turn, these groups brought their resources of knowledge and influence to the Company and provided crucial support to it, thereby assisting its rise to power.[81] This indigenous source of colonial rule in India reveals the woeful inadequacy of interpretations of colonialism which focus solely on the antagonisms between Indians and the British. From the earliest days of colonialism conflicts between Indians intersected with British power. It is this intersection which may account for the resilience of colonial rule in India.

The Company state and agriculture

Weavers were the first producers to bear the full brunt of Company disciplinary authority, but soon other forms of labor were caught in the same net. In the final decades of the century, the Company introduced measures to regulate the wages of craftsmen in a wide variety of occupations, ranging from carpentry to stone cutting. And in 1794, a cloth merchant in the Baramahal attempted to monopolize yarn spun by

[80] The expansion of British power may have been in part motivated by a desire to support these groups. In 1765 a Company servant in the Northern Sarkars argued that the Company must establish political authority in the district of Mustafanagar because "the business of the Company's merchants which is chiefly carried out there is liable to interruptions and impositions." K. Subba Rao, "Correspondence between the Hon. The East India Company and the Kandregula Family in the XIII Century," *Journal of the Andhra Historical Research Society*, 4 (1929–30), p. 63, cited in Bayly, *Indian Society*, p. 56.

[81] Of course this is not to deny the major conflicts between these Indians and the British.

peasant women.[82] However, some of the most strenuous efforts to reduce the power of laborers, and ones which were to have very grave consequences, took place in agriculture. The disciplining and weakening of agrarian producers were central to the colonial enterprise and these lay at the heart of the colonial transformation of South India.

In 1795, mirasidars in the jagir, the dominant agrarian class in the district, complained to the Company's collector, Lionel Place, that the proximity of Madras was placing upward pressures on wages, particularly those of artisans and laborers in agriculture. Place intervened on behalf of the mirasidars and negotiated lower wages with the artisans of the area. These were then publicized throughout the jagir as a "chattum" or schedule of wage maximums, very much modeled on English wage regulations. For the laborers in agriculture, Place recommended that wages be reduced under the direction of the judicial authority.[83] Both these responses are reminiscent of English policies. However, this was not the first time that the Company had attempted to put a ceiling on wages in South India. In 1759, to counter a recent wage inflation in Madras, a schedule of wages was promulgated and public notice was given that any laborer who "presume[d] to demand more" than stipulated on the schedule would be "severely punished on complaint."[84] In the early nineteenth century similar schedules of wage rates were issued in Tanjore. Carpenters, bricklayers, blacksmiths, chunam grinders and stone cutters were some of the occupations which came under the purview of these wage regulations.[85] In addition, in 1802 the collector of Tanjore ordered that laborers in agriculture were to be paid "at a regulated rate in grain and clothing."[86]

The mirasidars of the jagir also complained that there were not sufficient laborers to carry on the work of agriculture. To increase their numbers, the Company expelled all "pariahs" from the Madras army and prohibitions were placed on their recruitment in the future. In addition, to close off Madras as an alternative source of employment and as a haven for those fleeing the countryside, casual laborers were expelled from the city, a policy which was later extended to the other major towns of South India.[87] These measures were part of a larger attack on "untouchable"

[82] English East India Company, *The Baramahal Records*, Section VII, *Imposts* (Madras, 1920), p. 28.
[83] Board of Revenue Proceedings, 1796, vol. 144, pp. 562–3, 565–7, TNA. These measures to reduce the earnings and power of these agrarian producers may account for the major revolts in the jagir from the 1780s. See Sivakumar and Sivakumar, *Peasants and Nabobs*, chap. 4 and Irschick, *Dialogue and History*, chap. 1.
[84] *FSGDC*, 1759, p. 211.
[85] Madras Board of Revenue Proceedings, 1802, vol. P/286/80, pp. 2279–82, OIOC.
[86] Parliamentary Papers, 1841 (I), vol. xxviii, p. 121.
[87] Washbrook, "Land and Labor," p. 56.

laborers in South India, which was to dramatically reduce their status and position. Gyan Prakash has shown that in Bihar these producers were brought under a discourse of freedom and a relationship of dependence was interpreted as one of slavery and then bondage.[88] This transformation may also be traced for South India, but for our purposes what is more important is the weakened position of these laborers in the social and political order. This is evident from the testimony of T. H. Baber who served the English East India Company for thirty-two years "in every department of the public service":

How or whence this oppressive and cruel practice, not only of selling slaves off the estate where they were born and bred, but actually of separating husbands and wives, parents and children, and thus severing all the nearest and dearest associations and ties of our common nature, originated, it would be difficult to say; *but I have no doubt, and never had in my own mind, that it has derived support, if not its origin, from that impolitic measure, in 1798, of giving authority to the late Mr. Murdoch Brown, while overseer of the Company's plantation in Malabar, upon the representation of "the difficulties he experienced," even with "the assistance of the tehsildar," and "his own peons," "to procure workmen" and "of the price of free labor being more than he was authorized to give," to purchase indiscriminately as many slaves as he might require to enable him to carry on the works of that plantation.*[89]

Company state interventions to weaken the position of dependent laborers were also found in the Tamil country. Most importantly measures were enacted to limit the mobility of the adimai. In the Mayuram division of Tanjore, the Company in 1798 issued the following proclamation:

Notice is hereby given that the landholders in the villages dependent in the souba of Kumbakonam and Mayuram are permitted to take possession of all Pallar and Parayar properly belong to them, who have absconded from their masters, and are now employed under others in the division to the prejudice of the cultivation of the lands to which they immediately belong, and no person whatever is to object thereto or in any manner to prevent this order from having the fullest effect.

Notice is also further given that all Pallar and Parayar in the above-mentioned predicament are hereby peremptorily required to return immediately to their respective villages, and such of them as shall neglect to do so or any person who may attempt to conceal them or refuse to deliver them up on application being made to them by the proper owner, will on the fact being proved, be punished in the most exemplary manner.[90]

This order was followed with another in 1802 in which the collector

[88] Prakash, *Bonded Histories.*
[89] 'Papers Relative to Slavery in India," *Parliamentary Papers*, 1834, vol. xliv, p. 6.
[90] Tanjore District Records, vol. 3245, pp. 40–1, Diary of the Proceedings of the Collector of Mayuram Division, 6 July 1800, cited in Saraswati Menon, "Social Characteristics of Land Control in Thanjavur District During the 19th Century: A Sociological Study," unpublished Ph.D. Dissertation, Jawaharlal Nehru University, 1983, pp. 141–2.

decreed that throughout Tanjore "Slaves who have continued ten years with meerasidars or poragoodies, notwithstanding they may before [have] belonged to others will be considered as being with their proper masters."[91] To enforce this fixing of laborers the Company also announced that slaves who were not with their proper masters "will not be protected by the [Company] Circar" in case of mistreatment. In addition, corporal punishment was to be permitted to fix laborers: "For idleness or unjustifiable desertion labourers are to be moderately punished by the superintending peons or inhabitants who are not to use rattans but branches of the tamarind tree and never to stricke on the Head or arms."[92]

The Company's limits on mobility as well as its use of physical violence to enforce these limits were contrary to South Indian norms. The practices which prevailed in the late pre-colonial period are captured in the words of a Company servant who reported that in Masulipatnam slaves "can leave their masters at any time if they please, and no force can be used to recover them." Although there were a few dissenting voices, late eighteenth- and early nineteenth-century English observers largely concurred that the lash was rarely employed "by the master against his slave in the Tamil country."[93] Nevertheless, despite recognition on the part of Company servants that pre-colonial practices differed from colonial interpretations and innovations, by the second quarter of the nineteenth century adimai had been converted to slaves, with all the fixity and subordination the term implies. And as should be apparent this transformation occurred at the level not only of discourse, but also of practice.

The mobility of the agrarian producer not only created shortages of workers for agricultural operations, but also made it extremely difficult for the English to regularize the assessment and collection of revenue. Therefore, the settling of the agrarian producer became essential for the Company's settlement of the land revenue. The correspondence of Alexander Read, Thomas Munro and William MacLeod during the establishment of the revenue system in the Baramahal in the 1790s well illustrates the intimate connection between these two forms of settlement.

---

[91] Madras Board of Revenue Proceedings, 1802, vol. P/286/86, p. 2233, OIOC.
[92] Madras Board of Revenue Proceedings, 1802, vol. P/286/86, p. 2233–4, OIOC.
[93] Parliamentary Papers, 1841 (I), vol. xxviii, pp. 114, 122. Of course, this is not to deny that extreme violence was used at times against adimai. See for instance Irschick, *Dialogue and History*, p. 213, n. 44, for a discussion of a severe beating applied in 1727. I am not arguing in this work that late pre-colonial South India was the embodiment of the moral and the good. Rather, the norms of legitimate conduct were far different from those of the colonial period and that laborers had the means to enforce these norms from which they derived enormous benefits.

To avoid the toil and trouble of annual assessments, Munro and MacLeod fixed the level of the revenue demand for a period of several years. Despite the mobility of the *ryots*, they believed that they would be able to collect this sum "because the lease will fix them [the ryots] to their present habitations for at least five years."[94] Alexander Read, however, disagreed with this opinion:

You mention yourselves as one objection to your proposal that may be adduced, the diminishing the value of the districts belonging to the Company, by enticing away the inhabitants to your own farm and you answer it, by observing, that it would not be the case, because the lease would fix them to their present habitations for at least five years. It is clear that you can only mean such of them as enter into obligations with the Sirkar, by holding lands in farm by virtue of and immediately of the Collectors Putty but though their number exceeds 60,000 this year, by much the greater part who are Jeedgars and are commonly hired for the year, or the season only, are at liberty to move where they please, in quest of new service, during the *Calliwaddies*, or spring months.[95]

Other differences also existed among the collectors. In Munro's opinion, the Company should only constrain the movement of ryots in special cases, for instance if they neither relinquished their lands nor paid their revenues.[96] Nevertheless, Munro conceded that state authority had to be used to limit mobility when all other means had failed.[97] And Munro's fellow officer, James Graham, was of the opinion, in the words of Nilmani Mukherjee, that "some amount of restraint was essential to check this restless spirit [of the ryots] which was equally inimical to the interest of the State and that of the individuals."[98]

In the Baramahal, a variety of schemes were proposed to check mobility, including a proposal to make "farmers who shall entertain emigrants pay on demand a specific sum suppose 5 or 10 Pagodas for every man, or bullock as a compensation to the farmer, whose service or fields they quit."[99] At the end of the day, collectors often on their own initiative limited the freedom to move.[100] These attempts to fix the producer were the underside of the revenue settlement process, and have received little attention in the voluminous literature on the subject.[101]

---

[94] Board's Collections, 1795, vol. F/4/17, No. 752, pp. 15–16, OIOC.
[95] Board's Collections, 1795, vol. F/4/17, No. 752, pp. 22–3, OIOC.
[96] Munro was also outspoken against Company measures that limited the freedom of weavers. See MPP, 1794, vol. P/241/47, pp. 1679–87, OIOC.
[97] Nilmani Mukherjee, *The Ryotwari System in Madras* (Calcutta, 1962), p. 289.
[98] Mukherjee, *Ryotwari System*, p. 289.
[99] Board's Collections, 1795, vol. F/4/17, No. 752, p. 27, OIOC.
[100] According to Dharma Kumar, "Sometimes, indeed, collectors forced villagers who had fled to return to cultivate their lands till the Board of Revenue put a stop to this." See her "Agrarian Relations: South India," in Dharma Kumar (ed.), *CEHI*, vol. II, p. 220.
[101] Christopher Bayly has shown that the settled, self-sufficient village community was not a

Conclusion

With the fixing of producers in agriculture, agrarian society became far more settled in the nineteenth century.[102] F. W. Ellis noted this as early as 1816, when he observed that the dependent producers in the jagir rarely left their villages.[103] Evidence from later periods confirms these impressions of a great settling in nineteenth-century South India.[104] The emergence of the village community as the characteristic form of social and spatial organization further suggests the settled nature of life in British-ruled South India. With the elimination of the option to move, there was a sharp decline in the bargaining power of producers. This is apparent from the evolution of wages in nineteenth-century agriculture, which suggests a steady downward spiral. This is confirmed both by direct evidence regarding wage payments and by physical measures of body size which strongly indicate a deterioration in nutritional standards.[105]

The stagnation of agriculture in the nineteenth century which resulted from low rates of investment also contributed to the nineteenth-century fall in wages.[106] The collapse in investment, however, was itself closely connected to the weakening of agrarian producers. Neither the Company's servants nor their South Indian supporters may have intended it, but the settling of the direct producer eliminated what had been a major motive for undertaking agricultural improvement in pre-colonial South India: the competition for laborers.[107] Fluidity in the labor market fueled

timeless feature of South Asia, but a product of the colonial transformation. For Northern India, he has traced its creation to the decommercialization which occurred during the great depression of the second quarter of the nineteenth century. The perspective from labor modifies this picture. The creation of the settled village community has earlier roots in the transformation of the labor market and fixing of producers which was required for the functioning of the revenue system. Thus it was a product not solely of market operations, but of profound changes in the polity as well. See Bayly, *Rulers, Townsmen and Bazaars*, chap. 7.

[102] Factors such as the demilitarization of South India and the decline of internal trade also contributed to the settling of the agrarian society. This is not to imply that movement was eliminated altogether, but that in comparison with the eighteenth century South India was more settled.

[103] Bayley and Huddleston, *Papers on Mirasi Rights*, pp. 336–7.

[104] For some discussion of this see Washbrook, "Land and Labor," p. 85 and Irschick, *Dialogue and History*, pp. 191–5.

[105] Dharma Kumar, *Land and Caste in South India: Agricultural Labour in Madras Presidency in the Nineteenth Century* (Cambridge, 1965), chap. 9; Lance Brennan, John McDonald and Ralph Shlomowitz, "Trends in the Economic Well-Being of South Indians under British Rule: The Anthropometric Evidence," *Explorations in Economic History*, 31 (1994), pp. 225–60.

[106] For a discussion of this stagnation in the Tamil country, which became apparent by the late nineteenth and early twentieth century, see Baker, *Rural Economy*, chap. 3.

[107] The Company also did not share the imperative to invest in agricultural improvement which was an essential component of kingship and statecraft in the pre-colonial order.

agricultural improvement and South India's competitive position in the world economy rested upon a highly productive and efficient agriculture. With the rise of the English, however, Company state power, rather than agricultural investment, could now be drawn upon to attract and keep laborers. The long-term consequence was declining investment, and therefore stagnation, in agriculture.

Low levels of investment in nineteenth-century India have typically been attributed to a shortage of savings. According to nationalist critics of British rule, this lack of savings was due to the British drain of wealth from the subcontinent.[108] In a similar vein, David Ludden has argued that the heavy land revenue demand of the colonial state reduced the funds available for investment.[109] While not denying the devastating effects of the drain and the weight of the land revenue, I suggest that previous writers have analyzed the reasons for low rates of investment in the nineteenth century with little understanding of the investment process in late pre-colonial India. They have consequently failed to realize the enormous significance to agricultural stagnation in the nineteenth century of the social and political transformations which accompanied British rule. Attention to these social and political determinants of investment sheds light on several aspects of agricultural stagnation in nineteenth-century India.

First, the reasons for the failure of investment to increase after 1850 when inflation reduced the burden of the land revenue are made clearer. The continued stagnation in agriculture suggests that the problem was not simply lack of savings, but rather lack of demand for investment, which had its origins in the establishment of British power.[110] Second, such a focus on the demand for investment is also theoretically more satisfactory.[111] Finally, the recognition of investment itself as the key

[108] According to Amiya Bagchi, "the external drain from Bengal could be put at about 3 to 4 per cent of the gross domestic material product. If we add another 2 or 3 per cent as the expenditure on the wars of conquest incurred by the East India Company in this period, we can see that at least 5 to 6 per cent of resources of the ruled land were siphoned off from any possibility of investment. If we compare this waste with the 7 or 8 per cent of national income invested by Britain during the period of her Industrial Revolution, we can begin to gauge the magnitude of the damage inflicted by this period of British rule on the Indian economy." See his *Political Economy of Underdevelopment*, p. 81.

[109] Ludden, *Peasant History*, pp. 141–9.

[110] For central India Crispin Bates has found that profits were being made in agriculture, but these were not invested by landed groups. See his "Class and Economic Change in Central India: The Narmada Valley 1820–1930," in Clive Dewey (ed.), *Arrested Development in India* (New York, 1988), pp. 241–82.

[111] Since the work of Keynes, economists have understood that investment is not simply automatically determined by the availability of savings and, in fact, that the level of investment may itself determine the quantity of savings. In the case of nineteenth-century India, lack of investment resulted in low levels of output or income. Consequently the quantity of savings was small. For a discussion of these theoretical issues, see

variable makes it necessary to rethink the customary link between the drain and savings. Was there a shortage of savings in the nineteenth-century Indian economy?[112] If not, where did the land revenue, and the drain, come from? One possibility is that the drain was extracted by reducing consumption, particularly that of laborers in agriculture.[113] These questions and hypotheses, however, carry us into the nineteenth century, far beyond our focus on eighteenth-century South India.

The rise of English rule in South India meant the demise of a way of life for laborers. The rights which they possessed – in contract, in property, in community – were eroded and eliminated as the Company state had no respect for them. The Company state's fixing of laborers, in particular, had devastating consequences. The ability to move was central to the power of laborers in the political and economic order in pre-colonial South India. Migration, or its possibility, gave laborers a voice, as well as leverage, in that order. Therefore, the fixing of laborers meant far more than the creation of a geographically rooted society. Mobility was essential for laborers in pre-colonial South India to strike a balance with the forces which opposed them. As a consequence, when laboring classes were demobilized, they were also disenfranchised.

The Company's fixing of laborers, as well as its other interventions in the labor market, were modeled on English practices. However, the Company and its servants were selective in their transmission of English political customs and ideas. Of course, English political culture and institutions in their entirety could not be reproduced in South India, but the transfer that did take place was markedly one-sided. The Company freely introduced measures to discipline laborers. In the process, it took away the rights which laboring groups possessed as well as the methods with which they defended these rights, most importantly freedom of movement. However, the Company gave laborers nothing with which they could defend themselves. The Company's servants had no interest in planting the liberty tree, with which laborers in England defended themselves against both state and capital, in South India.[114] Thus eighteenth-century South India was the recipient of a highly regulatory state, but one of none of the political ideals and practices which countervailed such state

Stephen Marglin, *Growth, Distribution and Prices* (Cambridge, Mass., 1984).

[112] In Bengal Raja Rammohan Roy remarked that the conditions of the cultivators had not improved although the incomes of the proprietors had increased. See Ambirajan, *Classical Political Economy*, p. 111.

[113] Such a possibility would appear to receive support from David Washbrook, "Economic Development and the Making of 'Traditional' Society in Colonial India 1820–1855," *Transactions of the Royal Historical Society*, 6th Series, 3 (London, 1993), pp. 237–63.

[114] See E. P. Thompson, *The Making of the English Working Class* (New York, 1964).

power in England. Such a transformation left laborers in South India extremely weak, vulnerable and eventually impoverished and may help to explain the extreme despotism of the colonial state.

The forms and functions of the modern state are largely taken as self-evident. In particular, the modern state is conceived as an entity which intervenes in the lives of laborers to discipline them as well as to regulate the workings of the labor market. The motivations for these forms of state action may be diverse: whether it be supported as an instrument of capital, twentieth-century development or even socialist transformation. Common sense suggests that such a state is the universal form of polity in the modern period, and it is this common sense which allows the history of pre-colonial South Asia to be subsumed under the rubric of capitalism. However, as this book has shown, this is a doubtful claim.

To achieve this universal status the modern state triumphed over and then effaced the memory of alternative conceptions of sovereignty and statecraft. In Britain itself, which may be rightfully seen as the home of the modern state, the state's prerogatives to regulate labor coexisted with alternative conceptions of the relationship between the state, labor and property well into the eighteenth century. The modern state and its supporters had to battle against notions of property rights vested in communities, ideas of common rights, "undisciplined" work habits, and "embezzlement" and other violations of liberal, private property rights.[115]

The contrast with kingship in South India makes the exceptional nature of the eighteenth-century British state glaringly apparent. South India in the seventeenth and eighteenth centuries, before the rise of Company power, sustained a form of modernity which rested on vastly different political principles. These allowed laborers to maintain an enormously valuable set of rights, privileges and prerogatives and these were lost only as a consequence of the establishment of political power inspired by British ideas of statecraft. The British state is not in any way the natural form of the modern state, but emerged within the context of particular normative principles. Nor was the universalization of the British form of statecraft from the late eighteenth century a natural process, but rather, as illustrated in these pages, the outcome of both intense political conflict and deep political cooperation.

[115] See E. P. Thompson, *Customs in Common* (New York, 1993); Rule, "Property of Skill"; Linebaugh, *The London Hanged*; Jeanette Neeson, *Commoners: Common Right, Enclosure and Social Change in England, 1700–1820* (Cambridge, 1993).

Glossary

adimai dependent laborer in wet, rice-growing areas
amildar a collector or contractor for revenue
areca nut mildly narcotic nut chewed with betel leaves
artha prosperity
aumil subordinate revenue official
badam a bitter almond
bajra the Hindi word for kambu
Banjara a community of nomadic pack-bullock carriers
batta money for subsistence given by a creditor to a debtor
begar forced labor
betel leaf of a vine, chewed with areca nut
bhang hemp used for an intoxicating drink
burder a jati of potmakers
cadjan a palm leaf used for writing
call a measure of cloth quality which is literally the number of warp
    threads; one call equalled 240 threads
candy a unit of weight, in South India roughly 500 pounds
cash a copper coin used in South India; for much of the eighteenth
    century 80 cash equalled 1 fanam
chabuck (also chawbuck) to whip
chamar a jati of tanners
chana a pulse
chay a root which yields a red dye
chetty (also chitty) a term for several Tamil merchant castes
chucklers cobblers
chunam lime
churka a wooden roller used for cleaning cotton
circar (also sarkar, sircar, etc.) government or the state; used to distin-
    guish land under direct government authority from land under poligars
    or zamindars
cocanadas a reddish cotton cultivated in the coastal districts of Andhra
congee rice starch

corge   twenty pieces of cloth
cotu   a small hoe
cowle   a lease or grant in writing
Dasara   (also Navarattiri) great festival falling between mid-September and mid-October lasting nine nights and ten days
Deepavali   Hindu festival of lights, falls between October 15 and November 14
devanga   one of the four major weaving jatis in South India
dhair   (also dher) a jati of tanners
dhal   pulses
dharma   virtue
dub   copper coin used in the Northern Sarkars
dwipa   territory, island
fanam   a silver coin used in South India; for much of the eighteenth century 36 fanams equalled one pagoda
gadem   the forced sale of grain by the state
ganj   a fixed market center in North India
ghee   clarified butter
gingelly   sesame
goontika   a rake drawn by bullocks
gumastahs   (also gomastahs) a merchant's agent
havelly   land under direct government management
horse-womum   a spice
hundi   a credit note
inam   a tax-free grant of land by a ruler
jaggery   coarse brown sugar
jagir   an assignment of land revenue; used in the period of early Company rule to refer to the area around Madras
jati   kind, type, endogamous group which is the basic unit of caste
jeedgars   a class of peripatetic peasant cultivators
julaha   jati of Muslim weavers found in the Baramahal and Kongunad
junta   an instrument drawn by bullocks to rake and harrow
kaikolar   one of the four main weaving castes of South India
kalawedi   (also callawadie, etc.) movement of ryots during the summer months
kambu   bullrush, spiked or pearled millet
kannakapillai   (also conicoplies) a village accountant; brokers in the Company cloth procurement machinery
komaty   a Telugu merchant caste
kurchivar   a caste of tank diggers
kurumbars   a caste of shepherds
labbay   a Muslim trading community

lakh   one hundred thousand; used especially with money

longcloth   the ordinary staple calico of South India, esteemed for its length, which was approximately 36 yards

mahanadu   a local assembly composed of nattwars, or leaders from agrarian society

mamool   custom

manniwars   a jati of untouchable weavers in the Baramahal

marwaris   a community of merchants from Marwar, northwestern India

maund   a unit of weight; in South India approximately 25 pounds

mirasi   (also miras) inheritance, inherited property right

mirasidar   holder of superior mirasi rights; used to refer to agrarian elites in the wet, rice-growing areas of the Tamil country

mootah   administrative subdivision of a district

mung   a pulse

nadam   (also ladam) perennial cotton grown on red soils in the Tamil country

nayaka   warrior chief, ruler

oddar   a jati of tank diggers

pagoda   a gold coin used in South India

palaiyakkarar   a military chief, commander of a fortress

pallar   one of two major "untouchable" jais in the Tamil Country

parayar   (also pariah) one of the two major "untouchable" jatis in the Tamil country

paykett   district in which cloth or any other article of trade was provided; territorial unit in weaver social and political organization in parts of South India

poligar   palaiyakkarar

poragoodies   class of share-croppers in the wet, rice-growing areas; divided into a permanent and transitory categories

preta   ghost

punjam   a measure of cloth quality which is literally the number of warp threads; one punjam equalled 120 threads

putla vidhan   death ritual for an effigy, part of the repertoire of funerary rites

putty   (also pattah) lease, deed, contract, receipt; specifically a document specifying the land revenue due from a piece of land or a person

ragi   a food grain grown on dry (unirrigated) land

ryot   (also reyut) a cultivator, farmer or peasant

ryotwari   form of land-revenue settlement in which tax was levied on fields of individual landholders

sahukar   (also sowcar, sowkar) moneylender, banker

sale   one of the four main weaving jatis of South India

samayam   an association
seer   a unit of weight equal to 0.625 pounds
seniyar   one of the four main weaving jatis in South India
sepoy   a foot soldier
taccavi   a government advance or loan for agricultural production
tahsildar   a revenue official
taluk   an administrative subdivision of a district
tar-gur   an inferior form of sugar manufactured from the sap of palm trees
tennay   coconut
tope   a grove of trees, an orchard
tucu   a unit of weight equal to 10.1 pounds
tutee   a bamboo seed drill
uppam   annual cotton grown on black soils in the Tamil country
urad   a pulse
vis   a unit of weight equal to about 3 pounds
zamindar   a subordinate political official, often an independent little king; a landlord under British rule

Bibliography

PRIMARY SOURCES

MANUSCRIPT

In English
Madras Public Proceedings, 1761–1798, OIOC and TNA
District Records
  Bellary District Records, TNA
  Chingleput Collectorate Records, TNA
  Coimbatore Collectorate Records, TNA
  Godavari District Records, APSA
  Guntur Collectorate Records, APSA
  Madurai Collectorate Records, TNA
  Masulipatnam District Records, APSA
  North Arcot District Records, TNA
  Salem Collectorate Records, TNA
  South Arcot Collectorate Records, TNA
  Tanjore Collectorate Records, TNA
  Tinnevelly Collectorate Records, TNA
  Trichinopoly District Records, TNA
  Vizagapatnam District Records, APSA

The Paterson Diaries, MSS.Eur.E.379, OIOC
Board Miscellaneous, TNA
Board's Collections, OIOC
Home Miscellaneous Series, OIOC
Board of Revenue Proceedings, 1796–1802. TNA and OIOC

In Tamil
Mackenzie Collection, Government Oriental Manuscripts Library, Madras University

PRINTED

Bayley W. H. and W. Huddleston, *Papers on Mirasi Right Selected from the Records of the Madras Government* (Madras, 1862).
Bernier, François. *Travels in the Mogul Empire, 1656–68* (London, 1891).

Bidie, G. *Catalogue of Articles of the Madras Presidency and Travancore Collected and Forwarded to the Calcutta International Exhibition of 1883* (Madras, 1883).

Buchanan, Francis. *A Journey from Madras through the Countries of Mysore, Canara and Malabar* (3 vols., London, 1807).

Crisp, Burrish. *The Mysorean Revenue Regulations* (Calcutta 1792), in C. B. Greville, *British India Analyzed* (London, 1793).

Dubois, Abbé J. A. *Hindu Manners, Customs and Ceremonies*, trans. Henry K. Beauchamp, 3rd edn. (Oxford, 1924).

English East India Company. *The Baramahal Records*, Section III: *Inhabitants* (Madras, 1907).

The Baramahal Records, Section IV: *Products* (Madras, 1912).

The Baramahal Records, Section VII: *Imposts* (Madras, 1920).

Fort St. David Consultations 1696–1750 (Madras, 1933–5).

Fort St. George Diary and Consultation Book 1672–1760 (Madras, 1910–53).

Reports and Documents Connected with the Proceedings in Regard to the Culture and Manufacture of Cotton-wool, Raw Silk and Indigo in India (London, 1836).

Great Britain, House of Commons. *Parliamentary Papers.*

Havell, E. B. *Reports on the Arts and Industries of the Madras Presidency Submitted by Mr. E. B. Havell during Years 1885–88* (Madras, 1909).

Hoole, Elijah. *Madras, Mysore, and the South of India: A Personal Narrative of a Mission to those Countries* (London, 1844).

Kirkpatrick, William. *Select Letters of Tipu Sultan to Various Public Functionaries* (London, 1811).

Narayana Rao, D. *Report on the Survey of Cottage Industries in the Madras Presidency* (Madras, 1929).

Pelsaert, Francisco. *Jahangir's India*, trans. W. H. Moreland and P. Geyl (Cambridge, 1925).

Pillai, Ananda Ranga. *The Private Diary of Ananda Ranga Pillai* (12 vols., Madras, 1904).

Pringle, Arthur T. (ed.). *The Diary and Consultation Book of the Agent Governor and Council of Fort St. George 1682–1685* (Madras, 1894–5).

Rangasvami Sarasvati, A. "Political Maxims of the Emperor-Poet, Krishnadeva Raya," *JIH*, 4 (1926).

Tavernier, Jean-Baptiste. *Travels in India*, trans. V. Ball, ed. W. Crooke (2 vols., London, 1925).

Wagoner, Philip B. (trans.). *Tidings of the King* (Honolulu, 1993).

SECONDARY WORKS

Abraham, Meera. *Two Medieval Merchant Guilds of South India* (New Delhi, 1988).

Adas, Michael. "From Avoidance to Confrontation: Peasant Protest in Precolonial and Colonial Southeast Asia," *Comparative Studies in Society and History*, 23 (1981), pp. 217–47.

Ahuja, Ravi. "Labour Unsettled: Mobility and Protest in the Madras Region," *IESHR*, 35 (1998), pp. 381–404.

Alam, Muzaffar. "Aspects of Agrarian Uprisings in North India in the Early Eighteenth Century," in Sabyasachi Bhattacharya and Romila Thapar

(eds.), *Situating Indian History for Sarvepalli Gopal* (Delhi, 1986).
Ambirajan, S. *Classical Political Economy and British Policy in India* (Cambridge, 1978).
Appadurai, Arjun. "Gastro-Politics in Hindu South Asia," *American Ethnologist*, 8 (1981), pp. 494–511.
"Right and Left Hand Castes in South India," *IESHR*, 11 (1974), pp. 216–59.
Arasaratnam, S. "The Dutch East India Company and Its Coromandel Trade 1700–1740," *Bijdragen tot de Taal-Land-en Volkendunde*, 123 (1967), pp. 325–46.
Maritime Commerce and English Power: Southeast India 1750–1800 (Brookfield, Vt., 1996).
Merchants, Companies and Commerce on the Coromandel Coast (Delhi, 1986).
"Trade and Political Dominion in South India, 1750–1790: Changing British–Indian Relationships," *MAS*, 13 (1979), pp. 19–40.
"Weavers, Merchants and Company: The Handloom Industry in Southeastern India 1750–90," *IESHR*, 7 (1980), pp. 257–81.
Arokiaswami, M. *Kongunad* (Madras, 1956).
Bagchi, Amiya. "De-industrialization in India in the Nineteenth Century: Some Theoretical Implications," *Journal of Development Studies*, 12 (1976), pp. 135–64.
The Political Economy of Underdevelopment (Cambridge, 1982).
Bairoch, Paul. "International Industrialization Levels from 1750 to 1980," *Journal of European Economic History*, 11 (1982), pp. 269–333.
Baker, C. J. *An Indian Rural Economy 1880–1955: The Tamilnad Countryside* (Delhi, 1984).
Basu, Bhaskar Jyoti. "The Trading World of Coromandel and the Crisis of the 1730s," *Proceedings of the Indian History Congress*, 42nd Session, Bodh-Gaya (1981), pp. 333–9.
Bates, Crispin. "Class and Economic Change in Central India: The Narmada Valley 1820–1930," in Clive Dewey (ed.), *Arrested Development in India* (New York, 1988), pp. 241–82.
Bayly, C. A. *Indian Society and the Making of the British Empire* (Cambridge, 1988).
"Pre-Colonial Indian Merchants and Rationality," in Mushirul Hasan and Narayani Gupta (eds.), *India's Colonial Encounter: Essays in Memory of Eric Stokes* (Delhi, 1993).
Rulers, Townsmen and Bazaars: North Indian Society in the Age of European Expansion, 1770–1870 (Cambridge, 1983).
Beck, Brenda E. F. *Peasant Society in Konku: A Study of Right and Left Subcastes in South India* (Vancouver, 1972).
Berg, Maxine. *The Age of Manufactures 1700–1820* (London, 1985).
Breman, Jan. *Footloose Labour: Working in India's Informal Economy* (Cambridge, 1996).
Brennan, Lance, John McDonald and Ralph Shlomowitz. "Trends in the Economic Well-Being of South Indians under British Rule: The Anthropometric Evidence," *Explorations in Economic History*, 31 (1994), pp. 225–60.
Brennig, Joseph. "Joint-Stock Companies of Coromandel," in Blair B. Kling and M. N. Pearson (eds.), *The Age of Partnership: Europeans in Asia Before*

Dominion (Honolulu, 1979).

"Textile Producers and Production in Late Seventeenth Century Coromandel," *IESHR*, 23 (1986), pp. 333–56.

Briggs, John. *The Cotton Trade of India* (London, 1840).

Chakrabarty, Dipesh. *Rethinking Working Class History* (Princeton, 1989).

Chandra, Satish. "Some Institutional Factors in Providing Capital Inputs for the Improvement and Expansion of Cultivation in Medieval India," *Indian Historical Review*, 3 (1976), pp. 83–98.

Chaudhuri, K. N. *The Trading World of Asia and the English East India Company* (Cambridge, 1978).

Clark, Peter. "Migration in England during the Late Seventeenth and Early Eighteenth Centuries," *Past and Present*, no. 83 (1979), pp. 57–90.

Coats, A. W. "Changing Attitudes to Labour in the Mid-Eighteenth Century," *Economic History Review*, 11 (1958), pp. 35–51.

Das, Veena. *Structure and Cognition* (Delhi, 1977).

Das Gupta, Ashin. *Malabar in Asian Trade* (Cambridge, 1967).

Dirks, Nicholas. *The Hollow Crown: Ethnohistory of an Indian Kingdom* (Cambridge, 1987).

Dutt, Romesh. *The Economic History of India*, vol. I, *Under Early British Rule*, 2nd edn. (2 vols., London, 1906; repr. Delhi, 1990).

Dyer, Christopher and Simon A. C. Penn, "Wages and Earnings in Late Medieval England: Evidence from the Enforcement of the Labor Laws," in Christopher Dyer, *Everyday Life in Medieval England* (London and Rio Grande, Ohio, 1994).

Feldbaek, Ole. *India Trade under the Danish Flag 1772–1808* (Copenhagen, 1969).

Fisch, J. *Cheap Lives and Dear Limbs: The British Transformation of the Bengal Criminal Law* (Wiesbaden, 1983).

Francis, W. *Madura District Gazetteer* (2 vols., Madras, 1914).

Fukazawa, Hiroshi. "A Note on the Corvee System (Vethbegar)," in his *The Medieval Deccan: Peasants, Social Systems and States Sixteenth to Eighteenth Centuries* (Delhi, 1991).

Furber, Holden. *John Company at Work* (Cambridge, Mass., 1948).

Furniss, Edgar S. *The Position of the Laborer in a System of Nationalism* (Boston and New York, 1920; repr. New York, 1965).

Glamann, Kristoff. *Dutch-Asiatic Trade 1620–1740* (Copenhagen, 1958; repr. 'S-Gravenhage, 1981).

Gordon, Stewart. "The Slow Conquest: Administrative Integration of Malwa into the Maratha Empire," *MAS*, 11 (1978), pp. 1–40.

Marathas, Marauders, and State Formation in Eighteenth Century India (Delhi, 1994).

Greenough, Paul R. "Indulgence and Abundance as Asian Peasant Values: A Bengali Case in Point," *Journal of Asian Studies*, 42 (1983), pp. 831–50.

Gribble, J. D. B. *A Manual of the District of Cuddapah* (Madras, 1875).

Guha, Ranajit. *Dominance without Hegemony* (Cambridge, Mass., 1997).

Elementary Aspects of Peasant Insurgency in Colonial India (Delhi, 1983).

"The Prose of Counter-Insurgency," in Ranajit Guha (ed.), *Subaltern Studies II* (Delhi, 1983).

Guha, Sumit. "An Indian Penal Regime: Maharashtra in the Eighteenth Century," *Past and Present*, no. 147 (1995), pp. 101–26.

Gune, V. T. *The Judicial System of the Marathas* (Pune, 1953).

Habib, Irfan. *The Agrarian System of Mughal India* (Bombay, 1963).

Hossain, Hameeda. *The Company Weavers of Bengal* (Delhi, 1988).

Irschick, Eugene. *Dialogue and History: Constructing South India, 1795–1895* (Berkeley and Los Angeles, 1994).

Irwin, John and P. R. Schwartz, *Studies in Indo-European Textile History* (Ahmedabad, 1966).

Khan, Mohibbul Hasan. *History of Tipu Sultan* (Calcutta, 1951).

Kirmani, Mir Hussein Ali. *The History of the Reign of Tipu Sultan*, trans. Col. W. Miles, (London, 1864; repr. New Delhi, 1980).

Kumar, Dharma. "Agrarian Relations: South India," in Dharma Kumar (ed.), *CEHI*, vol. II, pp. 207–41.

Land and Caste in South India: Agricultural Labour in Madras Presidency in the Nineteenth Century (Cambridge, 1965).

Kumar, Dharma (ed.). *The Cambridge Economic History of India*, vol. II, c. 1757–c. 1970 (Cambridge, 1982).

Landes, David S. *Bankers and Pashas: International Finance and Economic Imperialism in Egypt* (Cambridge, Mass., 1958).

Linebaugh, Peter. *The London Hanged: Crime and Civil Society in the Eighteenth Century* (Cambridge, 1992).

Ludden, David. "Agrarian Commercialism in Eighteenth Century South India: Evidence from the 1823 Tirunelveli Census," *IESHR*, 25 (1988), pp. 493–519.

"Archaic Formations of Agricultural Knowledge in South India," in Peter Robb (ed.), *Meanings of Agriculture* (Delhi, 1996).

Peasant History in South India (Princeton, 1985).

McLane, John R. *Land and Local Kingship in Eighteenth-Century Bengal* (Cambridge, 1993).

Marglin, Stephen. *Growth, Distribution and Prices* (Cambridge, Mass., 1984).

Minchinton, W. E. (ed.). *Wage Regulation in Pre-Industrial England* (New York, 1972).

Mines, Mattison. *The Warrior Merchants: Textiles, Trade, and Territory in South India* (Cambridge, 1984).

Mitra, D. B. *The Cotton Weavers of Bengal* (Calcutta, 1978).

Mizushima,Tsukasa. *Nattar and Socio-Economic Change in South India in the 18th–19th Centuries* (Tokyo, 1986).

Moreland, W. H. *From Akbar to Aurangzeb* (London, 1923; repr. Delhi, 1990).

India at the Death of Akbar (London, 1920; repr. Delhi, 1990).

"Indian Exports of Cotton Goods in the Seventeenth Century," *Indian Journal of Economics*, 5 (1925), pp. 225–45.

Morris, Morris D. "Towards a Reinterpretation of Nineteenth-Century Indian Economic History," *Journal of Economic History*, 23 (1963), pp. 606–18.

Mukherjee, Nilmani. *The Ryotwari System in Madras* (Calcutta, 1962).

Mukhia, Harbans. "Illegal Extortions from Peasants, Artisans and Menials in Eighteenth Century Eastern Rajasthan," in his *Perspectives on Medieval His-*

tory (New Delhi, 1993).

Murton, Brian J. "Land and Class: Cultural, Social and Biophysical Integration in Interior Tamilnadu in the Late Eighteenth Century," in Robert E. Frykenberg (ed.), *Land Tenure and Peasant in South Asia* (Delhi, 1977), pp. 81–99.

Neeson, Jeanette. *Commoners: Common Right, Enclosure and Social Change in England, 1700–1820* (Cambridge, 1993).

Nicholson, F. A. *The Coimbatore District Manual* (Madras, 1898).

Nilakanta Sastri, K. A. *A History of South India* (Delhi, 1966).

Parry, Jonathan. "Sacrificial Death and the Necrophagous Ascetic," in Maurice Bloch and Jonathan Parry (eds.), *Death and the Regeneration of Life* (Cambridge, 1982).

Parshad, I. Durga. *Some Aspects of Indian Foreign Trade* (London, 1932).

Parthasarathi, Prasannan. "Merchants and the Rise of Colonialism," in Burton Stein and Sanjay Subrahmanyam (eds.), *Institutions and Economic Change in South Asia* (Delhi, 1996), pp. 85–104.

"Rethinking Wages and Competitiveness in the Eighteenth Century: Britain and South India," *Past and Present*, no. 158 (1998).

Pearse, Arno S. *Indian Cotton* (n.p., n.d.).

Perlin, Frank. "Concepts of Order and Comparison, with a Diversion on Counter Ideologies and Corporate Institutions in Late Pre-Colonial India," *Journal of Peasant Studies*, 12 (1985), pp. 87–165.

"Proto-Industrialization and Pre-Colonial South Asia," *Past and Present*, no. 98 (1983), pp. 30–95.

"State Formation Reconsidered," *MAS*, 19 (1985), pp. 415–80.

Postan, M. M. *The Medieval Economy and Society* (London, 1972).

Prakash, Gyan. *Bonded Histories: Genealogies of Labor Servitude in Colonial India* (Cambridge, 1990).

Prakash, Om. "Bullion for Goods: International Trade and the Economy of Early Eighteenth Century Bengal," *IESHR*, 13 (1976), pp. 159–87.

The Dutch East India Company and the Economy of Bengal 1630–1720 (Princeton, 1985).

Rajayyan, K. *Rise and Fall of the Poligars of Tamilnadu* (Madras, 1974).

Ramaswamy, Vijaya. "The Genesis and Historical Role of the Masterweavers in South Indian Textile Production," *Journal of the Economic and Social History of the Orient*, 28 (1985), pp. 294–325.

"Notes on Textile Technology in Medieval India with Special Reference to the South," *IESHR*, 17 (1980), pp. 227–41.

Textiles and Weavers in Medieval South India (Delhi, 1985).

Raychaudhuri, Tapan. *Jan Company in Coromandel 1605–1690* ('S-Gravenhage, 1962).

"The Mid-Eighteenth-Century Background," in Dharma Kumar (ed.). *CEHI*, vol. II, pp. 3–35.

"The State and the Economy: The Mughal Empire," in Tapan Raychaudhuri and Irfan Habib (eds.), *CEHI*, vol. I, pp. 172–93.

Raychaudhuri, Tapan and Irfan Habib (eds.), *The Cambridge Economic History of India*, vol. I, *c. 1200–1757* (Cambridge, 1982).

Rudner, David West. *Caste and Capitalism in Colonial India* (Berkeley, Calif., 1994).

Rule, John. *The Experience of Labor in Eighteenth-Century English Industry* (New York, 1981).

"The Property of Skill in the Period of Manufacture," in Patrick Joyce (ed.), *The Historical Meanings of Work* (Cambridge, 1987).

Schmidt, Arno. *Cotton Growing in India* (n.p., n.d.).

Sen, Ashok. "A Pre-British Economic Formation in India of the Late Eighteenth Century: Tipu Sultan's Mysore," in Barun De (ed.), *Perspectives in Social Sciences I* (Calcutta, 1977).

Sen, S. P. "The Role of Indian Textiles in Southeast Asian Trade in the Seventeenth Century," *Journal of Southeast Asian History*, 3 (1962), pp. 92–110.

Sivakumar, S. S. and Chitra Sivakumar. *Peasants and Nabobs* (Delhi, 1993).

Skinner, Quentin. *Liberty before Liberalism* (Cambridge, 1998).

Slack, Paul A. "Vagrants and Vagrancy in England, 1598–1664," *Economic History Review*, 27 (1974), pp. 360–79.

Smith, Adam. *The Wealth of Nations*, Canaan edn. (2 vols., Chicago, 1976).

Somers, Margaret R. "The 'Misteries' of Property. Relationality, Rural-Industrialization, and Community in Chartist Narratives of Political Rights," in John Brewer and Susan Staves (eds.), *Early Modern Conceptions of Property* (London, 1996).

Stein, Burton. *All the Kings' Mana: Papers on Medieval South Indian History* (Madras, 1984).

Peasant State and Society in Medieval South India (Delhi, 1980).

"State Formation and Economy Reconsidered," *MAS*, 19 (1985), pp. 387–413.

Thomas Munro: The Origins of the Colonial State and his Vision of Empire (Delhi, 1989).

Vijayanagar (Cambridge, 1989).

Stein, Burton (ed.). *The Making of Agrarian Policy in British India 1770–1900* (Delhi, 1992).

Subba Rao, K. "Correspondence between the Hon. The East India Company and the Kandregula Family in the XVIII Century," *Journal of the Andhra Historical Research Society*, 3 (1928), pp. 209–22; 4 (1929–30), pp. 61–71, 125–46; 10 (1936–7), pp. 194–208.

Subrahmanyam, Sanjay. *The Political Economy of Commerce: Southern India, 1500–1650* (Cambridge, 1990).

"Rural Industry and Commercial Agriculture in Late Seventeenth-Century South-eastern India," *Past and Present*, no. 126 (1989), pp. 76–114.

Subrahmanyam, Sanjay and C. A. Bayly. "Portfolio Capitalists and the Political Economy of Early Modern India," *IESHR*, 25 (1988), pp. 401–24.

Subramanian, Lakshmi. *Indigenous Capital and Imperial Expansion* (Delhi, 1996).

Sudhir P. and P. Swarnalatha. "Textile Traders and Territorial Imperatives: Masulipatnam, 1750–1850," *IESHR*, 29 (1992), pp. 145–69.

Teltscher, Kate. *India Inscribed* (Delhi, 1995).

Thirsk, Joan. "Industries in the Countryside," in F. J. Fisher (ed.), *Essays in the Economic and Social History of Tudor England* (Cambridge, 1961).

Thompson, E. P. *Customs in Common* (New York, 1993).
The Making of the English Working Class (New York, 1964).
"Time, Work-Discipline and Industrial Capitalism," *Past and Present*, no. 38 (1967), pp. 56–97.
Thurston, Edgar. *Castes and Tribes of Southern India* (7 vols., Madras, 1909).
Monograph on the Silk Fabric Industry of the Madras Presidency (Madras, 1899).
Monograph on the Woolen Fabric Industry of the Madras Presidency (Madras, 1898).
Washbrook, David. "Economic Development and the Making of 'Traditional' Society in Colonial India 1820–1855," *Transactions of the Royal Historical Society*, 6th Series, 3 (London, 1993), pp. 237–63.
"Land and Labour in Late Eighteenth-Century South India: The Golden Age of the Pariah?," in Peter Robb (ed.), *Dalit Movements and the Meanings of Labour in India* (Delhi, 1993).
"Progress and Problems: South Asian Economic and Social History *c.* 1720–1860," *MAS*, 22 (1988), pp. 57–96.
Wheeler, J. Talboys. *Handbook to the Cotton Cultivation in the Madras Presidency* (London, 1863).
Wink, André. *Land and Sovereignty in India* (Cambridge, 1986).

UNPUBLISHED WORKS

Brennig, Joseph. "The Textile Trade of Seventeenth Century Coromandel: A Study of a Pre-Modern Asian Export Industry," Ph.D. Dissertation, University of Wisconsin-Madison, 1975.
Menon, Saraswati. "Social Characteristics of Land Control in Thanjavur District During the 19th Century: A Sociological Study," Ph. D. Dissertation, Jawaharlal Nehru University, 1983.
Winzen, Kristina. "The Perception of Guildsmen by the City Representatives in the Imperial Diet of the Late Seventeenth Century," paper presented at the ESTER Seminar on Guilds and Guildsmen in European Towns 16th to 19th Centuries, International Institute of Social History, Amsterdam, November 1996.

Index

Books in this series

Printed in the United Kingdom
by Lightning Source UK Ltd.
117531UKS00001B/253

Cambridge Studies in Indian History and Society 7

Cambridge Studies in Indian History and Society publishes monographs on the history and anthropology of modern India. In addition to its primary scholarly focus, the series also includes work of an interdisciplinary nature which contributes to contemporary social and cultural debates about Indian history and society. In this way, the series furthers the general development of historical and anthropological knowledge to attract a wider readership than that concerned with India alone.

A list of titles which have been published in the series is featured at the end of the book

The Transition to a Colonial Economy

According to popular belief, poverty and low standards of living have been characteristic of India for centuries. In a challenge to this view, Prasannan Parthasarathi demonstrates that, until the late eighteenth century, laboring groups in South India, those at the bottom of the social order, were actually in a powerful position, receiving incomes well above subsistence. The subsequent decline in their economic fortunes, the author asserts, was a process initiated towards the end of that century, with the rise of British colonial rule. Building on recent scholarly reinterpretations of eighteenth-century India, he examines the transformation of Indian society and its economy under British rule through the prism of the laboring classes, arguing that their treatment during this transition had no precedent in the pre-colonial past and that poverty and low wages were a direct product of colonial rule. This represents a powerful revisionist statement on the role of Britain in India which will be of interest not only to students of the region, but also to economic and colonial historians.

Prasannan Parthasarathi is Assistant Professor in the Department of History, Boston College.